Algorithms and Networking
for Computer Games

Algorithms and Networking for Computer Games

Jouni Smed
Harri Hakonen
University of Turku, Finland

John Wiley & Sons, Ltd

Other Wiley Editorial Offices

John Wiley & Sons Inc., 111 River Street, Hoboken, NJ 07030, USA

Jossey-Bass, 989 Market Street, San Francisco, CA 94103-1741, USA

Wiley-VCH Verlag GmbH, Boschstr. 12, D-69469 Weinheim, Germany

John Wiley & Sons Australia Ltd, 42 McDougall Street, Milton, Queensland 4064, Australia

John Wiley & Sons (Asia) Pte Ltd, 2 Clementi Loop #02-01, Jin Xing Distripark, Singapore 129809

John Wiley & Sons Canada Ltd, 22 Worcester Road, Etobicoke, Ontario, Canada M9W 1L1

Wiley also publishes its books in a variety of electronic formats. Some content that appears
in print may not be available in electronic books.

British Library Cataloguing in Publication Data

A catalogue record for this book is available from the British Library

ISBN-13: 978-0-047-01812-5
ISBN-10: 0-470-01812-7

Typeset in 10/12pt Times by Laserwords Private Limited, Chennai, India
Printed and bound in Great Britain by Antony Rowe Ltd, Chippenham, Wiltshire
This book is printed on acid-free paper responsibly manufactured from sustainable forestry
in which at least two trees are planted for each one used for paper production.

In memory of

Timo Kaukoranta

and

Timo Raita

Contents

List of Figures

List of Tables

List of Algorithms

Preface

When students at MIT competed against each other in the first real-time graphical computer game *Spacewar* in 1962 (Graetz 1981), probably none of them could have dreamt how realistic and complex computer games would develop to be in four decades and how large a business would grow around them. Commercial arcade games such as *Pong* and *Space Invaders* arrived in the 1970s, and home computers brought computer games within the reach of all enthusiasts in the 1980s. Since then, game development and programming have turned from being small amateur enterprises into a more professional and larger-scale industry. Nowadays, the typical time span of development from an idea to a finished product is about two years and demands the work contribution of 20–50 persons. The current estimates of the annual revenue generated by computer games are around €25 billion and the annual growth is predicted to be over 10% over the next few years (Game Developers' Association of Australia 2003).

The game industry has slowly awakened to the possibilities of academic research. International Game Developers Association (2003) lists *game programming* among the eight core topics of game-related research areas. Game programming is defined to cover aspects of computer science relevant to gaming. This interest in novel solutions and improved methods is understandable, because the marketing of computer games is highly technology-driven. Earlier, the selling points were the amount of colours and real timeliness, then the amount of polygons and the frame update frequency, and now the amount of simultaneous players in a networked game and the realism of the simulation. These features also reflect what programming problems have been on the focus of the game developers at that time.

Apart from classical games with the likes of Chess, Backgammon and Go, computer games as a research topic remained on the margins of computer science for a long time. In fact, the turn of the new millennium saw the birth of several game-related academic conferences and journals and various game programming communities comprising also computer scientists. At the same time, the spectrum of the research topics has extended to cover problems encountered in real-time interactive computer games and networked multi-player games.

Game programming is not an isolated field of study but also includes many essential research areas of 'traditional' computer science. Solving an algorithmic or a networking problem is always more than just getting it done as quickly as possible; it is about analysing what is behind the problem and what possibilities there are to solve it. This is the direction where this book heads, and our intention is to provide the reader with a glance into the world of computer games as seen from the perspective of a computer scientist.

We assume that the reader is familiar with the fundamentals of algorithms and data structures (e.g. complexity analysis and graph theory). In case of uncertainty, they can be refreshed by revising basic textbooks such as *Introduction to Algorithms* (Cormen *et al.* 2001) and, of course, the ever so inspiring *The Art of Computer Programming* (Knuth 1998a,b,c). We describe classical game algorithms as well as review problems encountered in commercial computer games. For this reason, selecting material for this book has been arduous tightroping between these two worlds. The current selection may seem a bit of a ragbag, but the common factor in choosing the topics has been a combination of algorithmic and practical interest.

While preparing the manuscript, colleagues and students, intrigued by the words 'computer game', have asked us: 'Will it be a fun book to read'? After we have explained that it is really about algorithms and networking, they have concluded (perhaps somewhat disappointedly): 'Oh, it's a serious book then'. We hope the truth is neither black nor white (not that we are preferring dull grey), but we are sure this book will turn out to be both fun and serious – at least we have had serious fun while being funnily serious.

Turku, Finland   JOUNI SMED
April 2006   HARRI HAKONEN

Acknowledgements

First of all, we acknowledge the role of our colleague and dear friend Dr Timo Kaukoranta in gathering and analysing the topics that form the basis for this book. His untimely death was, at the same time, a devastating blow to our small research group as well as a waking call to realize in written form the ideas we have been tossing around for several years. Timo's spirit is present throughout this book, because while preparing the manuscript we often found ourselves thinking what he would have said about the topic at hand.

Many people have guided us through and led us into viewing the world as computer scientists. Professor Olli Nevalainen's pivotal role in steering us to the world of algorithms as well as the support from the late Professor Timo Raita have been both inspiring and invaluable to us. We are also grateful to Professor Timo Knuutila for lending his books, time, and expertise (and TeXpertise!) when we needed them.

We would like to thank our colleagues and co-authors – of whom we would like to mention here (alphabetically) Kai Kimppa, Tomi 'bgt' Mäntylä, Henrik Niinisalo, Pasi Uuppo, and Elina Valjanen – for widening our perspectives and sharpening our thoughts. We are also grateful for the feedback we have received from the students who have taken part in our various computer game-related courses and seminars in the Department of Information Technology, University of Turku and Turku Centre for Computer Science during 2001–2005. Also, we are indebted to the head of the department, Professor Ari Paasio, for his encouraging attitude towards our project.

It has been a pleasure to work with the people at Wiley. We thank Birgit Gruber for inviting us to write this book, and Richard Davies and Joanna Tootill for their support and guidance throughout the process.

Personal thanks and greetings go to our friends Antti Koski and Tommi Johtela for the countless hours of theoretical and (more often) practical computer game sessions, which sometimes provided us with new insights into various topics (and most of the time it was just fun to play).

Finally, Jouni wants to thank Iris for all the love and understanding, and Harri wants to thank Pyry for reminding dad when it was time to have a break.

1

Introduction

Let us play a little thought game: Get a pen and paper. Choose any game you know, and think about the elements required to make it work. Write down a list of these elements. Be as specific or indiscriminate as you want. Once you are finished, choose another game and think about it. Try to find items in the list of the first game that correspond to the second game and mark them. If there are features in the second game that the first one does not have, add them to the list. Repeat this procedure for two or three more games. Next, take the five most common items in your list and compare them to the following list. For each corresponding item you get one point.

The key elements of a game are as follows:

- Players who are willing to participate in the game

- Rules that define the limits of the game

- Goals that the players try to achieve during the game

- Opponents or opposing forces that prevent the player from achieving the goals

- A representation of the game in the real world.

How many points did you score?

J. Huizinga's definition for play from his classical work *Homo Ludens*, the playful human, captures most of the features:

> [Play] is an activity which proceeds within certain limits of time and space, in a visible order, according to rules freely accepted, and outside the sphere of necessity or material utility. The play-mood is one of rapture and enthusiasm, and is sacred or festive in accordance with the occasion. A feeling of exaltation and tension accompanies the action, and mirth and relaxation follow. (Huizinga 1955, p. 132)

A dictionary definition elaborates that 'game' is 'a universal form of recreation generally including any activity engaged in for diversion or amusement and often establishing a situation that involves a contest or rivalry' (Encyclopædia Britannica 2005). Crawford

Algorithms and Networking for Computer Games   Jouni Smed and Harri Hakonen
© 2006 John Wiley & Sons, Ltd

Figure 1.1 Components, relationships, and aspects of a game.

(1984, Chapter 1) defines game as 'a closed formal system that subjectively represents a subset of reality'. Accordingly, a game is self-sufficient, follows a set of rules, and has a representation in the real world. These observations are echoed by the definitions of Costikyan (2002, p. 24), who sees a game as 'an interactive structure of endogenous meaning that requires players to struggle toward a goal', and Salen and Zimmerman (2004, p. 80), to whom a game is 'a system in which players engage in an artificial conflict, defined by rules, that results in a quantifiable outcome'.

The five components we have listed seem to be present in every game, and the relationships between them form three aspects of a game, which are illustrated in Figure 1.1 (Smed and Hakonen 2003, 2005b):

(i) *Challenge*: Rules define the game and, consequently, the goal of the game. When players decide to participate in the game, they agree to follow the rules. The goal motivates the players and drives the game forwards, because achieving a goal in the game gives the players enjoyment.

(ii) *Conflict*: The opponent (which can include unpredictable humans and random processes) obstructs the players from achieving the goal. Because the players do not have a comprehensive knowledge of the opponent, they cannot precisely determine the opponent's effect on the game.

(iii) *Play*: The rules are abstract but they correspond to real-world objects. This representation concretizes the game for the players.

The challenge aspect alone is not enough for a definition of a game, because games are also about conflict. For example, a crossword puzzle may be a challenge in its own right but there is hardly any conflict in solving it – unless someone erases the letters or changes the hints or keeps a record of the time to solve the puzzle. Obviously, the conflict arises from the presence of an opponent, which aims at obstructing the player from achieving the goal. The opponent does not have to be a human but it can be some random process (e.g. throw of dice or shuffling of the deck of cards). The main feature of the opponent is that it is indeterministic for the player: Because the player cannot predict exactly what another human being or a random process will do, outwitting or outguessing the opponent becomes an important part of the game.

Challenge and conflict aspects are enough for defining a game in an abstract sense. However, in order to be played, the game needs to be concretized into a representation. This representation can be a cardboard and plastic pieces as well as three-dimensional graphics rendered on a computer screen. The players themselves can be the representation, such as in the children's game of tag. Regardless of the representation, there must exist a clear correspondence to the rules of the game.

Let us take the game of poker as an example. The players agree to follow the rules, which state (among other things) what cards there are in a deck, how many cards one can change, and how the hands are ranked. The rules also define the goal, having as good a hand as possible when the cards are laid on the table, which is the player's motivation. The other players are opponents, because they try to achieve a better hand to win. Also, the randomness of the deck caused by shuffling opposes the player, who cannot determine what cards will be dealt next. The game takes a concrete form in a deck of plastic-coated cards (or pixels on the screen), which represent the abstractions used in the rules.

Apart from these formal features, the game play also includes subjective elements such as immersion in the game world, a sense of purpose, and a sense of achievement from mastering the game. One could argue that the sense of purpose is essential for the immersion. What immerses us in a game (as well as in a book or a film) is the sense that there is a purpose or motive behind the surface. In a similar fashion, the sense of achievement is essential for the sense of purpose (i.e. the purpose of a game is to achieve goals, points, money, recognition etc.). From a human point of view, we get satisfaction in the process of nearing a challenging goal and finally achieving it. These aspects, however, are outside the scope of our current discussion, and we turn our focus to a subset of games, namely, computer games.

1.1 Anatomy of Computer Games

Computer games are a subset of games. To be more precise, let us define a computer game as a game that is carried out with the help of a computer program. This definition leaves us some leeway, since it does not implicate that the whole game takes place in the computer. For example, a game of chess can be played on the screen or on a real-world board, regardless of whether the opponent is a computer program. Also, location-based games (see Chapter 8) further obscure the traditional role of a computer game by incorporating real-world objects into the game world.

In effect, a computer program in a game can act in three roles:

(i) coordinating the game process (e.g. realizing a participant's move in a chess game according to the rules),

(ii) illustrating the situation (e.g. displaying the chessboard and pieces on screen), and

(iii) participating as a fellow player.

This role division closely resembles the *Model–View–Controller* (MVC) architectural pattern for computer programs. MVC was originally developed within the Smalltalk community

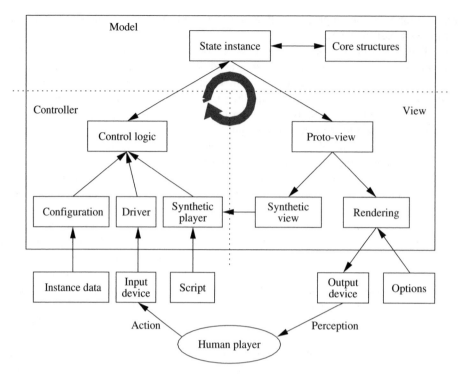

Figure 1.2 Model, View, and Controller in a computer game.

(Krasner and Pope 1988) and later on it has been adopted as a basis for object-oriented programming in general (Gamma *et al.* 1995). The basic idea is that the representation of the underlying application domain (Model) should be separated from the way it is presented to the user (View) and from the way the user interacts with it (Controller). Figure 1.2 illustrates the MVC components and the data flow in a computer game.

   The Model part includes software components that are responsible for the coordination role (e.g. evaluating the rules and upholding the game state). The rules and basic entity information (e.g. physical laws) form the core structures. It remains unchanged while the state instance is created and configured for each game process. The core structures need not cover all the rules, because they can be instantiated. For example, the core structures can define the basic mechanism and properties of playing cards (e.g. suits and values) and the instance data can provide the additional structures required for a game of poker (e.g. ranking of the hands, staking, and resolving ties).

   The View part handles the illustration role. A proto-view provides an interface into the Model. It is used for creating a synthetic view for a synthetic player or for rendering a view to an output device. The synthetic view can be pre-processed to suit the needs of the synthetic player (e.g. board coordinates rather than an image of the pieces on a board). Although rendering is often identified with visualization, it may as well include audification and other forms of sensory feedback. The rendering can have some user-definable options (e.g. graphics resolution or sound quality).

The Controller part includes the components for the participation role. Control logic affects the Model and keeps up the integrity (e.g. by excluding illegal moves suggested by a player). The human player's input is received through an input device filtered by a driver software. The configuration component provides instance data, which is used in generating the initial state for the game. The human player participates in the data flow by perceiving information from the output devices and performing actions through the input devices. Although the illustration in Figure 1.2 includes only one player, naturally there can be multiple players participating the data flow, each with thier own output and input devices. Moreover, the computer game can be distributed among several nodes rather than reside inside a single node. Conceptually, this is not a problem since the components in the MVC can as well be thought to be distributed (i.e. the data flows run through the network rather than inside a single computer). In practice, however, the networked computer games provide their own challenges (see Section 1.3).

1.2   Synthetic Players

A synthetic player is a computer-generated actor in the game. It can be an opponent, a non-player character (NPC) that participates limitedly (like a supporting actor), or a *deus ex machina*, which can control natural forces or godly powers and thus intervene or generate the game events.

Because everything in a computer game revolves around the human player, the game world is anthropocentric. Regardless of the underlying method for decision-making (see Chapter 6), the synthetic player is bound to show certain behaviour in relation to the human player, which can range from simple reactions to general attitudes and even complex intentions. As we can see in Figure 1.2, the data flow of the human player and the synthetic player resemble each other, which allows us to project human-like features to the synthetic player.

We can argue that, in a sense, there should be no difference between the players whether they are humans or computer programs; if they are to operate on the same level, both should ideally have the same powers of observation and the same capabilities to cope with uncertainties (see Chapter 7). Ideally, the synthetic players should be in a similar situation as their human counterparts, but of course a computer program is no match for human ingenuity. This is why synthetic players rarely display real autonomy but appear to behave purposefully (e.g. in *Grand Theft Auto III* pedestrians walk around without any real destination).

The more open (i.e. the less restrictive) the game world is, the more complex the synthetic players are. This trade-off between the Model and the Controller software components is obvious: If we remove restricting code from the core structures, we have to reinstate it in the synthetic players. For example, if the players can hurt themselves by walking into fire, the synthetic player must know how to avoid it. Conversely, if we rule out fire as a permitted area, path finding (see Chapter 5) for a synthetic player becomes simpler.

Let us take a look at two external features that a casual player is most likely to notice first in a synthetic player: humanness and stance. They are also relevant to the design of the synthetic player by providing a framework for the game developers and programmers.

1.2.1   Humanness

The success of networked multi-player games can be, at least in part, explained with the fact that the human players provide something that the synthetic ones still lack. This missing factor is the human traits and characteristics – flaws as much as (or even more than) strengths: fear, rage, compassion, hesitation, and emotions in general. Even minor displays of emotion can make the synthetic player appear more human. For instance, in *Half-Life* and *Halo* the synthetic players who have been taken by surprise do not act in superhuman coolness but show fear and panic appropriate to the situation. We, as human beings, are quite apt to read humanness into the decisions even when there is nothing but naïve algorithms behind them. Sometimes a game, such as *NetHack*, even gathers around a community that starts to tell stories of the things that synthetic players have done and to interpret them in human terms.

A computer game comprising just synthetic players could be as interesting to watch as a movie or a television show (Charles *et al.* 2002). In other words, if the game world is fascinating enough to observe, it is likely that it is also enjoyable to participate in – which is one of the key factors in games like *The Sims* and *Singles*, where the synthetic players seem to act (more or less) with a purpose and the human player's influence is, at best, only indirect.

There are also computer games that do not have human players at all. In the 1980s *Core War* demonstrated that programming synthetic players to compete with each other can be an interesting game by itself (Dewdney 1984). Since then some games have tried to use this approach, but, by and large, artificial intelligence (AI) programming games have only been the by-products of 'proper' games. For example, *Age of Empires II* includes a possibility to create scripts for computer players, which allows to organize games where programmers compete on who creates the best AI script. The whole game is then carried out by a computer while the humans remain as observers. Although the programmers cannot affect the outcome during the game, they are more than just enthusiastic watchers: They are the coaches and the parents, and the synthetic players are the protégès and the children.

1.2.2   Stance

The computer-controlled player can have different stances (or attitudes) towards the human player. Traditionally, the synthetic player has been seen only in the role of an enemy. As an enemy, the synthetic player must provide challenge and demonstrate intelligent (or at least purposeful) behaviour. Although the enemies may be omniscient or cheat when the human player cannot see them, it is important to keep the illusion that the synthetic player is at the same level as the human player.

When the computer acts as an ally, its behaviour must adjust to the human point of view. For example, a computer-controlled reconnaissance officer should provide intelligence in a visually accessible format rather than overwhelm the player with lists of raw variable values. In addition to accessibility, the human players require consistency, and even incomplete information (as long as it remains consistent) can have some value to them. The help can even be concrete operations like in *Neverwinter Nights* or *Star Wars: Battlefront* where the computer-controlled teammates respond to the player's commands.

The computer has a neutral stance when it acts as an observer (e.g. camera director or commentator) or a referee (e.g. judging rule violations in a sports game) (Siira 2004). Here, the behaviour depends on the context and conventions of the role. In a sports game, for example, the camera director program must heed the camera placements and cuts dictated by the television programme practice. Refereeing provides another kind of challenge, because some rules can be hard to judge. Finally, synthetic players can be used to carry on the plot, to provide atmosphere, or simply to act as extras. Nevertheless, as we shall see next, they may have an important role in assisting immersion in the game world and directing the game play.

1.3 Multi-playing

What keeps us interested is – surprise. Humans are extremely creative at this, whereas a synthetic player can be lacking in humaneness. One easy way to limit the resources dedicated to the development of synthetic players is to make the computer game a multi-player game.

The first real-time multi-player games usually limited the number of players to two, because the players had to share the same computer by dividing either the screen (e.g. *Pitstop II*) or the playtime among the participating players (e.g. *Formula One Grand Prix*). Also, the first networked real-time games connected two players over a modem (e.g. *Falcon A.T.*). Although text-based networked multi-player games started out in the early 1980s with Multi-user dungeons (MUDs) (Bartle 1990), real-time multi-player games (e.g. *Quake*) became common in the 1990s as local area networks (LANs) and the Internet became more widespread. These two development lines were connected when online game sites (e.g. *Ultima Online*) started to provide real-time multi-player games for a large number of players sharing the same game world.

On the technical level, networking in multi-player computer games depends on achieving a balance between the consistency and responsiveness of a distributed game world (see Chapter 9). The problems are due to the inherent technical limitations (see Chapter 8). As the number of simultaneous players increases, scalability of the chosen network architecture becomes critical. Although related research work on interactive real-time networking has been done in military simulations and networked virtual environments (Smed *et al.* 2002, 2003), cheating prevention is a unique problem for computer games (see Chapter 10).

Nowadays, commercially available computer games are expected to offer a multi-player option, and, at the same time, online game sites are expected to support an ever increasing number of users. Similarly, the new game console releases rely heavily on the appeal of online gaming, and a whole new branch of mobile entertainment has emerged with intention to develop distributed multi-player games for wireless applications.

The possibility of having multiple players enriches the game experience – and complicates the software design process – because of the interaction between the players, both synthetic and human. Moreover, the players do not have to be opponents but they can cooperate. Although more common in single-player computer games, it is possible to include a story-like plot in a multi-player game, where the players are cooperatively solving the story (e.g. *No One Lives Forever 2* and *Neverwinter Nights*). Let us next look at storytelling from a broader perspective.

1.4   Games and Storytelling

Storytelling is about not actions but reasons for actions. Human beings use stories to understand intentional behaviour and tend to 'humanize' the behaviour of the characters to understand the story (Spierling 2002). While 'traditional' storytelling progresses linearly, a game must provide an illusion of free will (Costikyan 2002). According to Aylett and Louchart (2003), computer games differ from other forms of storytelling in that the story time and real time are highly contingent, whereas in traditional forms of storytelling (e.g. cinema or literature) this dependency can be quite loose. Another differentiating factor is interactivity, which is non-existent or rather restricted in other forms of storytelling. Bringsjord (2001) lists four challenges to interactive storytelling: First, a plot and three-dimensional characters are not enough to produce a high-quality narrative but there has to be a theme (e.g. betrayal, self-deception, love, or revenge) behind them. Second, there should exist some element to make the story stay dramatically interesting. Third, apart from being robust and autonomous, the characters (i.e. synthetic players) have to be memorable personalities by themselves. Fourth, a character should understand the players – even to the point of inferring other characters' and players' beliefs on the basis of its own beliefs.

Anthropocentrism is reflected not only in the reactions but also in the intentions of the synthetic players. As a form of entertainment, amusement, or pastime, the intention of games is to immerse and engulf the human player fully in the game world. This means that the human player may need guidance while proceeding with the game. The goals of the game can get blurry, and synthetic players or events should lead the human players so that they do not stray too far from the intended direction set by the developers of the game. For this reason, the game developers are quite eager to include a story into the game. The usual approach to include storytelling into commercial computer games is to have 'interactive plots' (International Game Developers Association 2004). A game may offer only a little room for the story to deviate – like in *Dragon's Lair*, where, at each stage, the players can choose from several alternative actions of which all but one leads to a certain death. This linear plot approach is nowadays replaced by the parallel paths approach, where the story line is divided into episodes. The player has some freedom within the episode, which has fixed entry and exit points. At the transition point, the story of the previous episode is concluded and new story alternatives for the next episode are introduced. For instance, in *Max Payne* or *Diablo II*, the plot lines of the previous chapter are concluded at the transition point, and many new plot alternatives are introduced. Still, many games neither include a storyline nor impose a sequence of events. Granted that some of them can be tedious (e.g. *Frontier: Elite II*, in which the universe is vast and devoid of action whereas in the original *Elite* the goal remains clearer) – but so are many games that include a story.

Research on storytelling computer systems is mainly motivated by the theories of V. Propp (1968), because they help to reduce the task of storytelling to a pattern recognition problem; for example, see Fairclough and Cunningham (2002); Lindley and Eladhari (2002); Peinado and Gervás (2004). This pattern recognition approach can even be applied hierarchically to different abstraction levels. Spierling *et al.* (2002) decompose the storytelling system into four parts: story engine, scene action engine, character conversation engine, and actor avatar engine. These engines either rely on pre-defined data or act autonomously, and the higher level sets the outline for the level below. For example, on the basis of the current situation the story engine recognizes an adaptable story pattern and inputs instructions for the scene action engine to carry out. In addition to these implementation-oriented approaches, other methodological approaches to interactive storytelling have been suggested in the fields of narratology and ludology, but we omit a detailed discussion of them here.

The main problem with the often-used top-down approach is that the program generating the story must act like a human dungeon master. It must observe the reactions of the crowd as well as the situation in the game, and recognize what pattern fits the current situation: Is the game getting boring and should there be a surprising twist in the plot, or has there been too much action and the players would like to have a moment's peace to rest and regroup? Since we aim at telling a story to the human players, we must ensure that the world around them remains purposeful. We have general plot patterns that we try to recognize in the history and in the surroundings of a human player. This in turn determines how the synthetic players will act.

Instead of a centralized and omnipotent storyteller or dominant dungeon master, the plot could get revealed and the (autobiographical) 'story' of the game (as told by the players to themselves) could emerge from the interaction with the synthetic players. However, this bottom-up approach is, quite understandably, rarely used because it leaves the synthetic players alone with a grave responsibility: They must provide a sense of purpose in the chaotic world.

1.5   Other Game Design Considerations

Although defining what makes a game enjoyable is subjective, we can list some features that alluring computer games seem to have. Of course, our list is far from complete and open to debate, but we want to raise certain issues that are interesting in their own right but which – unfortunately – fall out of the scope of this book.

- *Customization*: A good game has an intuitive interface that is easy to learn. Because players have their own preferences, they should be allowed to customize the user interface to their own liking. For example, the interface should adapt dynamically to the needs of a player so that in critical situations the player has more detailed control. If a player can personalize her avatar (e.g. customize the characteristics to correspond to her real-world persona), it can increase the immersion of the game.

- *Tutorial*: The first problem a player faces is learning how the game works, which includes both the user interface and the game world. Tutorials are a convenient method for teaching the game mechanics to the player, where the player can learn the game by playing it in an easier and possibly assisted mode.

- *Profiles*: To keep the game challenging as the player progresses, it should support different difficulty levels that provide new challenges. Typically, this feature is implemented by increasing certain attributes of the enemies: their number, their accuracy, and their speed. The profile can also include the player's preferences of the type of game (e.g. whether it should focus on action or adventure).

- *Modifications*: Games gather communities around them, and members of the community start providing new modifications (or 'mods') and add-ons to the original game. A modification can be just a graphical enhancement (e.g. new textures) or it can enlarge the game world (e.g. new levels). Also, the original game developers themselves can provide extension packs, which usually include new levels, playing characters, and objects, and perhaps some improvement of the user interface.

- *Replaying*: Once is not enough. We take pictures and videotape our lives. The same also applies to games. Traditionally, many games provide the option to take screen captures, but replays are also an important feature. Replaying can be extended to cover the whole game, and the recordings allow the players to relive and memorize the highlights of the game, and to share them with friends and the whole game community.

It is important to recognize beforehand what software development mechanisms are published to the players and with what interfaces. The game developers typically implement special software for creating content for the game. These editing tools are a valuable surplus to the final product. If the game community can create new variations of the original game, longevity of the game increases. Furthermore, the inclusion of the developing tools is an inexpensive way – since they are already implemented – to enrich the contents of the final product.

Let us turn the discussion around and ask what factors are responsible for making a computer game bad. It can be summed in one word: *limitation*. Of course, to some extent limitation is necessary – we are, after all, dealing with limited resources. Moreover, the rules of the game are all about limitation, although their main function is to impose the goals for the game. The art of making games is to balance the means and limitations so that this equilibrium engrosses the human player. How do limitations manifest themselves in the program code? The answer is the lack of parameters: The more the things are hardcoded, the lesser the possibilities to add and support new features. Rather than shutting out possibilities, a good game – like any good computer program! – should be open and modifiable for both the developer and the player.

1.6   Outline of the Book

The intention of our book is to look at the algorithmic and networking problems present in commercial computer games from the perspective of a computer scientist. As the title implies, this book is divided into two parts: algorithms and networking. This emphasis on topic selection leaves out components of Figure 1.2 that are connected to the human-in-the-loop. Most noticeably, we omit all topics concerning graphics and human interaction – which is not to say that they are in any way less important or less interesting than the current selection of topics. Also, game design as well as ludological aspects of computer games fall out of the scope of this book.

The topics of the book are based on the usual problems that game developers encounter in game programming. We review the theoretical background of each problem and review the existing methods for solving them. The given algorithmic solutions are given not in any specific programming language but in pseudo-code format, which can be easily rewritten in any programming language and – more importantly – which emphasizes the algorithmic idea behind the solution. The algorithmic notation used is described in detail in Appendix A.

We have also included examples from real-world computer games to clarify different uses for the theoretical methods. In addition, each chapter is followed by a set of exercises, which go over the main points of the chapter and extend the topics by introducing new perspectives.

1.6.1 Algorithms

Part I of this book concentrates on typical algorithmic problems in computer games and presents solution methods. The chapters address the following questions:

- Chapter 2 – Random Numbers: How can we achieve indeterminism required by games using deterministic algorithms?

- Chapter 3 – Tournaments: How we can form a tournament to decide a ranking for a set of contestants?

- Chapter 4 – Game Trees: How can we build a synthetic player for perfect information games?

- Chapter 5 – Path Finding: How can we find a route in a (possibly continuous) game world?

- Chapter 6 – Decision-Making: How can we make a synthetic player act intelligently in the game world?

- Chapter 7 – Modelling Uncertainty: How can we model the uncertainties present in decision-making?

1.6.2 Networking

Part II turns the attention to networking. We aim at describing the ideas behind different approaches rather than get too entangled in the technical details. The chapters address the following questions:

- Chapter 8 – Communication Layers: What are the technical limitations behind networking?

- Chapter 9 – Compensating Resource Limitations: How can we cope with the inherent communication delays and divide the network resources among multiple players?

- Chapter 10 – Cheating Prevention: Can we guarantee a fair playing field for all players?

1.7 Summary

All games have a common basic structure comprising players, rules, goals, opponents, and representation. They form the challenge, play, and conflict aspects of a game, which are reflected, for instance, in the Model–View–Controller software architecture pattern. The computer can participate in the game as a synthetic player, which can act in the role of an opponent or a teammate or have a neutral stance. For example, synthetic player must take the role of a storyteller, if we want to incorporate story-like features into the game. Multi-playing allows other human players to participate in the same game using networked computers.

Game programming has matured from its humble beginnings and nowadays it resembles any other software project. Widely accepted software construction practices have been adopted in game development, and, at the same time, off-the-shelf components (e.g. 3D engines and animation tools) have removed the burden to develop all software components in house. This maturity, however, does not mean that there is no room for artistic creativity and technical innovations. There must be channels for bringing out novel and possibly radically different games, and, like music and film industry, independent game publishing can act as a counterbalance to the mainstream.

Nevertheless computer games are driven by computer programs propelled by algorithms and networking. Let us see what they have in store for us.

Exercises

1-1 Take any simple computer game (e.g. *Pac-Man*) and discern what forms its challenge aspect (i.e. player, rules and goal), conflict aspect, and play aspect.

1-2 A crossword puzzle is not a game (or is it?). What can you do to make it more game-like?

1-3 Why do we need a proto-view component in the MVC decomposition?

1-4 What kind of special skills and knowledge should game programmers have when they are programming

   (a) the Model part software components,

   (b) the View part software components, or

   (c) the Controller part software components?

1-5 Let us look at a first-person shooter (FPS) game (e.g. *Doom* or *Quake*). Discern the required software components by using the MVC. What kind of modelling does it require? What kind of View-specific considerations should be observed? How about the Controller part?

1-6 *Deus ex machina* (from Latin 'god from the machine') derives from ancient theater, where the effect of the god's appearance in the sky, to solve a crisis by divine intervention, was achieved by means of a crane. If a synthetic player participates in the game as a *deus ex machina*, what kind of role will it have?

1-7 What does 'anthropocentrism' mean? Are there non-anthropocentric games?

1-8 *The Sims* includes an option of free will. By turning it off, the synthetic players do nothing unless the player explicitly issues a command. Otherwise, they show their own initiative and follow, for example, their urges and needs. How much free will should a synthetic player have? Where would it serve the best (e.g. in choosing a path or choosing an action)?

1-9 Many games are variations of the same structure. Consider *Pac-Man* and Snake. Discern their common features and design a generic game that can be parameterized to be both the games.

1-10 Judging rules can be difficult – even for an objective computer program. In football (or soccer as some people call it), the official rules say that the referee can allow the play to continue 'when the team against which an offence has been committed will benefit from such an advantage' and penalize 'the original offence if the anticipated advantage does not ensue at that time' (Federation Internationale de Football Association 2003). How would you implement this rule? What difficulties are involved in it?

Part I

Algorithms

2

Random Numbers

One of the most difficult problems in computer science is implementing a truly random number generator – even D.E. Knuth devotes a whole chapter of his book *The Art of Computer Programming* to the topic (Knuth 1998b, Chapter 3). The difficulty stems partly from how we understand the word 'random', since no single number in itself is random. Hence, the task is not to simulate randomness but to generate a virtually infinite sequence of statistically independent random numbers uniformly distributed inside a given interval (Park and Miller 1988).

Because algorithms are deterministic, they cannot generate truly random numbers – except with the help of some outside device like processor-embedded circuits (Intel Platform Security Division 1999). Rather, the numbers are generated with arithmetic operations, and, therefore, the sequences are not random but *appear* to be so – hence, they are often said to be *pseudo-random*. It is quite easy to come up with methods like von Neumann's middle-square method, where we take the square of the previous random number and extract the middle digits; for example, if we are generating four-digit numbers, the sequence can include a subsequence:

$$r_i = 8269$$
$$r_{i+1} = 3763 \quad (r_i^2 = 68\underline{3763}61)$$
$$r_{i+2} = 1601 \quad (r_{i+1}^2 = 14\underline{1601}69)$$
$$\vdots$$

However, if we analyse this method more carefully, it will soon become clear why it is hardly satisfactory for the current purpose. This holds also for many other *ad hoc* methods, and Knuth sums up his own toils on the subject by exclaiming that 'random numbers should not be generated with a method chosen at random' (Knuth 1998b, p. 6).

Since every random number generator based on arithmetic operations has its inbuilt characteristic regularities, we cannot guarantee it will work everywhere. This problem is due to the fact that the pseudo-random number sequence produced is fixed and devised separately from the contexts of its actual use. Still, empirical testing and application-specific analysis can provide safety measures against deficiencies (Hellekalek 1998). The goal is

Algorithms and Networking for Computer Games   Jouni Smed and Harri Hakonen
© 2006 John Wiley & Sons, Ltd

to find such methods that produce sequences that are *unlikely* to get 'synchronized' to their contexts. Other aspects that may affect the design of random number generators are the speed of the algorithm, ease of implementation, parallelization, and portability across platforms.

Before submerging in the wonderful world of pseudo-random numbers, let us take a small sidetrack and acknowledge that sometimes we can do quite well without randomness. Most people hardly consider the sequence $S = \langle 0, 1, 2, 3, 4, 5, 6, 7 \rangle$ random, because it is easy to come up with a rule that generates it: $S_{i+1} = (S_i + 1) \bmod m$. But how about the sequence $R = \langle 0, 4, 2, 6, 1, 5, 3, 7 \rangle$? There seems to be no direct relationship between two consecutive values, but as a whole the sequence has a structure: even numbers precede odd numbers. A bit-aware reader may soon realize that $R_i = \text{BIT-REVERSE}(i, 3)$ is a simple model that explains R. Then, how about the sequence $Q = \langle 0, 1, 3, 2, 6, 7, 5, 4 \rangle$? It seems to have no general structure, but the difference between consecutive pairs is always one, which is typical for a binary-reflected Gray code. From these simple examples, we can see that sequences can have properties that are useful in certain contexts. If these characteristics are not used or observed – or not even discovered! – the sequence can *appear* to be random. To make a distinction, these random-like (or 'randomish') numbers are usually called *quasi-random numbers*. Quasi-randomness can be preferable to pseudo-randomness, for example, when we want to have a sequence that has a certain inherent behaviour or when we can calculate the bijection of a value and its index in the sequence.

2.1   Linear Congruential Method

At the turn of the 1950s, D.H. Lehmer proposed an algorithm for generating random numbers. This algorithm is known as the *linear congruential method*, and since its inception it has stood the test of time quite firmly. The algorithm is simple to implement and only requires a rigorous choice of four fixed integer parameters:

$$
\begin{array}{rll}
\text{modulus:} & m & (0 < m) \\
\text{multiplier:} & a & (0 \le a < m) \\
\text{increment:} & c & (0 \le c < m) \\
\text{starting value:} & X_0 & (0 \le X_0 < m)
\end{array}
$$

On the basis of these parameters, we can now obtain a sequence of random numbers by setting

$$X_{i+1} = (aX_i + c) \bmod m \quad (0 \le i). \tag{2.1}$$

This recurrence produces a repeating sequence of numbers denoted by $\langle X_i \rangle_{i \ge 0}$. More generally, let us define

$$b = a - 1$$

and assume that

$$a \ge 2, \quad b \ge 1.$$

We can now generalize Equation (2.1) to

$$X_{i+k} = (a^k X_i + (a^k - 1)c/b) \bmod m \quad (k \ge 0, \ i \ge 0), \tag{2.2}$$

which expresses the $(i + k)$th term directly in terms of the ith term.

Algorithm 2.1 describes two implementation variants of the linear congruential method defined by Equation (2.1). The first one can be used when $a(m - 1)$ does not exceed the largest integer that can be represented by the machine word. For example, if m is a one-word integer, the product $a(m - 1)$ must be evaluated within a two-word integer. The second variant can be applied when $(m \bmod a) \leq \lfloor m/a \rfloor$. The idea is to express the modulus in the form $m = aq + p$ to guarantee that the intermediate evaluations always stay within the interval $(-m, m)$. For a further discussion on implementation, see Wichmann and Hill (1982), L'Ecuyer (1988), Park and Miller (1988), L'Ecuyer and Côté (1991), Bratley et al. (1983, pp. 201–202), and Knuth (1998b, Exercises 3.2.1.1-9 and 3.2.1.1-10).

Because computer numbers have a finite accuracy, m is usually set close to the maximum value of the computer's integer number range. If we want to generate random floating point numbers where U_i is distributed between zero (inclusive) and one (exclusive), we can use the fraction $U_i = X_i/m$ instead and call this routine RANDOM-UNIT().

What if we want a random integer number within a given interval of length w ($0 < w \leq m$)? A straightforward solution would be to use the Monte Carlo approach and let $Y_i = X_i \bmod w$ or – to put it in another way – to let $Y_i = \lfloor U_i w \rfloor$. However, the problem with this method is that the distribution is not guaranteed to be uniform (see Figure 2.1), but Monte Carlo methods allow to reduce the approximateness of the solution at the cost of the running time. In this case, we could increase the range of the original random number, for example, by generating several random numbers and combining them, which would make the distribution more uniform but would require more computation.

The Las Vegas approach guarantees exactness and gives a simple solution, a uniform distribution, to our problem. This method partitions the original interval

$$[0, m - 1] = \bigcup_{i=0}^{w-1} \left[i \left\lfloor \frac{m}{w} \right\rfloor, (i + 1) \left\lfloor \frac{m}{w} \right\rfloor - 1 \right] \cup \left[w \left\lfloor \frac{m}{w} \right\rfloor, m - 1 \right],$$

where i gives the value in the new interval ($0 \leq i \leq w - 1$). The last interval (if existing) is excess and considered invalid (see Figure 2.2). Algorithm 2.2 implements this partitioning by using integer division. If a generated number falls within the excess range, a new one is generated until it is valid. The obvious downside is that the termination of the algorithm is not guaranteed. Nevertheless, if we consider the worst case where $w = \frac{m}{2} + 1$, the probability of not finding a solution after i rounds is of magnitude $1/2^i$.

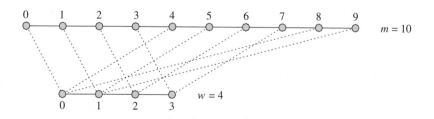

Figure 2.1   If $m = 10$ and $w = 4$, the Monte Carlo method does not provide a uniform distribution.

Algorithm 2.1 Linear congruential method for generating random integer numbers within the interval $[0, m)$.

RANDOM()
    out: random integer r ($0 \leq r \leq m - 1$)
    constant: modulus m; multiplier a; increment c; starting value X_0 ($1 \leq m \wedge 0 \leq$
                $a, c, X_0 \leq m - 1 \wedge a \leq i_{max}/(m - 1)$, where i_{max} is the largest possible in-
                teger value)
    local: previously generated random number x (initially $x = X_0$)
    1: $r \leftarrow (a \cdot x) \bmod m$
    2: $r \leftarrow$ MODULO-SUM(r, c, m)
    3: $x \leftarrow r$
    4: **return** r

RANDOM()
    out: random integer r ($0 \leq r \leq m - 1$)
    constant: modulus m; multiplier a; increment c; starting value X_0 ($1 \leq m \wedge 0 \leq$
                $a, c, X_0 \leq m - 1 \wedge (m \bmod a) \leq \lfloor m/a \rfloor$)
    local: previously generated random number x (initially $x = X_0$)
    1: $q \leftarrow m$ **div** a
    2: $p \leftarrow m$ **mod** a
    3: $r \leftarrow a \cdot (x \bmod q) - p \cdot (x \text{ div } q)$
    4: **if** $r < 0$ **then**
    5:     $r \leftarrow r + m$
    6: **end if**
    7: $r \leftarrow$ MODULO-SUM(r, c, m)
    8: $x \leftarrow r$
    9: **return** r

MODULO-SUM(x, y, m)
    in: addends x and y; modulo m ($0 \leq x, y \leq m - 1$)
    out: value $(x + y) \bmod m$ without intermediate overflows in $[0, m - 1]$
    1: **if** $x \leq m - 1 - y$ **then**
    2:    **return** $x + y$
    3: **else**
    4:    **return** $x - (m - y)$
    5: **end if**

2.1.1 Choice of parameters

Although the linear congruential method is simple to implement, the tricky part is choosing values for the four parameters. Let us have a look at how they should be chosen and how we can analyse their effect.

The linear congruential method generates a finite sequence of random numbers, after which the sequence begins to repeat. For example, if $m = 12$ and $X_0 = a = c = 5$, we get

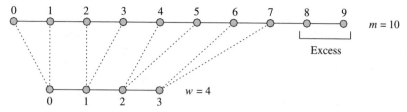

Figure 2.2 The Las Vegas method distributes the original interval uniformly by defining the excess area as invalid.

Algorithm 2.2 Las Vegas method for generating random integer numbers within the interval $[\ell, u)$.

RANDOM-INTEGER(ℓ, u)

    in: lower bound ℓ $(0 \leq \ell)$; upper bound u $(\ell < u \leq \ell + m)$

    out: random integer r $(\ell \leq r \leq u)$

    constant: modulus m used in RANDOM()

    local: the largest value w in the subinterval $[0, u - \ell] \subseteq [0, m - 1]$

    1: $w \leftarrow u - \ell$

    2: **repeat**

    3:    $r \leftarrow$ RANDOM() **div** (m **div** w)

    4: **until** $r < w$

    5: $r \leftarrow r + \ell$

    6: **return** r

---

the sequence

$$6, 11, 0, 5, 6, 11, 0, 5, \ldots$$

The repeating cycle is called a *period*, and, obviously, we want it to be as long as possible. Note that the values in the period of the linear congruential method are different, and it is impossible to have repetitions – unless we, for example, re-scale the interval with RANDOM-INTEGER(ℓ, u) or combine multiple sequences into one (Wichmann and Hill 1982). However, a long period does not guarantee randomness: The longest period of length m can always be reached by letting $a = c = 1$ (but you can hardly call the generated sequence random). Luckily, there are other values that reach the longest period, as the Theorem 2.1.1 shows.

Theorem 2.1.1 *The linear congruential sequence defined by integer parameters m, a, c, and X_0 has period length m if and only if*

  (i) *the greatest common divisor for c and m is 1,*

  (ii) *b is a multiple of each prime dividing m, and*

  (iii) *if m is a multiple of 4, then b is also a multiple of 4.*

We have denoted $b = a - 1$. For a proof, see (Knuth 1998b, pp. 17–19).

Modulus

Since the period cannot have more than m elements, the value of m should be large. Ideally m should be $i_{max} + 1$, where i_{max} is the maximum value of the integer value range. For example, if the machine word is unsigned and has 32 bits, we let $m = (2^{32} - 1) + 1 = 2^{32}$. In this case, the computation can eliminate the modulo operation completely. Similarly, if m is a power of two, the modulo operation can be replaced by a quicker bitwise-and operation. Unfortunately, these m values do not necessarily provide us with good sequences, not even if Theorem 2.1.1 holds.

Primes or Mersenne primes are much better choices for the value of m. A Mersenne prime is a prime of the form of $2^n - 1$; the first 10 Mersenne primes have $n = 2, 3, 5, 7, 13, 17, 19, 31, 61$, and 89 respectively. Quite conveniently, $2^{31} - 1$ is a Mersenne prime and thus it is often used with 32-bit machine words.

Multiplier

The multiplier a should be chosen so as to produce a period of maximum length. From Theorem 2.1.1 it follows that if m is the product of distinct primes, only when $a = 1$ we will get a full period. However, if m is divisible by a high power of some prime, we have more choices for a. There is a fundamental problem with small a values: If X_i is small, it is probable that X_{i+1} is also small. As a rule of thumb, the multiplier a should reside between 0.01 and $0.99m$, and its binary representation should not have a simple, regular bit pattern. For example, multipliers of the form $a = 2^x + 1$ $(2 \leq x)$ have a regular bit pattern and, therefore, tend to produce low-quality random sequences.

Increment

From Theorem 2.1.1 it also follows that the increment c can be chosen quite freely as long as it does not have a common factor with m (e.g. $c = 1$ or $c = a$). In many implementations $c = 0$, because it allows the elimination of one operation and makes the processing a bit faster. However, as Theorem 2.1.1 indicates, this cuts down the length of the period. Also, when $c = 0$, we must guarantee that $X_0 \neq 0$.

Starting value

The starting value (or *seed*) X_0 determines from where in the sequence the numbers are taken. A common oversight in the initialization is to always use the same seed value, because it leads to the same sequence of generated numbers. Usually this can be avoided by obtaining the seed value from the built-in clock of the computer, the last value from the previous run, user's mouse movements, previously handled keystrokes, or some other varying source.

2.1.2   Testing the randomness

Random number generators can be tested both empirically and theoretically. We omit the theoretical discussion and go through some rudiments of empirical tests; curious readers are referred to Knuth (1998b, Section 3.3). In most cases, the following tests are based on statistical tests (e.g. χ^2 or Kolmogorov–Smirnov) and they aim at providing some quantitative measures for randomness, when choosing between different parameter settings. Nevertheless, one should bear in mind that, although a random sequence might behave well in an existing test, there is no guarantee that it will pass a further test; each test gives us more confidence but can never banish our doubts.

Frequency test Are numbers distributed uniformly according to their frequencies?

Serial test Are pairs (triplets, quadruplets etc.) of successive numbers uniformly distributed in an independent manner?

Gap test Given a range of numbers, what is the distribution of the gaps between their occurrences in the sequence?

Poker test Group the sequence into poker hands each comprising five consecutive integers. Are the hands distributed as random poker hands should be?

Coupon collector's test What is the length of sequence required to get a complete set of given integers?

Permutation test Divide the sequence into groups of a given size. How often do different permutations occur?

Run test How long are the monotone segments (run-ups or run-downs of consecutive numbers) of the sequence?

Collision test If numbers are categorized with a hash function, how many collisions would occur?

Birthday spacings test If the numbers are hashed, how long are the spacings between them?

Spectral test If pairs (triplets, quadruples etc.) of successive numbers are treated as points in a hypercube, how uniformly would they fill it?

Spectral test is an important (and yet quite intuitive) test for analysing linear congruential random number generators. Moreover, we can rest assured that all good generators will pass the test and bad ones are likely to fail it. Although it is an empirical test and requires computation, it resembles theoretical tests in the sense that it deals with the properties of the full period.

Suppose we have a sequence of period m and we take t consecutive numbers of the sequence so that we have a set of points

$$\{(X_i, X_{i+1}, \ldots, X_{i+t-1}) \mid 0 \leq i < m\}$$

in t-dimensional space. For example, if $t = 2$, we can draw the points in a two-dimensional plane (see Figure 2.3). In this case, one can easily discern the parallel lines into which the points fall. This is an inherent property of the linear congruential methods: When t increases, the periodic accuracy decreases as there are fewer hyperplanes where the points can reside. In contrast, a truly random sequence would have the same accuracy in all dimensions.

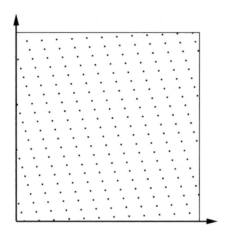

Figure 2.3 Two-dimensional spectral test results for the case where $m = 256$, $a = 21$, and $c = 11$.

2.1.3 Using the generators

Although the programmer implementing a random number generator must understand the theory behind the method, the user also has responsibilities. If one does not know the assumptions behind the linear congruential method, it can easily become a random number 'degenerator'. To prevent this from happening, let us go through some common pitfalls lurking in pseudo-random numbers generated by Equation (2.1).

- If $X_0 \neq 0$, the largest range of multiplicative linear congruential method $X_{i+1} = aX_i \bmod m$ is $[1, m - 1]$. However, the range of $U_i = X_i/m$ is not necessarily $(0, 1)$ if $1/m$ equals the value 0.0 or $(m - 1)/m$ equals the value 1.0, when rounded off. In other words, when converting random integers to decimal values, the characteristics of floating point arithmetic such as rounding must be considered and documented.

- Even if the sequence $\langle X_i \rangle_{i \geq 0}$ is well tested and appears to be random, it does not imply that $\langle f(X_i) \rangle_{i \geq 0}$ is also random. For this reason, one should not extract bits from X_i and expect them to have random properties. In fact, in linear congruential generators, the least significant bits tend to be less random than the most significant bits.

- The (pseudo-)randomness of a sequence $\langle X_i \rangle_{i \geq 0}$ does not imply any randomness for combinations (e.g. values in $\langle f(X_i, X_j) \rangle_{i,j \geq 0}$) or aggregations (e.g. pairs in $\langle (X_i, X_j) \rangle$). For example, if we take a bitwise exclusive-or of two pseudo-random numbers, the outcome can be totally non-random.

- If we select any subsequence of non-consecutive numbers from $\langle X_i \rangle_{i \geq 0}$, we cannot expect (without inspecting) this subsequence to have the same level of randomness. This is important especially when the same random number generator is shared among many sub-systems.

What is common to all of these situations is the fact that when the user modifies the sequence produced, he takes the role of the supplier with its accompanying responsibilities.

Although the theoretical and test results concerning a pseudo-random sequence do not automatically apply to a sequence derived from it, in practice long continuous blocks behave similarly to the whole sequence: When we test the pseudo-randomness of a sequence, the local inter-relationships are also measured and verified. This allows us to define multiple *parallel random number generators* from a single generator. Assume that the original generator $R = \langle X_i \rangle_{i \geq 0}$ has a period of length p and we need k parallel generators S_j $(j = 0, \ldots, k - 1)$. If we require that the parallel generators S_j must be disjoint and with equal lengths, they can have at most $\ell = \lfloor p/k \rfloor$ numbers from R. Now, if we define

$$S_j = \langle X_{\ell j}, X_{\ell j+1}, \ldots, X_{\ell j+(\ell-1)} \rangle = \langle X_{\ell j+i} \rangle_{i=0}^{\ell-1}, \tag{2.3}$$

subsequence S_j can be produced with the same implementation as R just by setting the seed to $X_{\ell j}$. Common wisdom says that the number of values generated from a linear congruential method should not exceed one thousandth of p (Knuth 1998b, p. 185), and thus we can have $k \geq 1000$ parallel generators from only one generator. For example, if $p = 2^{31} - 2$, we can define 1000 consecutive blocks of length $\ell = 2\,147\,483$ each. However, there are dependencies both within a block and between the blocks. Although a single block reflects the random-like properties of the original sequence, the block-wise correlations remain unknown until they are tested (Entacher 1999).

Table 2.1 presents five well tested multiplicative linear congruential methods and partitions them into 12 blocks of numbers. All of these generators have a Mersenne prime modulo $m = 2^{31} - 1 = 2\,147\,483\,647$, increment $c = 0$, and the same period length $p = 2^{31} - 2$. The multiplier $a = 16\,807 = 7^5$ is presented by Lewis et al. (1969), 39 373 by L'Ecuyer (1988), $41\,358 = 2 \cdot 3 \cdot 61 \cdot 113$ by L'Ecuyer et al. (1993), and both 48 271 and $69\,621 = 3 \cdot 23 \cdot 1009$ by Park and Miller (1988). All these generators can be implemented with the second variant of Algorithm 2.1. The blocks can be used as parallel generators, and we can draw about two million random numbers from each of them. For example, the seed of S_5 for the generator $X_{i+1} = 41\,358 \cdot X_i \bmod (2^{31} - 1)$ (where $X_0 = 1$) is $X_{894\,784\,850} = 9\,087\,743$. The values of Table 2.1 can also be used for verifying the implementations of these five generators.

2.2 Discrete Finite Distributions

Non-uniform random numbers are usually produced by combining uniform random numbers creatively (Knuth 1998b, Section 3.4). Distributions are usually described using a probability function. For example, if X is a random variable of n elementary events labelled as $\{0, 1, \ldots, n - 1\}$, the binomial distribution $\mathrm{Bin}(n, p)$ of X is defined as $p_k = P(X = k) = \binom{n}{k} p^k (1 - p)^{n-k}$ for $k = 0, 1, \ldots, n - 1$. A finite discrete distribution of n events can also be defined by listing the probabilities explicitly, $\{p_0, p_1, \ldots, p_{n-1}\}$, with the accompanying constraint $\sum_{i=0}^{n-1} p_i = 1$. However, if the probabilities are changing over time or if they are derived from separate calculations, the constraint may require an extra normalization step – but this can be avoided by relaxation: Instead of probabilities, each elementary event is given a weight value.

Algorithm 2.3 selects a random number r from a finite set $\{0, 1, \ldots, n - 1\}$. Each possible choice is associated with a weight, and the value r is selected with the probability

Table 2.1 Seed values X_{ℓ_j} of 12 parallel pseudo-random number generators S_j for five multiplicative linear congruential methods with multiplier a. The subsequences are $\ell = \lfloor (2^{31} - 2)/12 \rfloor = 178\,956\,970$ values apart from each others.

Block number j	Starting index ℓ_j	Multiplier a of the generator				
		16 807	39 373	41 358	48 271	69 621
0	0	1	1	1	1	1
1	178 956 970	1 695 056 031	129 559 008	289 615 684	128 178 418	1 694 409 695
2	357 913 940	273 600 077	1 210 108 086	1 353 057 761	947 520 058	521 770 721
3	536 870 910	1 751 115 243	881 279 780	1 827 749 946	1 501 823 498	304 319 863
4	715 827 880	2 134 894 400	1 401 015 190	1 925 115 505	406 334 307	1 449 974 771
5	894 784 850	1 522 630 933	649 553 291	9 087 743	539 991 689	69 880 877
6	1 073 741 820	939 811 632	388 125 325	1 242 165 306	1 290 683 230	994 596 602
7	1 252 698 790	839 436 708	753 392 767	1 088 988 122	1 032 093 784	1 446 470 955
8	1 431 655 760	551 911 115	1 234 047 880	1 487 897 448	390 041 908	1 348 226 252
9	1 610 612 730	1 430 160 775	1 917 314 738	535 616 434	2 115 657 586	1 729 938 365
10	1 789 569 700	1 729 719 750	615 965 832	1 294 221 370	1 620 264 524	2 106 684 069
11	1 968 526 670	490 674 121	301 910 397	1 493 238 629	1 789 935 850	343 628 718

$W_r / \Sigma_{i=0}^{n-1} W_i$. For example, for a uniform distribution $DU(n)$, each choice has the probability $1/n$, which is achieved using weights $W = \langle c, c, \ldots, c \rangle$ for any positive integer c. A simple geometric distribution $\text{Geom}(1/2)$ has the probability $1/2^{r+1}$ for a choice r, and it can be constructed using weights $W = \langle 2^{n-1}, 2^{n-2}, \ldots, 2^{n-1-r}, \ldots, 1 \rangle$. Note that W can be in any order, and $W_i = 0$ means that i cannot be selected.

Because the sequence S in Algorithm 2.3 is non-descending, line 10 can be implemented efficiently using a binary search that favours the leftmost of equal values (i.e. the one with the smallest index). Furthermore, lines 8 and 10 can be collapsed into one line by introducing a sentinel $S_{-1} \leftarrow 0$. Conversely, we can speed up the algorithm by replacing the sequence S with a Huffman tree, which gives an optimal search branching (Knuth 1998a, Section 2.3.4.5). If speed is absolutely crucial and many random numbers are generated from the same distribution, Walker's alias method can provide a better implementation (Kronmal and Peterson 1979; Matias *et al.* 1993).

Algorithm 2.3 Generating a random number from a distribution described by a finite sequence of weights.

RANDOM-FROM-WEIGHTS(W)
   in: sequence of n weights W describing the distribution ($W_i \in \mathbb{N}$ for $i = 0, \ldots, (n-1) \wedge 1 \le \Sigma_{i=0}^{n-1} W_i$)
   out: randomly selected index r according to W ($0 \le r \le m - 1$)
   1: $|S| \leftarrow n$ ▷ Reserve space for n integers.
   2: $S_0 \leftarrow W_0$
   3: **for** $i \leftarrow 1 \ldots (n-1)$ **do**   ▷ Collect prefix sums.
   4:    $S_i \leftarrow S_{i-1} + W_i$
   5: **end for**
   6: $k \leftarrow$ RANDOM-INTEGER($1, S_{n-1} + 1$)   ▷ Random $k \in [1, S_{n-1}]$.
   7: **if** $k \le S_0$ **then**
   8:    $r \leftarrow 0$
   9: **else**
   10:    $r \leftarrow$ smallest index i for which $S_{i-1} < k \le S_i$ when $i = 1, \ldots, n - 1$
   11: **end if**
   12: **return** r

2.3 Random Shuffling

In random shuffling we want to generate a *random permutation*, where all permutations have a uniform random distribution. We can even consider random shuffling as inverse sorting, where we are aiming at not permutations fulfilling some sorting criterion but all permutations. Although methods based on card shuffling or other real-world analogues can generate random permutations, their distribution can be far from uniform. Hence, better methods are needed.

Suppose we have an ordered set $S = \langle s_1, \ldots, s_n \rangle$ to be shuffled. If n is small, we can enumerate all the possible $n!$ permutations and obtain a random permutation quickly by generating a random integer between 1 and $n!$. Algorithm 2.4 produces all the permutations of $\langle 0, \ldots, n-1 \rangle$. To optimize, we can unroll the while loop at lines 23–28, because it is entered at most twice. For $3 \leq n$, the body of the while loop at lines 18–22 is entered at most $(n-2)$ times in every $(2n)$th iteration of the repeat loop. Also, line 29 is unnecessary when $n \geq 2$. For a further discussion and other solution methods, see Knuth (2005, Section 7.2.1.2) and Sedgewick (1977).

In most cases, generating all the permutations is not a practical approach (e.g. $9! > 2^{16}$, $13! > 2^{32}$ and $21! > 2^{64}$). Instead, we can shuffle S by doing random sampling without replacement: Initially, let an ordered set $R = \langle \rangle$. Select a random element from S iteratively and transfer it to R, until $S = \langle \rangle$. To convince ourselves that the distribution of the generated permutations is uniform, let us analyse the probabilities of element selections. Every element has a probability $1/n$ to become selected into the first position. The selected element cannot appear in any other position, and the subsequent positions are filled with the remaining $n-1$ elements. Because the selections are independent, the probability of any generated ordered set is

$$1/n \cdot 1/(n-1) \cdot 1/(n-2) \cdot \ldots \cdot 1/1 = 1/n!.$$

Hence, the generated ordered sets have a uniform distribution, since there are exactly $n!$ possible permutations. Algorithm 2.5 realizes this approach by constructing the solution in-place within the ordered set R.

Let us take a look at why the more 'naturalistic' methods often fail. Figure 2.4 illustrates a riffle shuffle, which is a common method when a human dealer shuffles playing cards. Knowledge about shuffling has been used by gamblers – which is why nowadays casinos use mechanisms employing other strategies, which, in turn, can turn out to be surprisingly inadequate (Mackenzie 2002) – and magicians in card tricks. Let us look at a simplification of a card trick named 'Premo' (Bayer and Diaconis 1992). Suppose we have a deck of cards arranged in the following order:

2 3 4 5 6 7 8 9 10 J Q K A 2 3 4 5 6 7 8 9 10 J Q K A
♡ ♡ ♡ ♡ ♡ ♡ ♡ ♡ ♡ ♡ ♡ ♡ ♡ ◇ ◇ ◇ ◇ ◇ ◇ ◇ ◇ ◇ ◇ ◇ ◇ ◇

2 3 4 5 6 7 8 9 10 J Q K A 2 3 4 5 6 7 8 9 10 J Q K A
♣ ♣ ♣ ♣ ♣ ♣ ♣ ♣ ♣ ♣ ♣ ♣ ♣ ♠ ♠ ♠ ♠ ♠ ♠ ♠ ♠ ♠ ♠ ♠ ♠ ♠

A magician gives the deck to a spectator and asks her to give it two riffle shuffles. Next, the spectator is asked to remove the top (here the leftmost) card, memorize its value, and

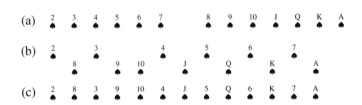

Figure 2.4 In riffle shuffle the deck is divided into two packets, which are riffled together by interleaving them.

Algorithm 2.4 Generating all permutations.

ALL-PERMUTATIONS(n)
  in: number of elements n ($1 \leq n$)
  out: sequence R containing all permutations of the sequence $\langle 0, 1, \ldots, (n-1) \rangle$
           ($|R| = n!$)
  local: index r of the result sequence
  1: $|R| \leftarrow n!$ ▷ Reserve space for $n!$ sequences.
  2: **for** $i \leftarrow 0 \ldots (n-1)$ **do**   ▷ Initialize C, O, and S of length n.
  3:    $C_i \leftarrow 0$; $O_i \leftarrow 1$; $S_i \leftarrow i$
  4: **end for**
  5: $r \leftarrow 0$
  6: **repeat**
  7:    $j \leftarrow n - 1$
  8:    $s \leftarrow 0$
  9:    $q \leftarrow C_j + O_j$

10:    **for** $i \leftarrow 0 \ldots (n-2)$ **do**
11:      $R_r \leftarrow$ **copy** S; $r \leftarrow r + 1$
12:      $\alpha \leftarrow j - C_j + s$; $\beta \leftarrow j - q + s$
13:      swap $S_\alpha \leftrightarrow S_\beta$
14:      $C_j \leftarrow q$
15:      $q \leftarrow C_j + O_j$
16:    **end for**
17:    $R_r \leftarrow$ **copy** S; $r \leftarrow r + 1$

18:    **while** $q < 0$ **do**
19:      $O_j \leftarrow -O_j$
20:      $j \leftarrow j - 1$
21:      $q \leftarrow C_j + O_j$
22:    **end while**
23:    **while** $q = (j + 1)$ **and** $j \neq 0$ **do**
24:      $s \leftarrow s + 1$
25:      $O_j \leftarrow -O_j$
26:      $j \leftarrow j - 1$
27:      $q \leftarrow C_j + O_j$
28:    **end while**
29:    **if** $j \neq 0$ **then**
30:      $\alpha \leftarrow j - C_j + s$; $\beta \leftarrow j - q + s$
31:      swap $S_\alpha \leftrightarrow S_\beta$
32:      $C_j \leftarrow q$
33:    **end if**
34: **until** $j = 0$
35: **return** R

Algorithm 2.5 Random shuffle.

SHUFFLE(S)
  in: ordered set S
  out: shuffled ordered set R
  1: $R \leftarrow$ **copy** S
  2: **for** $i \leftarrow 0 \ldots (|R| - 2)$ **do**
  3:   $j \leftarrow$ RANDOM-INTEGER$(i, |R|)$
  4:    swap $R_i \leftrightarrow R_j$
  5: **end for**
  6: **return** R

---

insert it into the pack. The magician has now a deck, which could look like this:

J 2 K Q A 3 2 K A A 3 4 2 2 4 5 K 3 3 5 4 4 6 6 5 5
♦ ♡ ♡ ♦ ♣ ♠ ♡ ♠ ♡ ♦ ♠ ♡ ♦ ♣ ♠ ♡ ♠ ♦ ♣ ♠ ♣ ♠ ♡ ♡ ♠ ♦

7 7 6 8 8 6 7 9 8 7 9 10 9 8 10 J 10 Q J 9 J K Q 10 Q A
♡ ♠ ♣ ♠ ♡ ♦ ♣ ♠ ♣ ♦ ♡ ♠ ♣ ♦ ♡ ♠ ♣ ♠ ♣ ♦ ♡ ♠ ♣ ♦ ♡ ♠

Glancing at the deck, the magician can easily determine which is the chosen card[1]. After two shuffles the deck has four rising sequences of cards (hint: look at each suit), and the inserted card is very likely to break one such run. In fact, if the magician has only one guess, the probability of success is 0.997. The original Premo trick allows the spectator to do three riffle shuffles. If the magician has one guess, the probability of success is still as high as 0.839; with two guesses it increases to 0.943. However, if the spectator does four riffle shuffles, the probability of success with one and two guesses drops to 0.288 and 0.471. This is known as a cut-off phenomenon, where the 'randomness' of the deck suddenly increases at some point during the shuffling (Aldous and Diaconis 1986). How should one then shuffle? For a deck of 52 cards, the consensus is that at least seven riffle shuffles is enough for most purposes – assuming the players have mere human cognitive and computational skills.

2.4 Creating Game Worlds

Despite the obvious uses for random numbers in computer games – such as generating events, monsters, or decisions – the deterministic nature of pseudo-random numbers allows us to utilize them in other contexts as well. In this section we study two cases, which use pseudo-random numbers for creating the game world. A third example case of pseudo-random numbers, synchronized simulation, is described in Section 9.5.

2.4.1 Starmap generation

In 1984 David Braben and Ian Bell released a computer game on interstellar trading. In addition to the trading system and three-dimensional space simulation, they managed to fit

---

[1] Answer: The King of clubs.

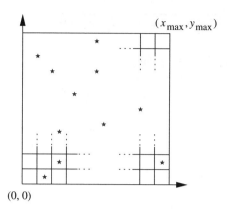

Figure 2.5 The positions in a two-dimensional galaxy are enumerated row by row starting from the origin.

eight galaxies filled with hundreds of stars, each with unique characteristics, into the 32 kB memory of a BBC Micro computer. The game is called *Elite*, and it uses pseudo-random number generation quite cleverly to compress the whole game world.

Suppose we have a two-dimensional galaxy that we want to populate with stars (see Figure 2.5). Further, suppose the galaxy is finite and discrete, where each position (x, y) can represent either a star or void space. Let d be the density of the galaxy (i.e. the ratio between the stars and the void). We can now enumerate each position, for example, row by row starting from the origin: $(0, 0)$, $(0, 1)$, ..., $(0, y_{max})$, $(1, 0)$, $(1, 1)$, ..., (x_{max}, y_{max}). By using this order, we generate a random number from the interval $[0, 1)$ for each position. If the generated number is greater than the density, the position is empty; otherwise, it is populated with a star and we generate a random number for it. This method is illustrated in the first part of Algorithm 2.6, which assumes that we have a function SET-SEED(v) for (re)setting the seed value used in Algorithm 2.1 (i.e. after the call $x = v$). If we want to conserve memory (as always, with the cost of computation time), we could use Equation (2.2) to generate a random number for a given position immediately without the need to generate the whole galaxy at once.

Each star is now associated with a random number, which is used as a new seed value when creating star-related characteristics such as name, size, and composition (see Figure 2.6). These characteristics can be extended to the planets in the star system, as the second part of Algorithm 2.6 illustrates. We could continue refining this hierarchy into smaller and smaller details (from a planet to continents to states to towns to citizens etc.), always using a seed value generated on the upper level as a basis for the next level (Lecky-Thompson 1999).

If we have constructed a galaxy in this way, we can compress it down to the initial seed value, which is then stored for later use. Since the pseudo-random numbers are deterministic, we can create the very same galaxy, down to the minute details, time and again from this one number.

Algorithm 2.6 Method for generating stars and planets.

CREATE-STARS(v)

    in: seed value v of the galaxy

    out: matrix G of seed values for the stars

    constant: maximum horizontal value x_{max}; maximum vertical value y_{max}; density d
              $(0 \le d \le 1)$

  1: $rows(G) \leftarrow x_{max} + 1$ ▷ Rows for the x-axis.

  2: $columns(G) \leftarrow y_{max} + 1$ ▷ Columns for the y-axis.

  3: SET-SEED(v)

  4: **for** $x \leftarrow 0 \ldots x_{max}$ **do**

  5:    **for** $y \leftarrow 0 \ldots y_{max}$ **do**

  6:      **if** RANDOM-UNIT() $< d$ **then**

  7:        $G_{x,y} \leftarrow$ RANDOM()   ▷ Create a star.

  8:      **else**

  9:        $G_{x,y} \leftarrow$ NIL   ▷ Void space.

10:      **end if**

11:    **end for**

12: **end for**

13: **return** G

CREATE-PLANETS(v)

    in: seed value v of the star system

    out: ordered set P of seed values for the planets

    constant: minimum number of planets p_{min}; maximum number of planets p_{max}

    local: number of planets p

  1: SET-SEED(v)

  2: $p \leftarrow$ RANDOM-INTEGER($p_{min}, p_{max} + 1$)

  3: **for** $i \leftarrow 0 \ldots (p - 1)$ **do**

  4:    $P_i \leftarrow$ RANDOM()

  5: **end for**

  6: **return** P

2.4.2 Terrain generation

Random numbers can be used to generate the terrain for a game world. To simplify this process, let us divide the terrain into discrete points (e.g. using a grid; see Section 5.1.1), each of which has a value representing the height of the terrain at that position. These points form a *height map*, which is a matrix comprising the height values (see Figure 2.7). Height maps are often illustrated with grey-scale pictures, where brightness is associated with the height (i.e. darker pixels represent lower ground and brighter pixels represent higher ground).

Algorithm 2.7 gives a straightforward implementation where a randomly generated number is assigned to each point in the height map. Unfortunately, the resulting terrain is too

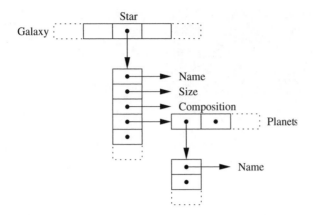

Figure 2.6 The seed value is used to create the characteristics of the star including the rest of the star system.

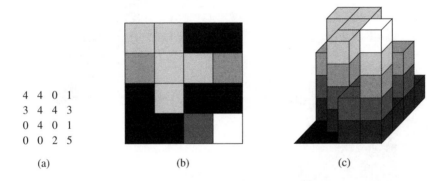

4	4	0	1
3	4	4	3
0	4	0	1
0	0	2	5

(a)   (b)   (c)

Figure 2.7 A height map divides the terrain into a grid: (a) the height values in a matrix, (b) the corresponding grey-scale picture, and (c) the corresponding isometric grey-scale picture.

Algorithm 2.7 Generating simple random terrain.

SIMPLE-RANDOM-TERRAIN()
    out: height map H (H is rectangular)
    constant: maximum height $h_{\max}$
    1: **for** $x \leftarrow 0 \ldots (columns(H) - 1)$ **do**
    2:   **for** $y \leftarrow 0 \ldots (rows(H) - 1)$ **do**
    3:     $H_{x,y} \leftarrow$ RANDOM-UNIT() $\cdot h_{\max}$ $\triangleright H_{x,y} \in [0, h_{\max})$.
    4:   **end for**
    5: **end for**
    6: **return** H

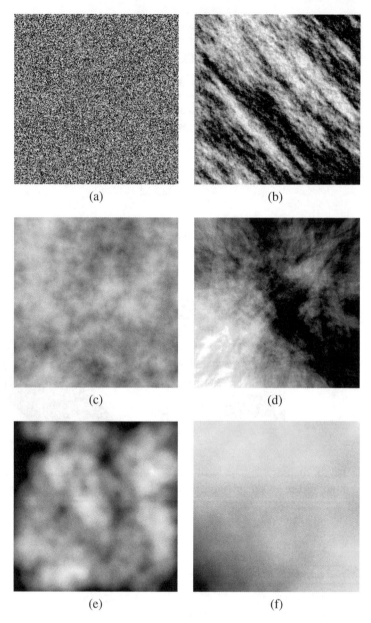

Figure 2.8 Randomly generated terrains where $h_{max} = 256$. (a) Simple random terrain. (b) Limited random terrain where $d_{max} = 64$. (c) Particle deposition terrain where $m = 10^7$, $i = 1$ and $b = 4$. (d) Fault line terrain where $f = 1000$ and $c = 2$. (e) Circle hill terrain where $c = 400$, $r = 32$ and $s = 16$. (f) Midpoint displacement terrain using diamond square where $d_{max} = 128$ and $s = 1$.

Algorithm 2.8 Generating limited random terrain.

LIMITED-RANDOM-TERRAIN()
    out: height map H (H is rectangular)
    local: average height of northern and western neighbours a; height h
    constant: maximum height h_{max}; maximum height difference d_{max}
  1: **for** $x \leftarrow 0 \ldots (columns(H) - 1)$ **do**
  2:   **for** $y \leftarrow 0 \ldots (rows(H) - 1)$ **do**
  3:     **if** $x \neq 0$ **and** $y \neq 0$ **then**
  4:       $a \leftarrow \left(H_{(x-1),y} + H_{x,(y-1)} \right) / 2$
  5:     **else if** $x \neq 0$ **and** $y = 0$ **then**
  6:       $a \leftarrow H_{(x-1),y}$
  7:     **else**
  8:       $a \leftarrow$ RANDOM-UNIT() $\cdot h_{max}$
  9:     **end if**
 10:     $h \leftarrow a + d_{max} \cdot ($RANDOM-UNIT$() - 1/2)$
 11:     $H_{x,y} \leftarrow \max\{0, \min\{h, h_{max}\}\}$ ▷ $H_{x,y} \in [0, h_{max}]$.
 12:   **end for**
 13: **end for**
 14: **return** H

---

noisy to resemble any landscape in the real world, as we can see in Figure 2.8(a). To smoothen the terrain, we can set a range within which the random value can vary (see Algorithm 2.8). Since the range depends on the heights already assigned (i.e. the neighbours to the west and the north), the generated terrain has diagonal ridges going to the south-east, as illustrated in Figure 2.8(b).

Instead of generating random height values, we can randomize the process of formation. In *particle deposition* method, 'grains' are dropped randomly on the terrain and they are allowed to pile up (see Algorithm 2.9). The height difference between neighbouring points is limited. If the grain dropped causes the height difference to exceed this limit, the grain falls down to a neighbouring point until it reaches an equilibrium (see Figure 2.9). The grains are dropped following Brownian movement, where the next drop point is selected randomly from the neighbourhood of the current drop point. The resulting terrain is illustrated in Figure 2.8(c).

Random numbers can also be used to select *fault lines* in the terrain. The height difference between the sides of a fault line is increased as shown in Figure 2.10. Algorithm 2.10 gives an implementation where we first randomly select two points (x_0, y_0) and (x_1, y_1). To calculate the fault line going through these points, we form a vector $\bar{v}$ with components $\bar{v}_x = x_1 - x_0$ and $\bar{v}_y = y_1 - y_0$. Thereafter, for each point (x, y) in the terrain, we can form a vector $\bar{w}$ for which $\bar{w}_x = x - x_0$ and $\bar{w}_y = y - y_0$. When we calculate the cross product $\bar{u} = \bar{v} \times \bar{w}$, depending on the sign of $\bar{u}_z$ we know whether the terrain at the point (x, y) has to be lowered or lifted:

$$\bar{u}_z = \bar{v}_x \bar{w}_y - \bar{v}_y \bar{w}_x.$$

An example of the fault line terrain can be seen in Figure 2.8(d).

Algorithm 2.9 Generating particle deposition terrain.

PARTICLE-DEPOSITION-TERRAIN(m)
  in: number of movements m
  out: height map H (H is rectangular)
  1: $p \leftarrow \langle$RANDOM-INTEGER$(0, columns(H))$, RANDOM-INTEGER$(0, rows(H))\rangle$
  2: **for** $i \leftarrow 1 \ldots m$ **do**
  3:    $\langle p', i'\rangle \leftarrow$ INCREASE(H, p) ▷ Increase i' that fits to $H_{p'}$.
  4:    $H_{p'} \leftarrow H_{p'} + i'$
  5:    $p \leftarrow$ BROWNIAN-MOVEMENT(H, p)
  6: **end for**
  7: **return** H

BROWNIAN-MOVEMENT(H, p)
  in: height map H; position p
  out: neighbouring position of p
  1: **case** RANDOM-INTEGER$(0, 4)$ **of**
  2:   0 : **return** EAST-NEIGHBOUR(H, p)
  3:   1 : **return** WEST-NEIGHBOUR(H, p)
  4:   2 : **return** SOUTH-NEIGHBOUR(H, p)
  5:   3 : **return** NORTH-NEIGHBOUR(H, p)
  6: **end case**

INCREASE(H, p)
  in: height map H; position p
  out: pair $\langle$position, increase$\rangle$
  constant: increase i; maximum height h_{max}
  1: $i' \leftarrow \min\{h_{max} - H_p, i\}$ ▷ Proper amount for increase.
  2: $n \leftarrow$ UNBALANCED-NEIGHBOUR(H, p, i')
  3: **if** $n = $ NIL **then return** $\langle p, i'\rangle$
  4: **else return** INCREASE(H, n)
  5: **end if**

UNBALANCED-NEIGHBOUR(H, p, i')
  in: height map H; position p; increase i' that fits to H_p
  out: neighbour of p which exceeds b or otherwise NIL
  constant: height difference threshold b
  1: $e \leftarrow$ EAST-NEIGHBOUR(H, p); $w \leftarrow$ WEST-NEIGHBOUR(H, p)
  2: $s \leftarrow$ SOUTH-NEIGHBOUR(H, p); $n \leftarrow$ NORTH-NEIGHBOUR(H, p)
  3: **if** $H_p + i' - H_e > b$ **then return** e
  4: **if** $H_p + i' - H_w > b$ **then return** w
  5: **if** $H_p + i' - H_s > b$ **then return** s
  6: **if** $H_p + i' - H_n > b$ **then return** n
  7: **return** NIL

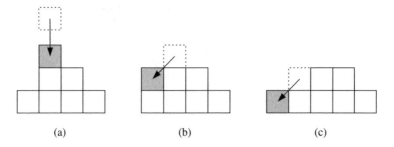

Figure 2.9 In particle deposition, each grain dropped falls down until it reaches an equilibrium. If the threshold $b = 1$, the grey grain moves downwards until the difference compared
to the height of neighbourhood is at most b.

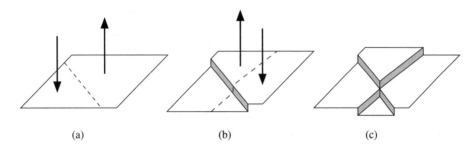

Figure 2.10 Fault lines are selected randomly. The terrain is raised on one side of the fault
line and lowered on the other.

Instead of fault lines, we can use *hills* to simulate real-world terrain formation. Random
numbers can be used to select the place for the hills. Algorithm 2.11 gives a simple method,
where every hill is in a circle with the same diameter and the height increase is based on
the cosine function. The resulting terrain is shown in Figure 2.8(e).

Random *midpoint displacement* method, introduced by Fournier *et al.* (1982), starts by
first setting the heights for the corner points of the terrain. After that, it subdivides the
region inside iteratively using two steps (see Figure 2.11):

 (i) *The diamond step*: Taking a square of four corner points, generate a random value
     at the diamond point (i.e. the centre of the square), where the two diagonals meet.
     The value is calculated by averaging the four corner values and by adding a random
     displacement value.

(ii) *The square step*: Taking each diamond of four corner points, generate a random value
     at the square point (i.e. the centre of the diamond). The value is calculated by averaging
     the corner values and by adding a random displacement value.

Variations on these steps are presented by Miller (1986) and Lewis (1987).

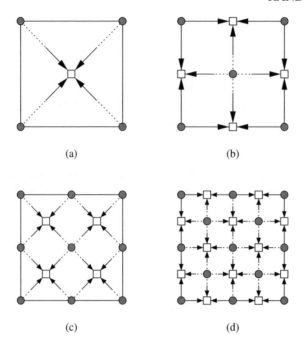

(a)   (b)

(c)   (d)

Figure 2.11 Midpoint displacement method consists of the diamond step, shown in subfigures (a) and (c), and the square step, shown in subfigures (b) and (d). The circles represent
the calculated values.

To make the implementation easier, we limit the size of the height map to $n \times n$, where

$$n = 2^k + 1$$

when the integer $k \geq 0$. Algorithm 2.12 gives an implementation, where the subroutine
DISPLACEMENT(H, x, y, S, d) returns the height value for position (x, y) in height map H

$$d + \frac{1}{4} \cdot \sum_{i=0}^{3} H_{(x+S_{2i}),(y+S_{2i+1})},$$

where S defines the point offsets from (x, y) in the square or diamond, and d is the current
height displacement.

   In addition to the methods described here, there are approaches such as fractal noise
(Perlin 1985) or stream erosion (Kelley *et al.* 1988) for terrain generation. Moreover, existing height maps can be modified using image processing methods (e.g. sharpening and
smoothing).

2.5 Summary

If we try to generate random numbers using a deterministic method, we end up generating pseudo-random numbers. The linear congruential method – which is basically just

---

Algorithm 2.10 Generating fault line terrain.

FAULT-LINE-TERRAIN()

    out: height map H (H is rectangular)

    constant: maximum height h_{max}; number of fault lines f; fault change c

 1: $H \leftarrow$ LEVEL-TERRAIN$(h_{max}/2)$ $\triangleright$ Initialize the terrain to flat.

 2: **for** $i \leftarrow 1 \ldots f$ **do**

 3:    $x_0 \leftarrow$ RANDOM-INTEGER$(0, columns(H))$

 4:    $y_0 \leftarrow$ RANDOM-INTEGER$(0, rows(H))$

 5:    $x_1 \leftarrow$ RANDOM-INTEGER$(0, columns(H))$

 6:    $y_1 \leftarrow$ RANDOM-INTEGER$(0, rows(H))$

 7:    **for** $x \leftarrow 0 \ldots (columns(H) - 1)$ **do**

 8:      **for** $y \leftarrow 0 \ldots (rows(H) - 1)$ **do**

 9:       **if** $(x_1 - x_0) \cdot (y - y_0) - (y_1 - y_0) \cdot (x - x_0) > 0$ **then**

10:         $H_{x,y} \leftarrow \min\{H_{x,y} + c, h_{max}\}$

11:       **else**

12:         $H_{x,y} \leftarrow \max\{H_{x,y} - c, 0\}$

13:       **end if**

14:      **end for**

15:    **end for**

16: **end for**

17: **return** H

Algorithm 2.11 Generating circle hill terrain.

CIRCLE-HILL-TERRAIN()

    out: height map H (H is rectangular)

    constant: maximum height h_{max}; number of circles c; circle radius r; circle height
                increase s

    local: centre of the circle (x', y')

 1: **for** $i \leftarrow 1 \ldots c$ **do**

 2:    $x' \leftarrow$ RANDOM-INTEGER$(0, columns(H))$

 3:    $y' \leftarrow$ RANDOM-INTEGER$(0, rows(H))$

 4:    **for** $x \leftarrow 0 \ldots (columns(H) - 1)$ **do**

 5:      **for** $y \leftarrow 0 \ldots (rows(H) - 1)$ **do**

 6:      $d \leftarrow (x' - x)^2 + (y' - y)^2$

 7:      **if** $d < r^2$ **then**

 8:        $a \leftarrow (s/2) \cdot (1 + \cos(\pi d / r^2))$

 9:        $H_{x,y} \leftarrow \min\{H_{x,y} + a, h_{max}\}$

10:      **end if**

11:      **end for**

12:    **end for**

13: **end for**

14: **return** H

Algorithm 2.12 Generating midpoint displacement terrain.

Midpoint-Displacement-Terrain()
    out: height map H ($columns(H) = rows(H) = n = 2^k + 1$ when $k \geq 0$)
    constant: maximum displacement d_{max}; smoothness s
1: initialize $H_{0,0}$, $H_{column(H)-1,0}$, $H_{0,row(H)-1}$ and $H_{column(H)-1,row(H)-1}$
2: $m \leftarrow (n - 1)$; $c \leftarrow 1$; $d \leftarrow d_{max}$
3: **while** $m \geq 2$ **do**
4:    $w \leftarrow m/2$; $x \leftarrow w$
5:    **for** $i \leftarrow 0 \ldots (c - 1)$ **do**   ▷ Centres.
6:      $y \leftarrow w$
7:      **for** $j \leftarrow 0 \ldots (c - 1)$ **do**
8:        $H_{x,y} \leftarrow$ Displacement$(H, x, y, \langle -w, -w, -w, +w, +w, -w, +w, +w \rangle, d)$
9:        $y \leftarrow y + m$
10:     **end for**
11:    $x \leftarrow x + m$
12:   **end for**
13:   $x \leftarrow x - w$; $t \leftarrow w$
14:   **for** $p \leftarrow 0 \ldots (c - 1)$ **do**   ▷ Borders.
15:     $H_{0,t} \leftarrow$ Displacement$(H, 0, t, \langle 0, -w, 0, +w, +w, 0, +w, 0 \rangle, d)$
16:     $H_{t,0} \leftarrow$ Displacement$(H, t, 0, \langle -w, 0, +w, 0, 0, +w, 0, +w \rangle, d)$
17:     $H_{t,x} \leftarrow$ Displacement$(H, t, x, \langle -w, 0, +w, 0, 0, -w, 0, -w \rangle, d)$
18:     $H_{x,t} \leftarrow$ Displacement$(H, x, t, \langle 0, -w, 0, +w, -w, 0, -w, 0 \rangle, d)$
19:     $t \leftarrow t + m$
20:   **end for**
21:   $x \leftarrow m$
22:   **for** $i \leftarrow 0 \ldots (c - 2)$ **do**   ▷ Middle horizontal.
23:     $y \leftarrow w$
24:     **for** $j \leftarrow 0 \ldots (c - 1)$ **do**
25:       $H_{x,y} \leftarrow$ Displacement$(H, x, y, \langle -w, 0, +w, 0, 0, -w, 0, +w \rangle, d)$
26:       $y \leftarrow y + m$
27:     **end for**
28:     $x \leftarrow x + m$
29:   **end for**
30:   $x \leftarrow w$
31:   **for** $i \leftarrow 0 \ldots (c - 1)$ **do**   ▷ Middle vertical.
32:     $y \leftarrow m$
33:     **for** $j \leftarrow 0 \ldots (c - 2)$ **do**
34:       $H_{x,y} \leftarrow$ Displacement$(H, x, y, \langle -w, 0, +w, 0, 0, -w, 0, +w \rangle, d)$
35:       $y \leftarrow y + m$
36:     **end for**
37:     $x \leftarrow x + m$
38:   **end for**
39:   $m \leftarrow m/2$; $c \leftarrow c \cdot 2$; $d \leftarrow d \cdot 2^{-s}$
40: **end while**
41: **return** H

---

a recursive multiplication equation – is one of the simplest, oldest, and the most studied of such methods. Pseudo-randomness differs in many respects from true randomness, and common sense does not always apply when we are generating pseudo-random numbers. For example, a pseudo-random sequence cannot usually be modified and operated as freely as a true random sequence. Therefore, the design of a pseudo-random number generator must be done with great care – and this implies that the user also has to understand the underlying limitations.

We can introduce randomness into a deterministic algorithm to have a controlled variation of its output. This enables us, for example, to create game worlds that resemble the real world but still include randomly varying attributes. Moreover, we can choose a deterministic algorithm randomly, which can be a good decision-making policy when we do not have any guiding information on what the next step should be. A random decision is the safest choice in the long run, since it reduces the likelihood of making bad decisions (as well as good ones).

Exercises

2-1 A friend gives you the following random number generator:

My-Random()

out:	random integer r
constant:	modulus m; starting value X_0
local:	previously generated random number x (initially $x = X_0$)

1: **if** $x \bmod 2 = 0$ **then**
2:    $r \leftarrow (x + 3) \cdot 5$
3: **else if** $x \bmod 3 = 0$ **then**
4:    $r \leftarrow (x + 5) \boxplus 314159265$ ▷ Bitwise exclusive-or.
5: **else if** $x \bmod 5 = 0$ **then**
6:    $r \leftarrow x^2$
7: **else**
8:    $r \leftarrow x + 7$
9: **end if**
10: $r \leftarrow r \bmod m$; $x \leftarrow r$
11: **return** r

How can you verify how well (or poorly) it works?

2-2 In the discussion on the design of random number generators (p. 24–25), parallelization and portability across platforms have been mentioned. Why are they considered as important issues?

2-3 The Las Vegas approach is not guaranteed to terminate. What is the probability that the repeat loop of Algorithm 2.2 continues after 100 rounds when $m = 100$ and $w = 9$?

2-4 An obvious variant to the linear congruential method is to choose its parameters randomly. Is the result of this new algorithm more random than the original?

2-5 Random number generators are as good as they perform on the tests. What would happen if someone comes up with a test where the linear congruential method performs poorly?

2-6 Does the following algorithm produce a unit vector (i.e. with length one) starting from the origin towards a random direction? Verify your answer by writing a program that visualizes the angle distributions with respect to the x-axis.

> My-Vector()
>
> **out:** unit vector (x', y') towards a random direction
> 1: $x \leftarrow 2 \cdot$ Random-Unit$() - 1$
> 2: $y \leftarrow 2 \cdot$ Random-Unit$() - 1$
> 3: $\ell \leftarrow \sqrt{x^2 + y^2}$ ▷ Distance from $(0, 0)$ to (x, y).
> 4: **return** $(x/\ell, y/\ell)$ ▷ Scale to the unit circle.

2-7 Let us define functions c and s from domain $(0, 1) \times (0, 1)$ to codomain $\mathbb{R}$:

$$c(x, y) = \sqrt{-2 \ln x} \cos(2\pi y), \qquad s(x, y) = \sqrt{-2 \ln x} \sin(2\pi y).$$

If we have two independent uniform random numbers $U_0, U_1 \in (0, 1)$, then $c(U_0, U_1)$ and $s(U_0, U_1)$ are independent random numbers from the standard normal distribution $N(0, 1)$ (i.e. with a mean of zero and a standard deviation of one) (Box and Muller 1958). In other words, if we aggregate combinations of independent uniform values, we have a normally distributed two-dimensional 'cloud' C of points around the origin:

$$C = \langle (c(U_{2i}, U_{2i+1}), s(U_{2i}, U_{2i+1})) \rangle_{i \geq 0}.$$

However, if we use any linear congruential method for generating these uniform values (i.e. $U_{2i} = X_{2i}/m$ and $U_{2i+1} = X_{2i+1}/m$), the independence requirement is not met. Curiously, in this case all the points in C fall on a single two-dimensional spiral and, therefore, cannot be considered normally distributed (Bratley *et al.* 1983). The effect can be analysed mathematically. To demonstrate how hard it is to recognize this defect experimentally, implement a program that draws the points of C using the linear congruential generator $a = 7^5$, $c = 0$, and $m = 2^{31} - 1$ (Lewis *et al.* 1969). Observe the effect using the following example generators:

- $a = 799$, $c = 0$, and $m = 2^{11} - 9$ (L'Ecuyer 1999)
- $a = 137$, $c = 187$, and $m = 2^8$ (Knuth 1998b, p. 94)
- $a = 78$, $c = 0$, and $m = 2^7 - 1$ (Entacher 1999).

What can be learned from this exercise?

2-8 Suppose we are satisfied with the linear congruential method with parameter values $a = 799$, $c = 0$, and $m = 2039 = 2^{11} - 9$ (L'Ecuyer 1999). If we change the multiplier a to value 393, what happens to the generated sequence? Can you explain why? What does this mean when we test randomness of these two generators?

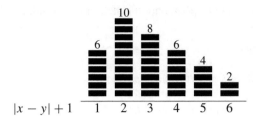

$$|x - y| + 1 \qquad 1 \quad 2 \quad 3 \quad 4 \quad 5 \quad 6$$

Figure 2.12 Probability distribution of a phantom die $|x - y| + 1$ when x and y are integers from [1, 6].

2-9 Explain why parallel pseudo-random number generators such as given in Equation (2.3) should not overlap?

2-10 Assume that we have a pseudo-random number sequence $R = \langle X_i \rangle_{i \geq 0}$ with a period of length p. We define k parallel generators S_j $(j = 0, \ldots, k - 1)$ of length $\ell = \lfloor p/k \rfloor$ from R:

$$S_j = \langle X_{\ell i + j} \rangle_{i=0}^{\ell - 1}.$$

Does S_j also have pseudo-random properties?

2-11 Let us call a die *phantom* if it produces the same elementary events – possibly with different probabilities – as an ordinary die. For example, if an ordinary hexahedron die gives integer values from [1, 6], equation $|x - y| + 1$ defines its phantom variant for integers $x, y \in [1, 6]$. The probability distribution of these phantom outcomes is depicted in Figure 2.12.

In the game Phantom Cube Die, a player can freely stack $6 \cdot 6 = 36$ tokens to six piles labelled with integers [1, 6]. The player casts two ordinary dice to determine the outcome e of the phantom die and removes one token from the pile labelled with e. The game ends when the phantom die gives the label of an empty pile. The score is the number of phantom die throws.

The challenge is to place the tokens so that the player can continue casting the die as long as possible. It is worth noting that although Figure 2.12 represents the probability distribution of the phantom die, it does not give the optimal token placement. Find out a better way to stack the tokens and explain this poltergeist phenomenon.

2-12 Interestingly, in the first edition of *The Art of Computer Programming* (1969) Knuth presents – albeit with some concern – Ulam's method, which simulates how a human shuffles cards. In the subsequent editions it has been removed and Knuth dismisses such methods as being 'miserably inadequate' (Knuth 1998b, p. 145). Ulam's method for shuffling works as follows:

ULAM-SHUFFLE(S)

    in: ordered set S
    out: shuffled ordered set R

constant: number of permutation generating subroutines p; number of repetitions r

```
 1: R ← copy S
 2: for i ← 1...r do
 3:    case RANDOM-INTEGER(1, p + 1) of
 4:       1: R ← PERMUTATION-1(R)
 5:       2: R ← PERMUTATION-2(R)
 6:       ...
 7:       p: R ← PERMUTATION-p(R)
 8:    end case
 9: end for
10: return R
```

The method uses a fixed number (p) of subroutines, each of which applies a certain permutation to the elements. Shuffling is done by selecting and applying randomly one of these permutations and by repeating this r times.

What is the fundamental problem of this method?

2-13 In Section 2.2, a discrete finite distribution is defined by listing the weight values W_r for each elementary event r. Obviously, W is not a unique representation for the distribution, because, for example, $W = \{1, 2, 3\}$ and $W' = \{2, 4, 6\}$ define the same distribution. This ambiguity can complicate, for example, equality comparisons. Design an algorithm CANONICAL-FORM-OF-WEIGHTS(W) that returns a unique representation for W.

2-14 When the number of elementary events n is small, we could implement row 10 in Algorithm 2.3 with a simple sequential search. The efficiency of the whole algorithm depends on how fast this linear search finds the smallest index i for which $S_{i-1} < k \leq S_i$. How would you organize the weight sequence W before the prefix sums are calculated? To verify your solution, implement a program that finds a permutation for the given weight sequence that minimizes the average number of the required sequential steps (i.e. increments of i). Also try out different distributions.

2-15 In Algorithm 2.4 the result sequence R is formed in lines 10–17. This locality can be used when designing an iterator variant NEXT-PERMUTATION(S). Describe this algorithm, which returns the next sequence of the previously generated sequence S.

2-16 In a perfect shuffle a deck of cards is divided exactly in half, which are interleaved alternately together. This can be done two ways: In an *in-shuffle* the bottom half is interleaved on top (1234 5678 → 51627384) and in an *out-shuffle* the top half is interleaved on top (1234 5678 → 15263748).

Take an ordinary deck of 52 cards and sort it into a recognizable order. Do consecutive out-shuffles for the deck and observe how the order changes (alternatively, if you feel more agile, write a computer program that simulates the shuffling). What happens eventually?

2-17 Casinos have devised different automated mechanical methods for shuffling the cards. One such method divides the deck into to seven piles by placing each card randomly either on the top or at the bottom of one pile (i.e. each card has 14 possible places to choose from). After that, the piles are put together to form the shuffled deck.

Is this a good method? Can a gambler utilize this information to his advantage?

2-18 An obvious continuation of Algorithm 2.6 is to use random numbers to create names for the stars and planets. Instead of creating random strings of characters, names usually follow certain rules. Select a set of real-world names (e.g. from J.R.R. Tolkien's world) and invent a set of rules that they follow. Design and implement a method that creates new names based on the set of rules and random numbers.

2-19 The starmap generation of Algorithm 2.6 creates a static galaxy. How would you implement a dynamic galaxy where every planet orbits around its star and rotates around its axis (i.e. at a given global startime the planet has a position and orientation)? What if we have an even more dynamic galaxy, where existing heavenly bodies can die and new ones can be born?

2-20 In Algorithm 2.9 routine UNBALANCED-NEIGHBOUR favours the neighbours in the order east, west, south, and north. Randomize the scanning order of the neighbourhood.

2-21 The midpoint displacement method limits the size of the terrain to $n \times n$, where $n = 2^k + 1$ when $k \geq 0$. How can we use it to generate arbitrary sized terrains?

2-22 In Algorithm 2.12, the double loops 'Middle horizontal' and 'Middle vertical' have similar loop indices (the ranges and the initial values differ only slightly). Collapse these loops together by introducing two extra loops with the range $i = 0, \ldots, (c - 1)$. Then collapse these two extra loops to include the loop 'Borders'. Implement these two variants and compare their running times.

The double loop 'Centres' generates every index pair in the array H. If the positions $H_{i,j}$ and $H_{j,i}$ are updated together and the diagonal of H is traversed separately, the range of the inner loop of 'Centres' can be cut to $j = 0, \ldots, (i - 1)$. Also, the diagonal loop can be embedded into the loop 'Borders'. Implement this third variant (with great care). Are these optimizations worth the effort? Continue this code tweaking until it becomes code pessimization. After that, give the fastest variant to your friends and let them ponder what it does.

3

Tournaments

The seven brothers of Jukola – Juhani, Tuomas, Aapo, Simeoni, Timo, Lauri, and Eero – have decided to find out which one is the best at the game of Kyykkä. To do this, the brothers need a series of matches, a *tournament*, and have to set down the rules for the form of the tournament (see Figure 3.1). They can form a scoring tournament, where everybody has one match against everybody else, in total 21 matches. To determine their relative order, a ranking, the brothers can agree to aggregate the match outcomes together by rewarding two points for the winner and zero points for the loser of a match, or one point each if the result is even and the match is a tie. When all the matches have been played, the brother with the most points will be the champion.

Another possibility is that they organize the event as a cup (or single elimination) tournament of three rounds and six matches, where the loser of each match (ties are resolved with armwrestling) is dropped from the competition, until there is only one contestant left. Apart from the champion, the rankings of the other players are not so obvious. Also, if the number of contestants is not a power of two, the incomplete pairing has to be handled fairly in the first round. Should the brothers have a ranking from the last year's tournament, the pairing can be organized so that the best-ranked players can meet only at the later stages of the tournament.

The brothers can settle the championship with a hill-climbing tournament, where the reigning champion from the last year's tournament has to defend his title in a series of six matches. If he loses a match, the winner becomes the new reigning champion and continues the series. The winner of the last match is crowned the champion of the whole tournament. Obviously, the last year's champion has a hard task of maintaining the title, because that requires six consecutive wins, whereas the last man in line can get championship by winning only one match.

Although the application area of tournament algorithms seems to be confined to sports games only, they provide us a general approach to determine a partial order between the participants and, therefore, we can apply them to a much wider range of problems. The (possibly incomplete) ranking information can be used, for instance, in game balancing (e.g. adjusting point rewarding schemes, or testing synthetic players by making them engage in

Algorithms and Networking for Computer Games   Jouni Smed and Harri Hakonen
© 2006 John Wiley & Sons, Ltd

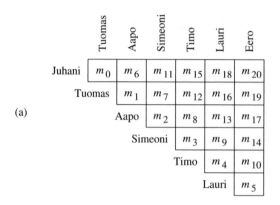

(a)

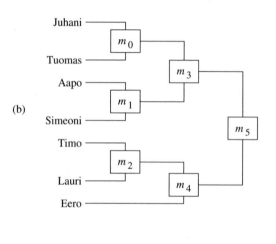

(b)

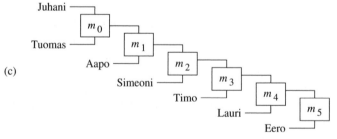

(c)

Figure 3.1 Tournaments for the seven brothers. (a) In a scoring tournament, everybody has one match against everybody else. (b) In an elimination tournament (or a cup), the remaining players are paired and only the winners get to the next round. (c) In a hill-climbing tournament, the reigning champion defends the title against players who have not yet had a possibility to become the champion.

a duel), in heuristic search (e.g. selecting sub-optimal candidates for a genetic algorithm or an evolving system), in group behaviour (e.g. modelling the pecking order in a flock), and in learning player characteristics (e.g. managing the overall historical knowledge about strengths and weaknesses).

Formally put, a tournament is a competition in which the players have one-on-one matches to resolve their relative fitness. Here, 'player' is a general term and can refer to an individual or a team. The result of a tournament is an ordering of the players' relative fitness. This information is often simplified into a *ranking* of the players, where the players are assigned a ranking number, and the smaller the rank, the better the player. Ranking can also be partial, which means that only some of the players can be ordered in comparison to the others. Even in these incomplete rankings, the result usually includes the player with the smallest rank, the *champion*, who is sometimes called – especially by scholars – the king.

Planning and organizing a tournament in the real world involves many constraints concerning costs, venue bookings, the time spent in travelling to the tournament sites, risk management, and other limited resources. In this chapter, we omit these practical concerns and limit our focus to scheduling the players of a tournament into matches of two players, which is called *pairing*.

As we saw earlier with the seven brothers' tournament, depending on how one match relates to the other matches, tournaments can be divided into three main categories:

- In a *rank adjustment tournament* (i.e. challenge or extended tournament), a match is a challenge for a rank exchange and is quite independent from the other challenges.

- In an *elimination tournament*, the purpose of a match is to eliminate the other player from the upcoming matches.

- In a *scoring tournament*, a player gets a reward if she succeeds in a match.

This categorization, however, is not strict, because these characterizing features are often combined together. For example, a season-wide ranking list can be used for assigning players either into preliminary qualifying rounds (i.e. elimination matches) or directly into the actual point awarding matches.

But before getting into the details of these tournaments, a few words about the notations we use in this chapter. Let us denote the set of n players in a tournament by P. We can label these players with indices $p_0, p_1, \ldots, p_{n-1}$, and player p_i can be referred to simply as player i. If player i has a rank, we denote it with $rank(i)$, and the ranks are enumerated consecutively starting from 0. The set of players having the same rank r is denoted with $rankeds(P, r)$ or $rankeds(r)$, if the set of players is known in the context. If this set is singleton (i.e. $rankeds(P, r) = \{p\}$), we simply use notation $ranked(r)$ to refer p directly. A match (or a duel) between players i and j, denoted as $match(i, j)$, has the outcomes i, j, or TIE for the cases where i wins, j wins, or there is no winner or loser. The *match* function itself does not change the ranks of the players, because the ranking rules are specific to the tournament. Furthermore, we assume that winning is transitive: If player q wins player r and p wins q, then we define that p also wins r. This indirect winning allows us to have different kinds of matching structures, especially in the elimination tournaments.

3.1   Rank Adjustment Tournaments

In a rank adjustment tournament, we have a set of players who already have a ranking and want to organize a tournament, where this ranking is adjusted according to the outcome of the match. Since the ranking can be updated immediately after each match, this kind of tournament suits ongoing (i.e., seasonless) competitions and the player pairings do not have to be coordinated in any specific way. A round in a rank adjustment tournament can have $0, 1, \ldots, \lfloor n/2 \rfloor$ independent matches at the same time. This makes it possible to insert or remove a tournament player without ruining the intuitiveness of the rank order.

We can set up the initial ranking of the players in P by using a ranking structure S (see Algorithm 3.1). The ranking structure S has the size $m = |S|$, which defines the number of different ranks, $0, 1, \ldots, m - 1$. Value S_i indicates how many players have the same rank i in the tournament. In other words, in a proper ranking $S_i = |rankeds(i)|$.

Algorithm 3.1 Constructing initial ranking in rank adjustment tournaments.

INITIAL-RANK-ADJUSTMENT(P, S)

> **in:**   set P of n unranked players in the tournament; sequence S of m non-negative integers in which S_i defines the number of players that have the same rank i ($\Sigma_{i=0}^{m-1} S_i = n$)
>
> **out:** set R of ranked players having the ranking structure S
>
> **local:** match sequences M and M' of players

1: $R \leftarrow$ **copy** P
2: $M \leftarrow enumeration(R)$ ▷ Order R to M in some way.
3: **for** $i \leftarrow 0 \ldots (S_0 - 1)$ **do**
4:    $rank(M_i) \leftarrow 0$ ▷ Declare M_i an initial champion.
5: **end for**
6: $c \leftarrow S_0$
7: **for** $r \leftarrow 1 \ldots (m - 1)$ **do**
8:    $W \leftarrow rankeds(R, r - 1)$ ▷ The runners-up.
9:    $M' \leftarrow enumeration(W)$
10:   **for** $i \leftarrow 0 \ldots (S_r - 1)$ **do**
11:      $rank(M_{c+i}) \leftarrow r$
12:      $j \leftarrow i$ **mod** $|M'|$
13:      **if** $rank(M'_j) \neq r$ **then**
14:         $R \leftarrow$ LADDER-MATCH(R, M'_j, M_{c+i})   ▷ Update ranks of M'_j and M_{c+i}.
15:      **end if**
16:   **end for**
17:   $c \leftarrow c + S_r$
18: **end for**
19: **return** R

Algorithm 3.1 uses routine *enumeration* to define some order to the given set, which can be, for example, a random order generated by function SHUFFLE described in Algorithm 2.5.

The algorithm also uses LADDER-MATCH described in Algorithm 3.2 to join the next subset of players into an existing rank structure (i.e. among the least successful players ranked so far). A new player exchanges rank with an already ranked opponent only if she wins the match. Because Algorithm 3.1 lets the players compete for the initial ranking, it is one of the simplest fair initialization methods. If fairness is unnecessary, the body of the algorithm becomes even simpler. For example, we can assign each player a random rank from structure S:

```
1: R ← SHUFFLE(P)
2: c ← 0
3: for r ← 0 ... (m − 1) do
4:    for i ← 0 ... (S_r − 1) do
5:       rank(R_{c+i}) ← r
6:    end for
7:    c ← c + S_r
8: end for
9: return R
```

Ladder tournaments

In a ladder tournament, a player can improve her rank by winning against another player who is ranked higher. A general ladder tournament orders the players P into a single chain according to their ranks: the first player in the chain, $ranked(0)$, is the champion, player $ranked(1)$ is the first runner-up, and so forth. Algorithm 3.2 describes the re-ranking rule LADDER-MATCH for two given players. A match can be arranged only between players whose ranks differ by one or two. Also, the possible rank exchange affects only the two players participating in the match. We can relax these two properties to allow less localized changes in the tournament ranking: The rank difference can be greater, or when a

---

Algorithm 3.2 Match in a ladder tournament.

LADDER-MATCH(P, p, q)

in: set P of players in the ladder structure; players p and q ($p, q \in P \land 1 \leq rank(q) − rank(p) \leq 2$)

out: set R of players after p and q have had a match

```
1: m ← match(p, q)
2: if m = TIE or m = p then        ▷ Nothing changes.
3:    return P
4: else                            ▷ Rank exchange.
5:    R ← P \ {p, q}
6:    p' ← copy p; q' ← copy q
7:    rank(p') ← rank(q)
8:    rank(q') ← rank(p)
9:    return R ∪ {p', q'}
10: end if
```

---

better-ranked player p loses to a worse-ranked player q, it also affects the ranks between them (i.e. to players $ranked(rank(p))$, $ranked(rank(p)+1)$, ..., $ranked(rank(q))$). To realize this generalized re-ranking we can use, for example, list update techniques (Albers and Mitzenmacher 1998; Bachrach and El-Yaniv 1997).

Hill-climbing tournament

A hill-climbing tournament – which is sometimes called a top-of-the-mountain tournament or a last man standing tournament – is a special ladder tournament, where the reigning champion defends the title against challengers. The tournament has $n-1$ rounds each having one match as described in Algorithm 3.3, which sequences the players and arranges a match between the reigning champion and the next player who has not yet participated. In other words, the matches obey the following invariant: After round $i = 0, \ldots, (n-1)-1$ we know that the player $ranked((n-1)-i-1)$ has won (directly or indirectly) against the players with ranks less than or equal to $(n-1)-i$. This reigning champion can be seen as a 'hill climber' among the other players.

Algorithm 3.3 Hill-climbing tournament.

HILL-CLIMBING-TOURNAMENT(P)
  in: set P of n unranked players ($1 \le n$)
  out: set R of ranked players which has a champion $ranked(R, 0)$
  local: ranking structure S; reigning champion c
  1: $S \leftarrow \langle 1, 1, \ldots, 1 \rangle$ ▷ Initialize n values.
  2: $R \leftarrow$ INITIAL-RANK-ADJUSTMENT(P, S)
  3: $c \leftarrow ranked(R, n-1)$ ▷ The tailender in R.
  4: **for** $r' \leftarrow 0 \ldots (n-2)$ **do**
  5:    $r \leftarrow (n-2) - r'$ ▷ For each rank from the bottom to the top.
  6:    $R \leftarrow$ LADDER-MATCH($R, ranked(R, r), c$)
  7:    $c \leftarrow ranked(R, r)$
  8: **end for**
  9: **return** R

Algorithm 3.3 assumes that the players are unranked and the initial order is generated using Algorithm 3.1. However, there are other ways to arrange the players into the match sequence. For example, we can produce a uniformly distributed random permutation SHUFFLE($\langle 0, 1, \ldots, n-1 \rangle$) and use it for the initial ranks. Alternatively, the initial ranking can be based on ranks from previous competitions. If the players are then arranged into a descending rank order, the reigning champion has only one match, the last one, whereas the bottom-ranked player has to win all the other players to clear her way to the championship match. Conversely, an ascending rank order requires that the reigning champion wins all $(n-1)$ matches to keep the title. Shortly put, we can set the reactivity of the championship race by initialization: Descending order is conservative, random order is democratic, and ascending order is challenging.

Pyramid tournaments

A general pyramid tournament relaxes the ladder tournament by allowing players to share the same rank. Assume that the ranks are $0, \ldots, m - 1$ and $m \leq n = |P|$. The pyramid ranking has usually a structure in which

$$1 = |rankeds\,(0)| < |rankeds\,(1)| < \ldots < |rankeds\,(m - 1)|$$

and

$$\sum_{i=0}^{m-1} |rankeds\,(i)| = n.$$

In this case, there is only one champion, and the set of ranked players grows as the rank index increases. Algorithm 3.4 defines re-ranking rule PYRAMID-MATCH for two players participating in a match. There are two kind of matches: In a peer match, both players have the same rank, and the winner gets the status *peerWinner*. A rank challenge match requires that the challenger has the *peerWinner* status; otherwise, the match is similar to LADDER-MATCH in Algorithm 3.2 with the difference that the rank difference is exactly one.

King of the hill tournament

A king of the hill tournament specializes the general pyramid tournament in the same way as the hill-climbing tournament specializes the general ladder tournament. Assume that the m level pyramid has the form $|rankeds\,(i)| = 2^i$ for all $i \in [0, m - 1]$, and $m \leq n$. This means that the number of player pairings at the level $(i + 1)$ is equal to the number of players at the level i. Algorithm 3.5 describes how the matches are organized into $2(m - 1)$ rounds. There are two rounds of matches for each pyramid level, except for the champion level 0. At the level $(i + 1)$, 2^i matches are held to find out the peer winners. After that, these winners face the players at the level i in a rank challenge match.

3.2 Elimination Tournaments

In an elimination tournament (or a knockout tournament) the loser of a match is eliminated from the tournament and the winner proceeds to the next round. This means that the match cannot end in a tie but has always a winner and a loser, which can be decided by an extra tiebreak competition such as overtime play and penalty kicks in football, or re-spotted black ball in snooker billiard. Also, multiple matches can be combined into a best-of-m match series (when m is odd), where the winner is the first one to win $(m + 1)/2$ matches.

Random selection tournament

The simplest elimination tournament is the random selection tournament, where a randomly selected player is declared a champion without any matches being played. The random selection is drawn from a distribution that can be given as a weight sequence for Algorithm 3.6 (for a details on assigning weight sequences, see Section 2.2).

Algorithm 3.4 Match in a pyramid tournament.

PYRAMID-MATCH(P, p, q)

    in: set P of players in the pyramid structure; players p and q ($p, q \in P \wedge$
              $((rank(p) = rank(q) \wedge \neg peerWinner(q)) \vee (rank(p) = rank(q) - 1 \wedge$
              $peerWinner(q))))$

    out: set R of players after p and q have had a match

    local: match outcome m

  1: $R \leftarrow P \setminus \{p, q\}$
  2: $m \leftarrow match(p, q)$
  3: **if** $rank(p) = rank(q)$ **then**   ▷ Peer match.
  4:   **if** ($m = p$ **and not** $peerWinner(p)$) **or**
           (($m = q$ **or** $m =$ TIE) **and** $peerWinner(p)$) **then**
  5:     $p' \leftarrow$ **copy** p
  6:     $peerWinner(p') \leftarrow (m = p)$
  7:   **else**
  8:     $p' \leftarrow p$
  9:   **end if**
 10:   **if** $m = q$ **then**
 11:     $q' \leftarrow$ **copy** q
 12:     $peerWinner(q') \leftarrow$ TRUE
 13:   **else**
 14:     $q' \leftarrow q$
 15:   **end if**
 16:   **return** $R \cup \{p', q'\}$
 17: **else**   ▷ Rank challenge match.
 18:   $q' \leftarrow$ **copy** q
 19:   $peerWinner(q') \leftarrow$ FALSE
 20:   **if** $m = p$ **or** $m =$ TIE **then**   ▷ No rank changes.
 21:     **return** $R \cup \{p, q'\}$
 22:   **else**   ▷ Rank exchange.
 23:     $p' \leftarrow$ **copy** p
 24:     $peerWinner(p') \leftarrow$ FALSE
 25:     $rank(p') \leftarrow rank(q)$
 26:     $rank(q') \leftarrow rank(p)$
 27:     **return** $R \cup \{p', q'\}$
 28:   **end if**
 29: **end if**

Random pairing tournament

In a random pairing tournament, the champion is decided by randomly selecting one of the first round winners. This is implemented in Algorithm 3.7, which uses Algorithm 3.6 for random drawing.

Algorithm 3.5 King of the hill tournament.

KING-OF-THE-HILL-TOURNAMENT(P)

    in: set P of n unranked players ($1 \leq n \wedge (n+1)$ is a power of two)

    out: set R of ranked players which has a champion $ranked(R, 0)$

    constant: number of pyramid levels m ($m = \lg(n+1)$)

    local: ranking structure S; match sequences M and M' of players

  1: $S \leftarrow \langle 2^0, 2^1, 2^2, \ldots, 2^{m-1} \rangle$ ▷ Initialize m values.

  2: $R \leftarrow$ INITIAL-RANK-ADJUSTMENT(P, S)

  3: **for** $r' \leftarrow 1 \ldots (m-1)$ **do**

  4:   $r \leftarrow (m-1) - (r'-1)$ ▷ From the bottom to the first runner-up.

  5:   $M \leftarrow enumeration(rankeds(R, r))$ ▷ Arrange the set into an order.

  6:   $\ell \leftarrow |M|$

  7:   **for** $i \leftarrow 0 \ldots (\ell/2 - 1)$ **do**   ▷ Determine the peer winners.

  8:     $peerWinner(M_{2i}) \leftarrow$ FALSE

  9:     $peerWinner(M_{2i+1}) \leftarrow$ FALSE

10:     $R \leftarrow$ PYRAMID-MATCH(R, M_{2i}, M_{2i+1})

11:   **end for**

12:   $M \leftarrow$ all peer winner players in $rankeds(R, r)$

13:   $M' \leftarrow enumeration(rankeds(R, r-1))$ ▷ Arrange the set into an order.

14:   **for** $i \leftarrow 0 \ldots (\ell/2 - 1)$ **do**   ▷ Determine the rank exchanges.

15:     $R \leftarrow$ PYRAMID-MATCH(R, M'_i, M_i)

16:   **end for**

17: **end for**

18: **return** R

Algorithm 3.6 Random selection tournament.

RANDOM-SELECTION-TOURNAMENT(P, W)

    in: sequence P of n unranked players ($1 \leq n$); sequence W of player weights ($|W| =$ $n \wedge W_i \in \mathbb{N}$ for $i = 0, \ldots, n-1 \wedge 1 \leq \Sigma_{k=0}^{n-1} W_k$)

    out: set R of ranked players which has a champion $ranked(R, 0)$ and the rest of the players have rank 1

  1: $R \leftarrow$ **copy** P

  2: $k \leftarrow$ RANDOM-FROM-WEIGHTS(W)

  3: $c \leftarrow R_k$

  4: $rank(c) \leftarrow 0$

  5: **for all** $p \in (R \setminus \{c\})$ **do**

  6:   $rank(p) \leftarrow 1$

  7: **end for**

  8: **return** R

Algorithm 3.7 Random pairing tournament.

RANDOM-PAIRING-TOURNAMENT(P)
    in: set P of n unranked players ($1 \leq n$)
    out: set R of ranked players which has a champion $ranked(R, 0)$ and the rest of the
             players have a rank 1
    local: match sequence M of players
    1: $W \leftarrow \langle 0, 0, \ldots, 0 \rangle$ ▷ Initialize n values.
    2: $M \leftarrow enumeration(P)$ ▷ Order P to M in some way.
    3: **for** $i \leftarrow 0 \ldots ((n \textbf{ div } 2) - 1)$ **do**
    4:    $m \leftarrow match(M_{2i}, M_{2i+1})$
    5:    $W_m \leftarrow 1$ ▷ Set the winner's weight to 1.
    6: **end for**
    7: $R \leftarrow$ RANDOM-SELECTION-TOURNAMENT(M, W)
    8: **return** R

Single elimination tournament

A single elimination tournament – which is perhaps better known as a *cup tournament* – resembles a complete binary tree: Leaf nodes represent the players and the internal nodes represent the matches. The winner of a match proceeds to the parent of the corresponding internal node (i.e. to the next match). The organization of the matches can be visualized with a diagram known as a *bracket*, which illustrated in Figure 3.2. By observing the binary tree structure, we obtain the following properties:

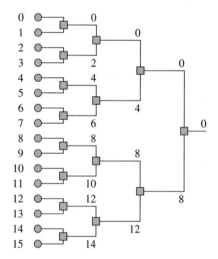

Figure 3.2 A bracket for an elimination tournament with 16 players (circles), which has 15 matches (squares).

- For $n = 2^x$ players, where $x = 0, 1, \ldots$, we have $n - 1$ matches organized into $\lg n = x$ rounds.

- If the rounds are indexed from 0, round i has $2^{x-1-i} = n/2^{i+1}$ matches.

- After each round, the number of the remaining participants is halved.

Round $x - 3$, which has four matches, is called the *quarter-final*, round $x - 2$ with two matches is the *semifinal*, and the last round $x - 1$ having only one match is the *final*.

If the number of players n is not a power of two, we cannot pair the players in every round. This means that some players may proceed to the next round without a match, and such a player is said to receive a *bye*. If we handle the byes by adding them as virtual players that automatically lose their matches, we can increase n to the nearest higher power of two by including $2^{\lceil \lg n \rceil} - n$ byes into the tournament bracket.

Because of the hierarchical organization of matches, the future player pairings depend strongly on the initial pairings. For instance, if the players are assigned to the matches as in Figure 3.2, it is not possible to have both $match(0, 2)$ and $match(1, 3)$. This inherent property of the single elimination tournament becomes a problem if we have some *a priori* knowledge about the player strengths and expect that it is possible for all of the t top-ranked players to reach the round $\lg (n/t)$. To analyse this reachability criterion we must first consider how initial pairing is done.

The process of assigning the players into the initial match pairs is called *seeding*. We can formulate it as follows: Given a bracket with consecutively indexed placeholders for the n players, the seeding is an arrangement of player indices $\{0, 1, \ldots, n - 1\}$ to a sequence R so that the player R_i is put into the bracket position i. The bracket positions define the first round matches to be $match(R_{2i}, R_{2i+1})$ for $i \in [0, n/2 - 1]$. Now, we can analyse the reachability criterion by setting the player index to be equal to the player's rank.

When the pre-tournament ranking cannot be estimated, we can use a random seeding. Hence, the probability that the two best players are able to reach the final is $\frac{1}{2} \cdot \frac{n}{n-1}$. A simple implementation for RANDOM-SEEDING(n) is

1: **return** SHUFFLE$(\langle 0, 1, \ldots, n - 1 \rangle)$

Table 3.1 presents the three most commonly used deterministic seedings for 16 player ranks, which fulfil the reachability criterion (i.e. the top-ranked players have the best possibilities to proceed to the next round). The first column contains the place index in the bracket (as a decimal number and a binary radix). The *standard seeding* is bijective (i.e. $S_{S_i} = i$) and it can be generated with Algorithm 3.8. In the *ordered standard seeding*, the mapping sequence of the standard seeding is sorted such that it is in ascending order as far as possible without violating the reachability criterion. Quite surprisingly, Algorithm 3.9 produces this sequence with a simple control flow. Both of these standard seedings reward the past success by pairing the top-ranked players with the bottom-ranked ones: The initial matches are $match(ranked(i), ranked(n - 1 - i))$ for $i \in [0, n/2 - 1]$. If this is considered to be unfair play, Algorithm 3.10 provides a method for *equitable seeding*, where each initial match has the same rank difference $n/2$. Bit enthusiasts may appreciate the observation that this sequence can be generated easily by reversing the bits of the placeholder indices – perhaps this property could be called 'bitectivity'.

The allocation of byes in the elimination bracket is another possible source of unfairness. There are two practical suggestions:

Table 3.1 Three common deterministic seeding types for an elimination tournament of 16 players. Instead of player indices, the seedings are defined by predetermined ranks.

Placeholder index	Standard	Ordered standard	Equitable
0 (0000)	0	0	0 (0000)
1 (0001)	15	15	8 (1000)
2 (0010)	8	7	4 (0100)
3 (0011)	7	8	12 (1100)
4 (0100)	4	3	2 (0010)
5 (0101)	11	12	10 (1010)
6 (0110)	12	4	6 (0110)
7 (0111)	3	11	14 (1110)
8 (1000)	2	1	1 (0001)
9 (1001)	13	14	9 (1001)
10 (1010)	10	6	5 (0101)
11 (1011)	5	9	13 (1101)
12 (1100)	6	2	3 (0011)
13 (1101)	9	13	11 (1011)
14 (1110)	14	5	7 (0111)
15 (1111)	1	10	15 (1111)

(i) The byes should have the bottom ranks (i.e. they are paired with the best players).

(ii) The byes should be restricted to the first round (i.e. the number of the remaining players in the second round is a power of two).

While this seems sensible for both of the standard seedings, realizing it in the equitable seeding turns out to be different, because the $\ell = 2^{\lceil \lg n \rceil} - n$ byes should have ranks $n/2, \ldots, n/2 + \ell - 1$.

Let us revert to the single elimination tournament, which is implemented in Algorithm 3.11. It assumes that the players P are already ranked, and the function call A-SEEDING produces a rank ordering, for example, by applying one of the four seeding algorithms described earlier. Although the players have unique ranks initially, the tournament deciding the champion only. It is clear why the runners-up are hard to decide; for instance, the first runner-up has lost to the champion in some round (not necessary in the final). To sort the runners-up we would have to organize a mini tournament of $\lg n$ players before we know the silver medallist. Naturally, we can give credit to the players with a score for each match won, which is then used to adjust the already existing ranking, especially if there are many tournaments in a season.

In the real-world sports games, a fair assessment of ranks for all players before the tournament can be too demanding a task. To compensate for and to reduce the effect of seeding, we can introduce a random element into the pairing. For example, if we are able to

Algorithm 3.8 Standard seeding for an elimination bracket.

STANDARD-SEEDING(n)

in: number of players n ($2 \leq n \wedge n$ is a power of two)

out: sequence R of n ranks indicating the initial match pairings between players $ranked(R_{2i})$ and $ranked(R_{2i+1})$, when $i = 0, \ldots, n/2 - 1$

1: $R \leftarrow \langle 0, -1, -1, \ldots, -1 \rangle$ ▷ Initialize n values.

2: **return** INTERNAL-STANDARD-SEEDING($R, 2, 0, n - 1$)

INTERNAL-STANDARD-SEEDING(R, n', α, ω)

in: sequence R of n ranks; number of players n' at the current bracket level ($1 \leq n' \wedge$ n' is a power of two); interval $[\alpha, \omega]$ of R under construction ($0 \leq \alpha \leq \omega < |R|$)

out: sequence of ranks R

1: **if** $\alpha = \omega$ **then return** R **end if**

2: **if** $R_\alpha = -1$ **then**

3:     $R_\alpha \leftarrow (n' - 1) - R_\omega$

4: **else**

5:     $R_\omega \leftarrow (n' - 1) - R_\alpha$

6: **end if**

7: $\mu \leftarrow (\omega - \alpha - 1)/2$

8: $R \leftarrow$ INTERNAL-STANDARD-SEEDING($R, 2 \cdot n', \alpha, \alpha + \mu$)

9: $R \leftarrow$ INTERNAL-STANDARD-SEEDING($R, 2 \cdot n', \alpha + \mu + 1, \omega$)

10: **return** R

Algorithm 3.9 Ordered standard seeding for an elimination bracket.

ORDERED-STANDARD-SEEDING(n)

in: number of players n ($2 \leq n \wedge n$ is a power of two)

out: sequence R of n ranks indicating the initial match pairings between players $ranked(R_{2i})$ and $ranked(R_{2i+1})$, when $i = 0, \ldots, n/2 - 1$

1: $|R| \leftarrow n$ ▷ Reserve space for n integers.

2: $R_0 \leftarrow 0$

3: **return** INTERNAL-ORDERED-STANDARD-SEEDING($R, 2, 0, n - 1$)

INTERNAL-ORDERED-STANDARD-SEEDING(R, n', α, ω)

in: sequence R of n ranks; number of players n' at current bracket level ($1 \leq n' \wedge n'$ is a power of two); interval $[\alpha, \omega]$ of R under construction ($0 \leq \alpha \leq \omega < |R|$)

out: sequence of ranks R

1: **if** $\alpha = \omega$ **then return** R **end if**

2: $\mu \leftarrow (\omega - \alpha - 1)/2$

3: $R \leftarrow$ INTERNAL-ORDERED-STANDARD-SEEDING($R, 2 \cdot n', \alpha, \alpha + \mu$)

4: $R_{\alpha+\mu+1} \leftarrow (n' - 1) - R_\alpha$

5: $R \leftarrow$ INTERNAL-ORDERED-STANDARD-SEEDING($R, 2 \cdot n', \alpha + \mu + 1, \omega$)

6: **return** R

Algorithm 3.10 Equitable seeding for an elimination bracket.

EQUITABLE-SEEDING(n)
in: number of players n ($2 \leq n \wedge n$ is a power of two)
out: sequence R of n ranks indicating the initial match pairings between players
         $ranked(R_{2i})$ and $ranked(R_{2i+1})$, when $i = 0, \ldots, n/2 - 1$
1: $w \leftarrow 1 + \lfloor \lg(n-1) \rfloor$ ▷ Bits required for the value $(n-1)$.
2: $|R| \leftarrow n$ ▷ Reserve space for n integers.
3: **for** $i \leftarrow 0 \ldots (n-1)$ **do**
4:     $R_i \leftarrow$ BIT-REVERSE(i, w)
5: **end for**
6: **return** R

BIT-REVERSE(x, w)
in: λ-bit integer value x with bit representation $b_{\lambda-1} \ldots b_1 b_0$; number of the lower-
         most bits w ($0 \leq w \leq \lambda$)
out: integer value in which the w lowermost bits are reversal of the w lowermost bits
         in x
1: **return** λ-bit integer value $0 \ldots 0 b_0 b_1 \ldots b_{w-1}$

---

determine the best four players (regardless of their relative ranking), we can place them in
the sub-brackets of the tournament according to a deterministic seeding after which the rest
of the (unranked) players are randomly seeded to the whole bracket. Another possibility
is to re-seed the players before each round, the rationale being that wins provide us with
information on the players' current strength.

When the players are equally matched (i.e. there is not much difference in their level
of fitness), the single elimination tournament has the disadvantage that the outcome of the
matches are susceptible to mistakes, relapses, accidents, and other unpredictable mishaps.
To compensate for this 'randomness', the player can of course have multiple matches (e.g.
a best-of-m matches) but there are also variants of the elimination tournament that provide
a more robust result. In a *double elimination tournament* the player is eliminated from the
competition after she has lost two matches. The matches are organized into a winners'
bracket and a losers' bracket (or a consolation bracket) – naturally there are specific rules
for assigning a loser in the losers' bracket. The brackets are then used like in the single
elimination tournament, and the winner of each bracket gets to the final.

3.3   Scoring Tournaments

Instead of adjusting the ranking directly, the ranks can be decided on the basis of a scoring
table. The winner of a match is rewarded by giving scoring points, whereas the loser gets
none, and in a tie both players score points. These scoring tournaments measure the overall
fitness among the players better, and the matches are less dependent on one another. We
can even arrange the same pairs have multiple matches during the season, which, in the
long run, should make the ranking reflect the true fitness order of the players better.

Algorithm 3.11 Single elimination tournament.

SINGLE-ELIMINATION-TOURNAMENT(P)

   in: sequence P of n ranked players ($1 \leq n \wedge n$ is a power of two $\wedge$ P is a permutation of $\langle 0, 1, \ldots, n - 1 \rangle$)

   out: set R of ranked players which has a champion $ranked(R, 0)$ and the rest of the players have rank 1; attribute $wins(i)$ indicates the number of wins for player i

   local: sequence S of initial match indices

  1: $R \leftarrow$ **copy** P

  2: $S \leftarrow$ A-SEEDING(n)   ▷ Seeding as a rank order.

  3: $|M| \leftarrow n$ ▷ Reserve space for n players.

  4: **for** $i \leftarrow 0 \ldots (n - 1)$ **do**   ▷ Assign the initial order.

  5:   $M_i \leftarrow ranked(R, S_i)$ ▷ The player with rank S_i.

  6: **end for**

  7: **for** $r \leftarrow 0 \ldots ((\lg n) - 1)$ **do**   ▷ For each round.

  8:   $|M'| \leftarrow n/2^{r+1}$ ▷ Reserve space for the winners.

  9:   **for** $i \leftarrow 0 \ldots (n/2^{r+1} - 1)$ **do** ▷ For each match.

10:     $M'_i \leftarrow match(M_{2i}, M_{2i+1})$

11:   **end for**

12:   **for all** $p \in (M \setminus M')$ **do**   ▷ The runners-up.

13:     $rank(p) \leftarrow 1$

14:     $wins(p) \leftarrow r$

15:   **end for**

16:   $M \leftarrow M'$

17: **end for**

18: $p \leftarrow$ the single value in M

19: $rank(p) \leftarrow 0$ ▷ The champion.

20: $wins(p) \leftarrow \lg n$

21: **return** R

Scoring can be included in any type of tournament, and it provides an easy way to combine different types of tournaments into one hybrid tournament. For example, in the preliminary matches, the players can be grouped into 16 disjoint *pools* where they play three random pairing tournaments. A match win rewards the player with one point and a tie, half points. If several players share the highest score of a pool, the pool champion is selected randomly. The preliminary champions are then seeded in an elimination tournament, which decides the champion of the whole tournament.

Let us begin with the *round robin tournament*, which is the base for many scoring tournaments. The round robin tournament itself does not impose any specific scoring mechanism but describes how to organize the matches where every player meets the other players exactly once with a minimum number of rounds. To describe the idea behind the algorithm, we convert the match allocation to a graph problem.

An undirected graph $G = (V, E)$ with vertices V and edges E is called *complete* if every vertex is connected to another vertex by an edge and no vertex has a loop. In other words, for all $v \in V$ we have $|neighbourhood(v)| = |V| - 1 \wedge (v, v) \notin E$. A complete graph with

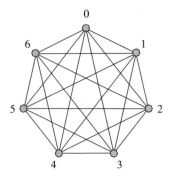

Figure 3.3 A clique graph representation of the matches in a round robin tournament with seven players.

n vertices is called a *clique*, and it is denoted as K_n. Without a loss of generality, we can place the vertices on the perimeter of a circle so as to have a polygonal representation of the graph and enumerate the vertices clockwise as in Figure 3.3. Let us identify a vertex with its number. If we set a vertex to be a player and an edge to be a match, K_n represents all the match pairings in a round robin tournament for n players.

Because the players are allowed to participate in at most one match at a time, we still have to schedule the matches into the rounds. If n is odd, the edges E of K_n can be partitioned into $(n-1)/2$ disjoint sets. Let us define a perimeter distance π of the edge (p, q) as $\pi(p, q) = \min\{|p - q|, n - |p - q|\}$. If we define a subset of undirected edges with a perimeter distance i as

$$\Pi(V, i) = \{(p, q) \mid \pi(p, q) = i \wedge p, q \in V\}, \tag{3.1}$$

the edge set of K_n becomes a disjoint union

$$E = \bigcup_{i=1}^{(n-1)/2} \Pi(V, i), \tag{3.2}$$

where each $\Pi(V, i)$ has exactly n members. In other words, if n is odd, Equation (3.2) provides us with a convenient way to partition all the $n(n-1)/2$ possible pairings into n rounds with $(n-1)/2$ matches each. When assigning matches for a round, we select only the unused pairings with different perimeter distances. Because a player faces the other players exactly once and each player 'rests' one match (i.e. has a bye for one round), this scheduling gives a solution with a minimum number of rounds.

We have some leeway when selecting the unused player pairings for a round. We can partition the sets $\Pi(V, i)$ to n rounds as illustrated in Figure 3.4. In round $r \in [0, n-1]$, the player with the index r is given a bye, and the matches for the round are

$$match((r + k) \bmod n, (r + n - k) \bmod n) \tag{3.3}$$

for $k \in [1, (n - 1)/2]$ (note that k is just a match enumeration, not a perimeter length). As Figure 3.4 illustrates, each edge belongs to one round only and every edge gets selected

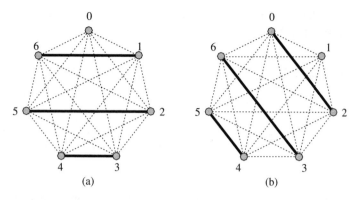

Figure 3.4 A partition of the matches into two rounds of a round robin tournaments with seven players: (a) the matches for the initial round, and (b) the matches for the next round.

Table 3.2 A straightforward organization of matches in a round robin tournament with seven players.

Round	Matches			Resting
0	1 – 6	2 – 5	3 – 4	0
1	2 – 0	3 – 6	4 – 5	1
2	3 – 1	4 – 0	5 – 6	2
3	4 – 2	5 – 1	6 – 0	3
4	5 – 3	6 – 2	0 – 1	4
5	6 – 4	0 – 3	1 – 2	5
6	0 – 5	1 – 4	2 – 3	6

to some round. Table 3.2 lists the whole schedule round by round for seven players. The column 'resting' shows the player with the bye, and, as already mentioned, it equals the round index.

An observant reader might have already noticed that the method presented does not work at all if the number of players is even. Fortunately, we can easily transform the scheduling problem with an even n to a problem with an odd n: If n is even, we divide the set of players $P = \{p_0, p_1, \ldots, p_{n-1}\}$ into two sets:

$$P = S \cup P', \tag{3.4}$$

where set S is a singleton and set P' equals $P \setminus S$. We can always let $S = \{p_{n-1}\}$. Because set P' has an odd number of players, Equation (3.3) provides a schedule of their matches. The resting player of P' is then paired with the player in S. For example, to determine the matches for eight players, we pair the eighth player p_7 with the resting player as per Table 3.2.

Algorithm 3.12 returns the matches in a round robin tournament, when the round index and the number of players is given. The resulting sequence R consists of $\lfloor n/2 \rfloor$ pairs of player indices that define the matches. If n is odd, the sequence also includes an extra entry R_{n-1} for the resting player.

Algorithm 3.12 Straightforward pairings for a round robin tournament.

SIMPLE-ROUND-ROBIN-PAIRINGS(r, n)

in: round index r ($0 \le r \le 2 \cdot \lfloor (n-1)/2 \rfloor$); number of players n ($1 \le n$)

out: sequence R of n player indices indicating the match pairings between players R_{2i} and R_{2i+1}, when $i = 0, \dots, \lfloor n/2 \rfloor - 1$; if n is odd, R_{n-1} indicates the resting player.

1: $|R| \leftarrow n$ ▷ Reserve space for n player indices.
2: $R_{n-1} \leftarrow r$ ▷ The resting player when n is odd.
3: $n' \leftarrow n$
4: **if** n is even **then**
5:   $R_{(n-1)-1} \leftarrow n-1$ ▷ The player in the singleton set.
6:   $n' \leftarrow n-1$ ▷ Transform the problem to 'n is odd'.
7: **end if**
8: **for** $k \leftarrow 1 \dots ((n'-1)/2)$ **do**
9:   $i \leftarrow 2(k-1)$
10:   $R_i \leftarrow (r+k) \bmod n'$
11:   $R_{i+1} \leftarrow (r + n' - k) \bmod n'$
12: **end for**
13: **return** R

If the players face each other once, the round robin tournament has $n(n-1)/2$ matches in total. For instance, if $n = 100$, a full tournament requires 4950 matches. Instead of generating and storing the match pairings into a data structure, it would be more convenient to have a combination rule linking the player indices and the round index. On the basis of this rule, we could answer directly to questions such as the following:

(i) Who is the resting player (i.e. the opponent of the player in the singleton set in Equation (3.4)) in the given round?

(ii) Given two players, state in which round they will face one another?

Since Algorithm 3.12 is based on Equation (3.3), we have a simple invariant for a round r: The sum of the player indices equals to $2r \bmod n$ whenever n is odd. Unfortunately, this regularity does not seem to give a direct answer to question (ii) (e.g. if $n = 7$, the sums are $0, 2, 4, 6, 1, 3, 5$ for rounds $0, 1, \dots, 6$ respectively). However, we can use the sum to define the organization of the match. For example, sorting the rounds listed in Table 3.2 according to the sum of player indices modulo n gives us the schedule as in Table 3.3. Let us call this match schedule as *normalized round robin pairings*.

Algorithm 3.13 describes a method for generating pairings for a round in a normalized round robin tournament. Also, it defines the function RESTING that gives an answer to the question (i), and the function ROUND answering the question (ii).

Table 3.3 A normalized organization of matches in a round robin tournament with seven players.

Round	Matches			Resting	Modulo
0	1 – 6	2 – 5	3 – 4	0	0
1	5 – 3	6 – 2	0 – 1	4	1
2	2 – 0	3 – 6	4 – 5	1	2
3	6 – 4	0 – 3	1 – 2	5	3
4	3 – 1	4 – 0	5 – 6	2	4
5	0 – 5	1 – 4	2 – 3	6	5
6	4 – 2	5 – 1	6 – 0	3	6

An algorithm generating the match pairings is in key position in the algorithm that organizes the round robin tournament. The concept of *sorted sequence of kings* approximates the player rankings in a round robin tournament without having to resort to a scoring mechanism (Wu and Sheng 2001). Nevertheless, it is quite common to reward the players when they excel in the matches, and Algorithm 3.14 realizes such a tournament. The algorithm uses a function A-ROUND-ROBIN-PAIRINGS, which can be any method that generates proper pairings (e.g. Algorithm 3.12 and Algorithm 3.13).

3.4 Summary

Tournaments compare the participants to rank them into a relative order or, at least, to find out who is the best among them. The comparison of two competitors is carried out in a match, and its outcome contributes in a specified way to the rankings. Since there are no regulations on how the matches and the ranks should affect each other, we are free to compose a tournament that suits our needs. However, if we want both a simple tournament structure and an effective comparison method, we can choose from three different approaches: rank adjustment, competitor elimination, and point scoring. In practice, a tournament event often combines these concepts so that consecutive rounds have a justifiable assignment of one-to-one matches.

In a rank adjustment tournament, a match is seen as a challenge where the winner gets the better rank and the looser the lower one. Because ranks are persistent, this approach suits the case in which the rank order must be upheld constantly, the set of participants changes often, and there are no competition seasons. In an elimination tournament, a match win provides an entrance to the next round, while the looser gets excluded from the tournament. The tournament structure can include random elements, for instance, in making the initial pairings or the final drawings. Because the participants can be ordered only partially, the purpose of the event is often to determine only the champion. A scoring tournament makes the matches more independent from one another by accumulating the outcomes using a point rewarding system. Since the participants are ranked according to their point standing, we can balance the amount of the matches and the fairness of the final ordering.

Table 3.4 summarizes the characteristic properties of four types of tournaments. Their overall structure can be measured in terms of the amount of the matches in total, the amount of the rounds required to determine the champion, the amount of matches before one can

---

Algorithm 3.13 Normalized pairings for a round robin tournament.

NORMALIZED-ROUND-ROBIN-PAIRINGS(r, n)

   in: round index r $(0 \le r \le 2 \cdot \lfloor (n-1)/2 \rfloor)$; number of players n $(1 \le n)$

   out: sequence R of n player indices indicating the match pairings between players R_{2i} and R_{2i+1}, when $i = 0, \ldots, \lfloor n/2 \rfloor - 1$; if n is odd, R_{n-1} indicates the resting player.

  1: $|R| \leftarrow n$ ▷ Reserve space for n player indices.

  2: $s \leftarrow$ RESTING(r, n)   ▷ The resting player when n is odd.

  3: $R_{n-1} \leftarrow s$

  4: $n' \leftarrow n$

  5: **if** n is even **then**

  6:   $R_{(n-1)-1} \leftarrow n - 1$ ▷ The player in the singleton set.

  7:   $n' \leftarrow n - 1$ ▷ Transform the problem to 'n is odd'.

  8: **end if**

  9: **for** $k \leftarrow 1 \ldots ((n'-1)/2)$ **do**

10:   $i \leftarrow 2(k-1)$

11:   $R_i \leftarrow (s+k) \bmod n'$

12:   $R_{i+1} \leftarrow (n - (s+k) + r) \bmod n'$

13: **end for**

14: **return** R

RESTING(r, n)

   in: round index r $(0 \le r \le 2 \cdot \lfloor (n-1)/2 \rfloor)$; number of players n $(1 \le n)$

   out: index of the resting player (when n is odd) or the opponent of the singleton player (when n is even)

  1: **return** $(r \cdot ((n+1) \textbf{ div } 2)) \bmod n$

ROUND(p, q, n)

   in: player indices p and q $(0 \le p, q \le n-1 \wedge p \ne q)$; number of players n $(1 \le n)$

   out: index of the round where the players p and q have a match

  1: **if** n is even **and** $(p = n-1$ **or** $q = n-1)$ **then**

  2:   $o \leftarrow p + q - (n-1)$ ▷ Opponent of the singleton player.

  3:   **return** $(2o) \bmod (n-1)$

  4: **else**

  5:   $t \leftarrow 2 \cdot ((n-1) \textbf{ div } 2) + 1$ ▷ Number of rounds.

  6:   **return** $(p+q) \bmod t$

  7: **end if**

---

become the champion, and the amount of matches in a given round. The hill-climbing tournament is the simplest because of the linear scheduling of the matches. The king of the hill and the elimination tournament are based on a tree-like structure and, thus, they have a logarithmic number of rounds with respect to the number of players. The round robin tournament is the most demanding by all measures because every player has a match with the other players.

Table 3.4 Characteristic features of tournaments for n players. The matches for initial rank adjustments are not taken into account. However, we assume that the single elimination tournament is set up by a standard seeding order. In general, we assume $2 \leq n$, except that for the king of the hill tournament we require that $n + 1$ is a power of two. The round index i is from the interval $[0, r - 1]$.

	Hill climbing	King of the hill	Single elimination	Round robin
All matches	$n - 1$	$n - 1$	$n - 1$	$n(n - 1)/2$
All rounds ($= r$)	$n - 1$	$2(\lg(n + 1) - 1)$	$\lceil \lg n \rceil$	n if n is odd; $n - 1$ otherwise
Matches of the champion	$\in [1, r]$	$\in [1, r]$	$\in [r - 1, r]$	$n - 1$
Matches in round i	1	$2^{\lfloor (r-1-i)/2 \rfloor}$	$n - 2^{\lceil \lg n \rceil - 1} - 1$ if $i = 0$; $2^{\lceil \lg n \rceil - (i+1)}$ if $i \geq 1$	$\lceil n/2 \rceil$

Algorithm 3.14 Round robin tournament including a scoring for the match results.

ROUND-ROBIN-TOURNAMENT(P)

   in: sequence P of n players ($1 \leq n$)

   out: sequence R of n players with attribute $score(i)$

   constant: score points for a winner w, for a loser ℓ, for a tie t

   local: number of rounds t

  1: $R \leftarrow$ **copy** P

  2: **for all** $p \in R$ **do**

  3:   $score(p) \leftarrow 0$

  4: **end for**

  5: **if** n is even **then**

  6:   $t \leftarrow n - 1$

  7: **else**

  8:   $t \leftarrow n$

  9: **end if**

10: **for** $r \leftarrow 0 \ldots (t - 1)$ **do**

11:   $M \leftarrow$ A-ROUND-ROBIN-PAIRINGS(r, n)

12:   **for** $i \leftarrow 0 \ldots ((n \textbf{ div } 2) - 1)$ **do**

13:      $p \leftarrow M_{2i}$

14:      $q \leftarrow M_{2i+1}$

15:      $m \leftarrow match(R_p, R_q)$

16:      **if** $m = p$ **then**

17:         $score(p) \leftarrow score(p) + w$

18:         $score(q) \leftarrow score(q) + \ell$

19:      **else if** $m = q$ **then**

20:         $score(p) \leftarrow score(p) + \ell$

21:         $score(q) \leftarrow score(q) + w$

22:      **else**

23:         $score(p) \leftarrow score(p) + t$

24:         $score(q) \leftarrow score(q) + t$

25:      **end if**

26:   **end for**

27:   **if** n is odd **then**

28:      player R_{n-1} receives a bye

29:   **end if**

30: **end for**

31: **return**

Although the tournaments are often associated with sports games, they can be used in any context that evaluates a set of objects against each other. These methods have intuitive consequences, they are very customizable, and they have an inherent property of managing partial ordering.

Exercises

3-1 Draw a bracket for a hill-climbing tournament (see Algorithm 3.3) and for a king of the hill tournament (see Algorithm 3.5).

3-2 Algorithm 3.3 organizes a hill-climbing tournament and ranks the players. If we want to find out only the champion, the algorithm can be simplified by unfolding the function calls INITIAL-RANK-ADJUSTMENT and LADDER-MATCH and by removing the unnecessary steps. Realize these changes and name the algorithm SIMPLE-HILL-CLIMBING-TOURNAMENT(P).

3-3 Draw a bracket of match pairings for SIMPLE-HILL-CLIMBING-TOURNAMENT(P) when $|P| = 8$ (see Exercise 3-2).

3-4 Algorithm 3.5 uses routine *enumeration* to arrange the players into some order so that they can be paired to the matches. If the order is random, the operation resembles RANDOM-SEEDING (see p. 57). Rewrite Algorithm 3.5 by substituting *enumeration* with RANDOM-SEEDING.

3-5 Algorithm 3.5 defines the king of the hill tournament. Simplify the algorithm for finding out only the champion (see Exercise 3-2). Call this new algorithm as SIMPLE-KING-OF-THE-HILL-TOURNAMENT(P).

3-6 Draw a bracket for SIMPLE-KING-OF-THE-HILL-TOURNAMENT(P) when $|P| = 15$ (see Exercise 3-5).

3-7 In the real world, a player p can decline a rank adjustment tournament match with a less-ranked player q. After d rejections, the player p is considered as having lost to q. We have considered only the case where $d = 0$. Generalize Algorithm 3.2 for the case $d > 0$.

3-8 In a rank adjustment tournament, the number of revenge matches r is usually limited. This means that a player cannot face the same player more than r times in a row. We have considered only the case where $r = \infty$. Generalize Algorithm 3.2 to account finite r values.

3-9 Removing a player p from a rank adjustment tournament empties the rank $rank(p)$. Devise at least three different strategies to handle the empty slots in a ranking structure.

3-10 A ladder tournament L can be split into two separate ladder tournaments L' and L'' by assigning each player either to L' or to L''. The new ranks of the players are adjusted so that they do not contradict the relative rankings in L. However, there are many ways to define the inverse operation, joining two tournaments of disjoint players. Design algorithm JOIN-LADDER-TOURNAMENTS(L', L'') that gives both tournaments an equal value. This means, for example, that the joining does not force the champion of L'' to compete against the worst players in L' before she can have a match with the champion of L'.

3-11 Exercise 3-10 tackles the problem of splitting and joining of ladder tournaments. How can these operations be defined in an elimination tournament?

3-12 In the pyramid tournament, the player status *peerWinner* can be seen as a token that is assigned to the player p, and it can be only lost in a match. If the players' ranks change often, this tokenization can be unfair: If p competes only occasionally, he keeps the *peerWinner* status even if all the other peer players have been re-ranked. Devise a better strategy for controlling *peerWinner* status in such situations.

3-13 Solving the organization of the matches of a tournament resembles the (parallel) selection algorithms. For example, the structure of the hill-climbing tournament is similar to searching for a maximum of n values sequentially (see Exercise 3-2). Algorithm 3.15 describes how to search for a maximum value in parallel. What tournament structure does it resemble?

Algorithm 3.15 Maximum value in parallel.

PARALLEL-MAX(P)
  in: sequence P of n values $(1 \leq n)$
  out: maximum value of P
  local: amount of pairs h
  1: **if** $n = 1$ **then**
  2:    **return** P_0
  3: **else**
  4:    $h \leftarrow n$ **div** 2
  5:    **if** n is odd **then**   ▷ Reserve space for Q.
  6:       $|Q| \leftarrow h + 1$
  7:       $Q_h \leftarrow P_{n-1}$
  8:    **else**
  9:       $|Q| \leftarrow h$
 10:   **end if**
 11:   **for** $i \leftarrow 0 \ldots (h - 1)$ **do**   ▷ In parallel for each i.
 12:      $Q_i \leftarrow \max\{P_{2i}, P_{2i+1}\}$
 13:   **end for**
 14:   **return** PARALLEL-MAX(Q)
 15: **end if**

3-14 In a best-of-m match series of two players (e.g. p and q) the winner is the first one to win $\lceil (m + 1)/2 \rceil$ matches. Suppose we have in total n players ranked uniquely from $[0, n - 1]$ so that $ranked(0)$ is the champion and $ranked(n - 1)$ is the tailender. If we define that for one match

$$P(match(p, q) = p) = \frac{1}{2} \cdot \left(1 + \frac{rank(q) - rank(p)}{n}\right)$$

when $rank(p) < rank(q)$, what is the probability that p wins the best-of-m series.

3-15 The random selection tournament (see Algorithm 3.6) and the random pairing tournament (see Algorithm 3.7) provide similar types of results. However, the latter method seems to be under-defined because the pairwise matches provide us with information about the relative strengths between the players. Should we rephrase the result as follows: 'set R of ranked players that have the champion $ranked(R, 0)$, the initial match winners with rank 1, and the rest of the players with rank 2'?

3-16 If you have answered 'yes' to Exercise 3-15, redesign the elimination tournament algorithms presented. Especially, remove attribute $wins(\bullet)$ from Algorithm 3.11. If you have answered 'no', complement all the elimination tournament algorithms with attribute $wins(\bullet)$. Finally, give the opposing answer to Exercise 3-15 and redo this exercise.

3-17 The three common deterministic seeding methods – the standard seeding, the ordered standard seeding, and the equitable seeding – for an elimination tournament are listed in Table 3.1. To prevent the same matches from taking place in the successive tournaments (and to introduce an element of surprise), we can apply these seeding methods only partially. The $t = 2^x$ top players are seeded as before, but the rest are placed randomly. Refine the deterministic seeding algorithms to include the parameter t.

3-18 In a single elimination tournament (see Algorithm 3.11), the seeding initializes the match pairs for the first round. Design algorithm SINGLE-ELIMINATION-SEEDING-TOURNAMENT(P), where the seeding is applied before every round. Analyse and explain the effects of different seeding methods.

3-19 In the bracket of a single elimination tournament we have allocated the players for the initial matches by labelling the player placeholders with player indices or equivalently by ranks (see Figure 3.2 and Table 3.1). In practice, it would be convenient to also identify the matches. Design an algorithm that gives a unique label for each match in the bracket so that the label is independent of the actual players in the match.

3-20 Design and describe a general *m-round winner tournament*, ROUND-WINNER-TOURNA-MENT(P, m), for players P, where in each round $0, 1, \dots, m - 1$ the players are paired randomly and the winners proceed to the next round. After round $m - 1$, the champion is selected randomly from the remaining players. Interestingly, this tournament structure has the following special cases: $m = 0$ is a random selection tournament, $m = 1$ is a random pairing tournament, and $m = \lg |P|$ is a single elimination seeding tournament as in Exercise 3-18.

3-21 Assume that a single elimination tournament has $n = 2^x$ players and the number of rounds is x. How many single elimination tournaments should we have so that the total number of matches equals the matches in a round robin tournament?

4

Game Trees

Many classical games such as Chess, Draughts and Go are *perfect information games*, because the players can always see all the possible moves. In other words, there is no hidden information among the participants but they all know exactly what has been done in the previous turns and can devise strategies for the next turns from equal grounds. In contrast, poker is an example of a game in which the players do not have perfect information, since they cannot see the opponents' hands. Random events are another source of indeterminism: Although there is no hidden information in Backgammon, dice provide an element of chance, which changes the nature of information from perfect to probabilistic. Because perfect information games can be analysed using combinatorial methods, they have been widely studied and were the first games to have computer-controlled opponents.

This chapter concentrates on two-player perfect information zero-sum games. A game has a *zero-sum* property when one player's gain equals another player's loss, whereas in a non-zero sum game (e.g. Prisoner's Dilemma) one player gains more than the other loses. All possible plays of a perfect information game can be represented with a *game tree*: The root node is the initial position, its successors are the positions the first player can reach in one move, their successors are the positions resulting from the second player's replies, and so forth. Alternatively, a game position can be seen as a state from the set of all legal game positions, and a move defines the transition from one state to another. The leaves of the game tree represent terminal positions in which the outcome of the game – win, loss, or draw – can be determined. Each path from the root to a leaf node represents a complete play instance of the game. Figure 4.1 illustrates a partial game tree for the first two moves of Noughts and Crosses.

In two-player perfect information games, the first player of the round is commonly called MAX and the second player MIN. Hence, a game tree contains two types of nodes, MAX nodes and MIN nodes, depending on who is the player that must make a move at the given situation. A *ply* is the length of the path between two nodes (i.e. the number of moves required to get from one node to another). For example, one round in a two-player game equals two plies in a game tree. Considering the root node, MAX nodes have even plies and MIN nodes have odd plies. Because of notational conventions, the root node has no ply

Algorithms and Networking for Computer Games   Jouni Smed and Harri Hakonen
© 2006 John Wiley & Sons, Ltd

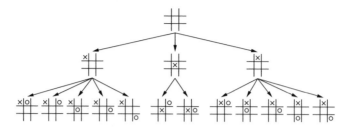

Figure 4.1 Partial game tree for the first two moves of Noughts and Crosses. The tree has been simplified by removing symmetrical positions.

number (i.e. the smallest ply number is one), and the leaves, despite having no moves, still are labelled as MAX or MIN nodes. In graphical illustrations, MAX nodes are often represented with squares and MIN nodes with circles. Nevertheless, we have chosen to illustrate MAX and MIN nodes with triangles ▽ and △, because these glyphs bear a resemblance to the equivalent logical operators ∨ and ∧.

Having touched upon the fundamentals, we are now ready for the problem statement: Given a node v in a game tree, find a winning strategy for the player MAX (or MIN) from the node v, or, equivalently, show that MAX (or MIN) can force a win from the node v. To tackle this problem we review in the following sections the minimax method, which allows us to analyse both whole and partial game trees, and alpha-beta pruning, which often reduces the number of nodes expanded during the search for a winning strategy. Finally, we take a look at how we can include random elements in a game tree for modelling games of chance.

4.1 Minimax

Let us start by thinking of the simplest possible subgame in which we have a MAX node v whose children are all leaves. We can be sure that the game ends in one move if the game play reaches the node v. Since the aim is (presumably) to win the game, MAX will choose the node that leads to the best possible outcome from his perspective: If there is a leaf leading to a win position, MAX will select it and win the game; if a win is not possible but a draw is, he will choose it; otherwise, MAX will lose no matter what he does. Conversely, because of the zero-sum property if v belongs to MIN, she will do her utmost to minimize MAX's advantage. We know now the outcome of the game for the nodes one ply above the leaves, and we can analyse the outcome of the plies above that recursively using the same method until we reach the root node. This strategy for determining successive selections is called the *minimax* method, and the sequence of moves that minimax deduces to be the optimal for both sides is called the *principal variation*. The first move in the principal variation is the best decision for the player who is assigned to the root of the game tree.

We can assign numeric values to the nodes: MAX's win with $+1$, MIN's win with -1, and a draw with 0. Because we know the outcome of the leaves, we can immediately assign values to them. After that, minimax propagates the value up the tree according to the following rules:

(i) If the node is labelled MAX, assign the maximum value of its children to it.

(ii) If the node is labelled MIN, assign the minimum value of its children to it.

The assigned value indicates the value of the best outcome that a player can hope to achieve – assuming the opponent also uses minimax.

As an example, let us look at a simplification of the game of Nim called *Division Nim*. Initially, there is one heap of matches on the table. On each turn a player must divide one heap into two non-empty heaps that have a different number of matches (e.g. for a heap of six matches the only allowed divisions are 5–1 and 4–2). The player who cannot make a move loses the game. Figure 4.2 illustrates the complete game tree for a game with seven matches.

Figure 4.3 illustrates the same game tree but now with values assigned. The two leaves labelled with MIN are assigned to +1, because in those positions MIN cannot make a move and loses; conversely, the only MAX leaf is assigned to −1, because it represents a position

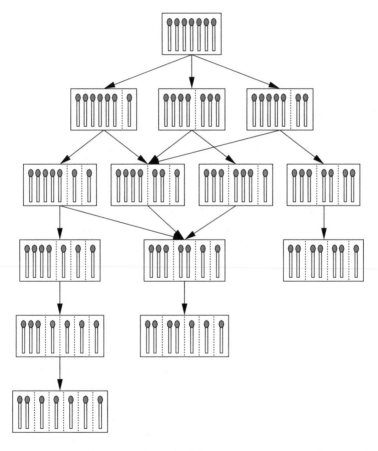

Figure 4.2 Game tree for Division Nim with seven matches. To reduce size, identical nodes in a ply have been combined.

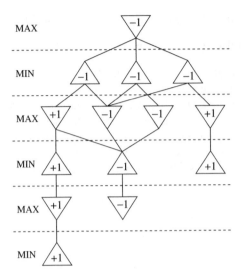

Figure 4.3 Complete game tree with valued nodes for Division Nim with seven matches.

in which MAX loses. By using the aforementioned rules, we can assign values to all internal nodes, and, as we can see in the root node, MAX, who has the first move, loses the game because MIN can always force the game to end in the MAX leaf node.

The function that gives a value to every leaf node is called a *utility function* (or pay-off function). In many cases, this value can be determined solely from the properties of the leaf. For example, in Division Nim if the leaf's ply from the root is odd, its value is $+1$; otherwise, the value is -1. However, as pointed out by Michie (1966), the value of a leaf can also depend on the nodes preceding it up to the initial root. When assigning values to a leaf node v_i, we take MAX's perspective and assign a positive value for MAX's win, a negative value for his loss, and zero for a draw. Let us denote this function with $value(v_i)$. Now, the minimax value for a node v can be defined with a simple recursion

$$minimax(v) = \begin{cases} value(v), & \text{if } v \text{ is a leaf;} \\ \min_{u \in children(v)} \{minimax(u)\}, & \text{if } v \text{ is a MIN node;} \\ \max_{u \in children(v)} \{minimax(u)\}, & \text{if } v \text{ is a MAX node,} \end{cases} \tag{4.1}$$

where $children(v)$ gives the set of successors of node v. Algorithm 4.1 implements this recurrence by determining backed-up values for the internal nodes after the leaves have been evaluated.

Both Equation (4.1) and its implementation Algorithm 4.1 have almost similar subparts for the MIN and MAX nodes. Knuth and Moore (1975) give a more compact formulation for the minimax method called *negamax*, where both node types are handled identically. The idea is to first negate the values assigned to the MIN nodes and then to take the maximum value as in the MAX nodes. Algorithm 4.2 gives an implementation for the negamax method.

Algorithm 4.1 Minimax.

MINIMAX(v)
  in: node v
  out: utility value of node v
  1: **if** *children*(v) = Ø **then**   ▷ v is a leaf.
  2:   **return** *value*(v)
  3: **else if** *label*(v) = MIN **then**   ▷ v is a MIN node.
  4:   $e \leftarrow +\infty$
  5:   **for all** $u \in$ *children*(v) **do**
  6:     $e \leftarrow \min\{e, \text{MINIMAX}(u)\}$
  7:   **end for**
  8:   **return** e
  9: **else**   ▷ v is a MAX node.
10:   $e \leftarrow -\infty$
11:   **for all** $u \in$ *children*(v) **do**
12:     $e \leftarrow \max\{e, \text{MINIMAX}(u)\}$
13:   **end for**
14:   **return** e
15: **end if**

Algorithm 4.2 Negamax.

NEGAMAX(v)
  in: node v
  out: utility value of node v
  1: **if** *children*(v) = Ø **then**   ▷ v is a leaf.
  2:   $\ell \leftarrow$ *value*(v)
  3:   **if** *label*(v) = MIN **then** $\ell \leftarrow -\ell$ **end if**
  4:   **return** ℓ
  5: **else**   ▷ v is a MAX or MIN node.
  6:   $e \leftarrow -\infty$
  7:   **for all** $u \in$ *children*(v) **do**
  8:     $e \leftarrow \max\{e, -\text{NEGAMAX}(u)\}$
  9:   **end for**
10:   **return** e
11: **end if**

4.1.1   Analysis

When analysing game tree algorithms, some simplifying assumptions are made about the features of the game tree. Let us assume that each internal node has the same branching factor (i.e. the number of children), and we search the tree to some fixed depth before which the game does not end. We can now estimate how much time the minimax (and negamax) method uses, because it is proportional to the number of expanded nodes. If the branching factor is b and the depth is d, the number of expanded nodes (the initial node included) is

$$1 + b + b^2 + \ldots + b^d = \frac{1 - b^{d+1}}{1 - b} = \frac{b^{d+1} - 1}{b - 1}.$$

Hence, the overall running time is $O(b^d)$.

There are two ways to speed up the minimax method: We can try to reduce b by pruning the game tree, which is the idea of alpha-beta pruning described in Section 4.2, or we can try to reduce d by limiting the search depth, which we shall study next.

4.1.2   Partial minimax

Minimax method gives the best zero-sum move available for the player at any node in the game tree. This optimality is, however, subject to the utility function used in the leaves and the assumption that both players utilize the same minimax method for their moves. In practice, the game trees are too large for computing the perfect information from the leaves up, and we must limit the search to a *partial game tree* by stopping the search and handling internal nodes as if they were leaves. For example, we can stop after sequences of n moves and guess how likely it is for the player to win from that position. This depth-limiting approach is called an *n-move look-ahead* strategy, where n is the number of plies included in the search.

In a *partial minimax* method, such as n-move look-ahead, the internal nodes in which the node expansion is stopped are referred as *frontier nodes* (or horizon nodes or tip nodes). Because the frontier nodes do not represent the final positions of the game, we have to estimate whether they lead to a win, loss, or draw by using a heuristic *evaluation function* (or static evaluation function or estimation function). Naturally, it can use more than the values $+1, 0, -1$ to imply the likelihood of the outcome. After the evaluation, the estimated values are propagated upwards through the tree using minimax. At best, the evaluation function correctly estimates the backed-up utility function values and the frontier node behaves as a leaf node. Unfortunately, this is rarely the case and we may end up selecting non-optimal moves.

Evaluation function

Devising an apt evaluation function is essential for the partial minimax method to be of any use. First, it conveys domain-specific information to the general search method by assigning a merit value to a game state. This means that the range of the evaluation function must be wide enough so that we can distinguish relevant game situations. Second, theoretical analysis of the partial minimax shows that errors in the evaluation function start to dominate the root value when the look-ahead depth n increases, and to tackle this the evaluation function should be derived using a suitable methodology for the problem. Also, static evaluation functions often analyse just one game state at a time, which makes it hard to identify strategical issues and to maintain consistency in consecutive moves, because strategy is about setting up goals with different time scales.

We can also define an evaluation function for the leaf nodes. This can be accomplished simply by including (and possibly by rescaling the range) the utility function to it. An evaluation function $e(s, p)$ for a player p is usually formed by combining numerical measurements $m_i(s, p)$ of the most important properties in the game state s. These measurements define terms $t_k(s, p)$ that often have one of the following substructures:

- Single measurement $m_i(s, p)$ alone defines a term value. These measurements are mainly derived from a game state, but nothing prevents us from using the move history as a measurement. For example, the ply number of the game state can be used to emphasize the effect of a measurement for more offensive or defensive play.

- The difference in measurements, $m_i(s, p) - m_j(s, q)$, is used to estimate opposing features between players p and q, and often the measure is about the balance of the same property (i.e. $i = j$). For example, if $m_i(s, p)$ gives the mass centre of p's pieces, term $|m_i(s, p) - m_i(s, q)|$ reflects the degree of conflicting interests in the game world. In Noughts and Crosses, the evaluation function can estimate the number of win nodes in the non-leaf subtrees of the current node (see Figure 4.4).

- Ratio of measurements $m_i(s, p)/m_j(s, q)$ combines properties that are not necessarily conflicting, and the term often represents some form of an advantage over the other player. In Draughts, for example, a heuristic can consider the piece advantage, because it is likely that having more pieces than your opponent leads to a better outcome.

The evaluation function aggregates these terms maintaining the zero-sum property: $e(s, \text{MAX}) = -e(s', \text{MIN})$, where s' is a state that resembles state s but where MIN and MAX roles are reversed. For example, A.L. Samuel's classical heuristic for Draughts (Samuel

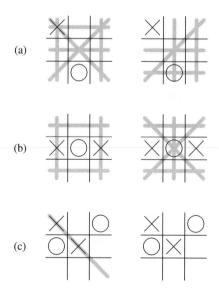

Figure 4.4 Evaluation function $e(\bullet)$ for Noughts and Crosses. (a) MAX (crosses) has six possible winning lines, whereas MIN (noughts) has five: $e(\bullet) = 6 - 5 = 1$ (b) MAX has four possible winning lines and MIN has five $e(\bullet) = 4 - 5 = -1$ (c) Forced win to MAX, hence $e(\bullet) = +\infty$.

1959) evaluates board states with a weighted sum of 16 heuristic measures (e.g. piece locations, piece advantage, centre control, and piece mobility). Evaluation function as a weighted linear sum

$$e(s, p) = \sum_k w_k t_k(s, p) \tag{4.2}$$

suits the cases in which the terms are independent best. In practice, such terms are hard to devise, because a state can present many conflicting advantages and disadvantages at the same time. Samuel (1959, 1967) describes different ways to handle terms that are dependent, interacting, non-linear, or otherwise combinational.

Apart from the selection of measurements and terms, evaluation functions akin to Equation (4.2) pose other questions:

- How many terms should we have? If there are too few terms, we may fail to recognize some aspects of the play, leading to strategical mistakes. On the other hand, too many terms can result in erratic moves, because a critical term can be overrun by a group of irrelevant ones.

- What magnitude should the weights have? Samuel (1959) reduces this problem to determining how to orient towards the inherent goals and strategies of the game: The terms that define the dominant game goals (e.g. winning the game), should have the largest weights. A medium weight indicates that the term relates to subgoals (e.g. capturing enemy pieces). The smallest weights are assigned to terms that force to achieve intermediate goals (e.g. moving pieces to opportunistic positions).

- Which are weight values that lead to the best outcome? Determining the weights can be seen as an optimization problem for the evaluation function over all possible game situations. For simple games, assigning the weights manually can lead to satisfactory evaluation, but more complex games require automatized weight adjusting as well as proper validation and verification strategies.

- How can the losing of 'tendency' information be avoided? For example, in turn-based games the goodness or badness of a given game situation depends on whose turn it is. This kind of information gets easily lost when the evaluation function is based on a weighted sum of terms.

The partial minimax method assumes that game situations can be ranked by giving them a single numeric value. In the real world, decision-making is rarely this simple: Humans are – at least on their favourite expertise domain – apt to ponder on multi-dimensional 'functions' and can approximately grade and compare the pros and cons of different selections. Moreover, humans tend to consider the positional and material advantages and their balance. Moves that radically change both of these measurements are hard to evaluate and compare using any general single-value scheme. For example, losing the queen in Chess usually weakens winning possibilities radically, but in certain situations sacrificing the queen can lead to a better end game.

Controlling the search depth

Evaluation up to a fixed ply depth can be seriously misleading, because a heuristically promising path can lead later on to an unfavourable situation. This is called the *horizon effect*, and a usual way to counteract it is to do a *staged search*, where we search several plies deeper from nodes that look exceptionally good (one should always look a gift horse in the mouth).

If the game has often-occurring game states, the time used in the search can be traded for larger memory consumption by storing triples ⟨state, state value, best move from state⟩ in a *transposition table*. Transposition table implements one of the simplest learning strategies, *rote learning*: If the frontier node's value is already stored, the effective search depth is increased without extra stage searches. Transposition table also gives an efficient implementation for *iterative deepening*, where the idea is to apply n-move look-ahead with increasing values for $n = 1, 2, \ldots$ until time or memory constraints are exceeded.

The look-ahead depth need not to be the same for every node, but it can vary according to the phase of the game or the branching factor. A chain of unusually narrow subtrees is easier to follow to a deeper level, and these subtrees often relate to tactical situations that do not allow mistakes. Moreover, games can be divided into phases (e.g. opening, mid-game, and end game) that correlate to the number of pieces and their positions on the board. The strategies employed in each phase differ somewhat, and the search method should adapt to these different requirements.

No matter how cleverly we change the search depth, it does not entirely remove the horizon effect – it only widens the horizon. Another weakness of the look-ahead approach is that the evaluations that take place deep in the tree can be biased by their very depth: We want to have an estimate of minimax but, in reality, we get a minimax of estimates. Also, the search depth introduces another bias, because the minimax value for the root node gets distorted towards win in odd plies and towards loss in even plies, which is caused by errors in the evaluation function. A survey of other approaches to cope with the horizon effect – including identification of quiescent nodes and using null moves – is presented by Abramson (1989).

At first sight, it seems that the deeper the partial minimax searches the game tree, the better it performs. Perhaps counter-intuitively, the theory derived for analysing partial minimax method warns that this assumption is not always justified. Assume that we are using n-move look-ahead heuristic in a game tree that has a uniform branching factor b and depth d, and the leaf values are generated from a uniform random distribution. Now, we have three theorems about the partial search, which can be summarized as follows:

- *Minimax convergence theorem*: As n increases, it is likely that the root value converges to only one value that is given by a function of b and d.

- *Last player theorem*: The root values backed up from odd and even n frontiers cannot be compared with each other. In other words, values from different plies can be compared only if the same player has made the last move.

- *Minimax pathology theorem*: When n increases, the probability for selecting a non-optimal move increases. This result seems to be caused by the combination of the uniformity assumptions on branching, depth, and leaf value distribution. Removing any of these assumptions seems to result in non-pathology. Fortunately, this is often the case in practice.

Although the partial minimax method is easy to derive from the minimax method by just introducing one count-down parameter to the recursion, the theoretical results show that these two methods differ considerably. Theory also cautions us not to assume too much, and the development of partial minimax methods belongs more to the area of experimentation, verification, and hindsight.

4.2 Alpha-Beta Pruning

When we are expanding a node in minimax, we already have available more information than what the basic minimax uses because of the depth-first search order. For example, if we are expanding MIN's node, we know that in order to end up in this node MAX has to choose it in the previous ply. Assume that the MAX node in the previous ply has already found a choice that provides a result four (see Figure 4.5). Therefore, the MIN node we are currently expanding will not be selected by MAX if its result is smaller than four. With this in mind, we descend to its children, and because we are expanding a MIN node, we want to find the minimum among them. If at any point this minimum becomes smaller than or equal to four, we can stop immediately and prune this branch of the game tree. This is because in the previous ply MAX has a choice that leads to at least as good a result and hence this part of the tree will not be selected. Thus, by removing branches that do not offer good move candidates, we can reduce the actual branching factor and the number of expanded nodes.

Alpha-beta pruning is a search method that keeps track of the best move for each player while it proceeds in a depth-first fashion in the game tree. During the search it observes and updates two values, alpha and beta. Alpha value is associated with MAX and it can never decrease; beta value is associated with MIN and it can never increase. If in a MAX node alpha has value four, it means that MAX does not have to consider any of the children that have a value less than or equal to four; alpha is the worst result that MAX can achieve from that node. Similarly, a MIN node that has a beta value six can omit children that have a value of six or more. In other words, the value of a backed-up node is not less than alpha and not greater than beta. Moreover, the alpha value of a node is never less than the alpha

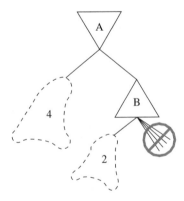

Figure 4.5 Pruning the game tree. MAX node A has the maximum value four when it expands node B. If the minimum value of node B gets below four, node B can be discarded from search and unexpanded children can be omitted.

value of its ancestors, and the beta value of a node is never greater than the beta value of its ancestors.

The alpha-beta method prunes subtrees off the original game tree observing the following rules:

(i) Prune below any MIN node having a beta value less than or equal to the alpha value of any of its MAX ancestors.

(ii) Prune below any MAX node having an alpha value greater than or equal to the beta value of any of its MIN ancestors.

Algorithm 4.3 describes a minimax method that employs alpha-beta pruning. Initially, the algorithm is called with the parameter values $\alpha = -\infty$ and $\beta = +\infty$. Algorithm 4.4 describes a variant of alpha-beta pruning using negamax instead.

Algorithm 4.3 Alpha-beta pruning using minimax.

MINIMAX-ALPHA-BETA(v, α, β)
  in: node v; alpha value α; beta value β
  out: utility value of node v
  1: **if** $children(v) = \emptyset$ **then**   ▷ v is a leaf.
  2:    **return** $value(v)$
  3: **else if** $label(v) = $ MIN **then**   ▷ v is a MIN node.
  4:    **for all** $u \in children(v)$ **do**
  5:      $e \leftarrow$ MINIMAX-ALPHA-BETA(u, α, β)
  6:      **if** $e < \beta$ **then**
  7:        $\beta \leftarrow e$
  8:      **end if**
  9:      **if** $\beta \leq \alpha$ **then**
10:        **return** β ▷ Prune.
11:      **end if**
12:    **end for**
13:    **return** β
14: **else**   ▷ v is a MAX node.
15:    **for all** $u \in children(v)$ **do**
16:      $e \leftarrow$ MINIMAX-ALPHA-BETA(u, α, β)
17:      **if** $\alpha < e$ **then**
18:        $\alpha \leftarrow e$
19:      **end if**
20:      **if** $\beta \leq \alpha$ **then**
21:        **return** α ▷ Prune.
22:      **end if**
23:    **end for**
24:    **return** α
25: **end if**

Algorithm 4.4 Alpha-beta pruning using negamax.

NEGAMAX-ALPHA-BETA(v, α, β)
  in: node v; alpha value α; beta value β
  out: utility value of node v
  1: **if** $children(v) = \emptyset$ **then**   ▷ v is a leaf.
  2:    $\ell \leftarrow value(v)$
  3:    **if** $label(v) = \text{MIN}$ **then** $\ell \leftarrow -\ell$ **end if**
  4:    **return** ℓ
  5: **else**   ▷ v is a MAX or MIN node.
  6:    **for all** $u \in children(v)$ **do**
  7:       $e \leftarrow -\text{NEGAMAX-ALPHA-BETA}(u, -\beta, -\alpha)$
  8:       **if** $\beta \le e$ **then**
  9:          **return** e ▷ Prune.
10:      **end if**
11:      **if** $\alpha < e$ **then**
12:         $\alpha \leftarrow e$
13:      **end if**
14:    **end for**
15:    **return** α
16: **end if**

Let us go through an example, which is illustrated in Figure 4.6. First, we recurse through nodes A and B passing the initial values $\alpha = -\infty$ and $\beta = +\infty$, until for the MAX node C we get values -3 and -2 from the leaves. We return $\alpha = -2$ to B, which calls D with parameters $\alpha = -\infty$ and $\beta = -2$. Checking the first leaf gives $\alpha = +5$, which fulfils the pruning condition $\alpha \ge \beta$. We can prune all other leaves of node D, because we know MIN will never choose D when it is in node B. In node B, $\beta = -2$, which is returned to node A as a new α value. Second, we call node E with parameters $\alpha = -2$ and $\beta = +\infty$. The leaf value -5 below node F has no effect, and F returns -2 to node E, which fulfils the pruning condition $\beta \le \alpha$. Third, we recurse nodes leaving from G with $\alpha = -2$ and $\beta = +\infty$. In node H, we update $\alpha = +1$, which becomes the β value for G. Because the first leaf node of I fulfils the pruning condition, we can prune all other branches omitting it. Finally, node G returns the β value to the root node A, which becomes its α value and $+1$ is the result for the whole tree.

4.2.1 Analysis

The efficiency of alpha-beta pruning depends on the order in which the children are expanded. Preferably, we would like to consider them in non-decreasing value order in MIN nodes and in non-increasing order in MAX nodes. If the orders are reversed, it is possible that alpha-beta cannot prune anything and reduces back to plain minimax.

Reverting to the best case, let us analyse using the negamax variant how many nodes alpha-beta pruning expands. Suppose that at depth $d - 1$ alpha-beta can prune as often as possible so that each node at depth $d - 1$ needs to expand only one child at depth

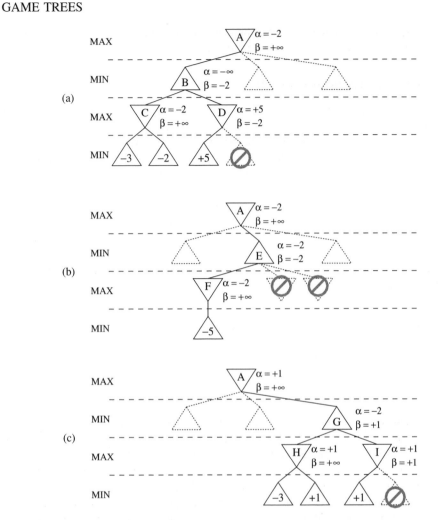

Figure 4.6 An example of alpha-beta pruning: (a) searching the subtree B, (b) searching the subtree E, and (c) searching the subtree G. The values for α and β represent the situation when a node has been searched.

d before the rest gets pruned away. The only exceptions are the nodes belonging to the principal variation (or the optimum path) but we leave them out in our analysis. At depth $d-2$ we cannot prune any nodes, because no child returns a value less than the value of beta that was originally passed to it, which at $d-2$ is negated and becomes less than or equal to alpha. Continuing upwards, at depth $d-3$ all nodes (except the principal variation) can be pruned, at depth $d-4$ no nodes can be pruned, and so forth.

If the branching factor of the tree is b, the number of nodes increases by a factor of b at half of the plies of the tree and stays almost constant at the other half. Hence, the total number of expanded nodes is $\Omega(b^{d/2}) = \Omega(\sqrt{b^d})$. In other words, in the best case

alpha-beta allows to reduce the number of branches to the square root of its original value
and lets minimax to search twice the original depth in the same time.

4.2.2   Principal variation search

For the alpha-beta pruning to be more effective, the interval (α, β) should be as small as
possible. In *aspiration search*, we limit the interval artificially and are ready to handle cases
in which the search fails and we have to revert to the original values. The search fails at
internal node v if all of its subtrees have their minimax values outside the assumed range
(α', β') (i.e. every subtree value $e \notin (\alpha', \beta')$). Because minimax (and negamax) method
with alpha-beta pruning always returns values within the search interval, the out-of-range
value e can be used to recognize a failed search. As noted by Fishburn (1983), we can add
a *fail-soft* enhancement to the search by returning a value e that gives the best possible
estimate of the actual alpha-beta range (i.e. e is as close as possible to it with respect to
the information gathered in the failed search).

   Principal variation search (PVS) – introduced by Finkel and Fishburn (1982) and re-
named by Marsland and Campbell (1982) – does the search even more intelligently. A node
in a game tree belongs to one of the following types:

  (i) α-node, where every move has $e \le \alpha$ and none of them gets selected;

 (ii) β-node, where every move has $e \ge \beta$;

(iii) principal variation node, where one or more moves has $e > \alpha$ but none of them has
      $e \ge \beta$.

PVS assumes that whenever we find a principal variation move when searching a node,
we have a principal variation node. This assumption means that we will not find a better
move for the node in the remaining children. Simply put, once we have found a good move
(i.e. which is between α and β), we search the rest of the moves assuming that they are
all bad, which can be done much quicker than searching for a good move among them.
This can be verified by using a narrow alpha-beta interval $(\alpha, \alpha + \varepsilon)$, which is called a *null
window*. The value ε is selected so that the encountered values cannot fall inside the interval
$(\alpha, \alpha + \varepsilon)$. If this principal variation assumption fails and we find a better move, we have
to re-search it normally without assumptions, but this extra effort is often compensated by
the savings gained. Algorithm 4.5 concretizes this idea.

4.3   Games of Chance

Diced Noughts and Crosses is a generalization of the ordinary Noughts and Crosses. The
game is played on an $m \times m$ grid with a die of n equally probable sides. The player who
has ℓ tokens in a row is the winner. In each turn, a player first selects a subset S of empty
squares on the grid and then distributes n 'reservation marks' to them. The amount for
marks in an empty square s is denoted by $marks(s)$. Next, the player casts the die for
each $s \in S$. Let us assume that the outcome of the die is d. The player places her token

Algorithm 4.5 Principal variation search using negamax.
___

PRINCIPAL-VARIATION-SEARCH(v, α, β)
 in: node v; alpha value α; beta value β
 out: utility value of node v
 local: value t for null-window test
 1: **if** $children(v) = \emptyset$ **then**   ▷ v is a leaf.
 2: $\ell \leftarrow value(v)$
 3: **if** $label(v) =$ MIN **then** $\ell \leftarrow -\ell$ **end if**
 4: **return** ℓ
 5: **else**   ▷ v is a MAX or MIN node.
 6: $w \leftarrow$ some node $w' \in children(v)$
 7: $e \leftarrow -$PRINCIPAL-VARIATION-SEARCH($w, -\beta, -\alpha$)
 8: **for all** $u \in children(v) \setminus \{w\}$ **do**
 9:   **if** $\beta \leq e$ **then**
10:    **return** e ▷ Prune.
11:   **end if**
12:   **if** $\alpha < e$ **then**
13:    $\alpha \leftarrow e$
14:   **end if**
15:   $t \leftarrow -$PRINCIPAL-VARIATION-SEARCH($u, -(\alpha + \varepsilon), -\alpha$)
16:   **if** $e < t$ **then**
17:    **if** $t \leq \alpha$ **or** $\beta \leq t$ **then**
18:     $e \leftarrow t$
19:    **else**   ▷ Not a principal variation node.
20:     $e \leftarrow -$PRINCIPAL-VARIATION-SEARCH($u, -\beta, -t$)
21:    **end if**
22:   **end if**
23: **end for**
24: **return** e ▷ Fail-soft enhancement.
25: **end if**
___

to s if $d \leq marks(s)$. In other words, each mark on a square increases the probability for capturing it by $1/n$, and if $marks(s) = n$, the capture is certain. To compare, in Noughts and Crosses a legal move is always certain, but in Diced Noughts and Crosses a move is only the player's suggestion that can get rejected with the probability $1 - d/marks(\bullet)$. We get the ordinary Noughts and Crosses with parameters $m = \ell = 3$ and $n = 1$. The variant in which $n = 2$ can be played using a coin and we name it Copper Noughts and Crosses.

Owing to indeterministic moves, the game tree of Copper Noughts and Crosses cannot be drawn as a *minimax tree* as in Figure 4.1. However, the outcome of a random event can be accounted by considering its expected value. This idea can be used to generalize the game trees by introducing *chance nodes* (Michie 1966). Figure 4.7 illustrates how a move in Copper Noughts and Crosses may be evaluated from the perspective of MAX.

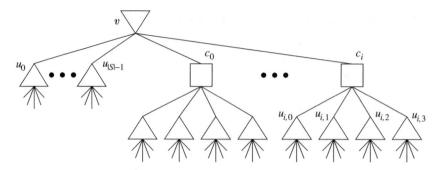

Figure 4.7 An extract from a general game tree for Copper Noughts and Crosses consists of a MAX node (the labile triangle), MIN nodes (the stable triangles) and CHANCE nodes (the squares).

Suppose that the grid has $|S|$ empty squares. The player can select $|S|$ certain moves $u_0, \ldots, u_{|S|-1}$ that can be evaluated as in an ordinary minimax tree. The coin tossing is used when the player's marks m_0 and m_1 are on different squares. Because we do not have to care about the identity of the marks, there are $|S|(|S| - 1)/2$ combinations to consider. A chance node c_i $(i \in [0, \ldots, |S|(|S| - 1)/2 - 1])$ has four possible outcomes: the token can be placed on both marks, only on m_0, only on m_1, or both marks are void. Because each of these events happens with the probability $1/4$, the value for c_i can be calculated by $1/4 \cdot (e(u_{i,0}) + e(u_{i,1}) + e(u_{i,2}) + e(u_{i,3}))$, where $e(\bullet)$ represents the utility value of the subtree.

The game trees resembling Figure 4.7 are called *-minimax trees (Ballard 1983). Their utility values can be obtained from Equation (4.3), which is a generalization of Equation (4.1). Here, $emm(\bullet)$ is an abbreviation for the *expectiminimax* value.

$$emm(v) = \begin{cases} value(v), & \text{if } v \text{ is a leaf;} \\ \min_{u \in children(v)} \{emm(u)\}, & \text{if } v \text{ is a MIN node;} \\ \max_{u \in children(v)} \{emm(u)\}, & \text{if } v \text{ is a MAX node,} \\ \sum_{u \in children(v)} (P(u) \cdot emm(u)), & \text{if } v \text{ is a CHANCE node,} \end{cases} \qquad (4.3)$$

The chance nodes often cause a combinatorial explosion in the branching factor of the game trees, which prevents us from implementing Equation (4.3) similarly to Algorithm 4.1. Because the chance nodes do not affect the evaluation of MIN and MAX nodes, the evaluation method can use alpha-beta pruning, but even this observation does not help much if the chance nodes have the largest branching factor. Interestingly, it is possible to utilize the information gathered by the depth-first searching order also in the chance nodes. To do this, we assume that for the leaf nodes $value(\bullet)$ can be bounded to a constant interval $[\ell_{\min}, \ell_{\max}]$ (Ballard 1983). Suppose we are calculating the value of a chance node c within the given interval (α, β) and we are about to descend to its child node u_i. In other words, we have already evaluated the child nodes $u_0, \ldots, u_{i-1}$ and nodes $u_{i+1}, \ldots$ will be evaluated later. Node c will not be selected by its parent if either Equation (4.4) or

Equation (4.5) holds.

$$\sum_{k=0}^{i-1}(P(u_k) \cdot emm(u_k)) + P(u_i) \cdot emm(u_i) + \ell_{max} \cdot \left(1 - \sum_{k=0}^{i} P(u_k)\right) \leq \alpha, \qquad (4.4)$$

$$\sum_{k=0}^{i-1}(P(u_k) \cdot emm(u_k)) + P(u_i) \cdot emm(u_i) + \ell_{min} \cdot \left(1 - \sum_{k=0}^{i} P(u_k)\right) \geq \beta. \qquad (4.5)$$

The first Σ-term of the summation is already known, the middle term is to be calculated next, and the last one gives the worst estimate for the remaining nodes. By reorganizing the terms, we get Equation (4.6) and Equation (4.7), respectively, and because of the direction of these inequalities the expressions on the right-hand side can be used as alpha-beta values for the node u_i.

$$emm(u_i) \leq \frac{\alpha - \sum_{k=0}^{i-1}(P(u_k) \cdot emm(u_k)) - \ell_{max} \cdot \left(1 - \sum_{k=0}^{i} P(u_k)\right)}{P(u_i)}, \qquad (4.6)$$

$$emm(u_i) \geq \frac{\beta - \sum_{k=0}^{i-1}(P(u_k) \cdot emm(u_k)) - \ell_{min} \cdot \left(1 - \sum_{k=0}^{i} P(u_k)\right)}{P(u_i)}. \qquad (4.7)$$

The alpha-beta values for the child nodes can be calculated incrementally from the following recurrences:

$$\begin{cases} E_0 = 0 \\ E_k = E_{k-1} + P(u_{k-1}) \cdot emm(u_{k-1}) \end{cases} \qquad \begin{cases} D_0 = 1 - P(u_0) \\ D_k = D_{k-1} - P(u_k) \end{cases}$$

In other words, for the child node u_i we get the interval bounds

$$\alpha_i = \frac{\alpha - E_i - \ell_{max} \cdot D_i}{P(u_i)}, \qquad (4.8)$$

$$\beta_i = \frac{\beta - E_i - \ell_{min} \cdot D_i}{P(u_i)}. \qquad (4.9)$$

Note that $E_k + P(u_k) \cdot emm(u_k)$ also gives the final result of c at the last child node u_k. Algorithm 4.6 implements this alpha-beta pruning for every node in a $*$-minimax tree with the fail-soft enhancement.

The drawback of Algorithm 4.6 is that it expects the worst from the un-visited children of the chance nodes and, thus, the alpha-beta pruning begins to affect only later in the evaluation. However, in practice these children tend to have the same properties. This is why Ballard (1983) considers Algorithm 4.6 as a starting point (called *Star1*) and presents various effective sampling (or probing) strategies for the child nodes that supplement the depth-first idea and lead to narrower alpha-beta intervals. Also Hauk *et al.* (2005) provide further insights into the topic.

4.4 Summary

In zero-sum perfect information games, the minimax method provides us with the optimal game play. However, if we cannot build the whole game tree for the game, we have to

Algorithm 4.6 Expectiminimax using alpha-beta pruning and fail-soft enhancement.

EXPECTI-ALPHA-BETA(v, α, β)
    in: node v; alpha value α; beta value β
    out: utility value of node v
    constant: the range of $value(\bullet)$ for a leaf node is $[\ell_{min}, \ell_{max}]$
1: **if** $children(v) = \emptyset$ **then**   ▷ v is a leaf.
2:   **return** $value(v)$
3: **else if** $label(v) =$ CHANCE **then**   ▷ v is a CHANCE node.
4:   $d \leftarrow 1$
5:   $s \leftarrow 0$
6:   **for all** $u \in children(v)$ **do**
7:     $d \leftarrow d - P(u)$
8:     $\alpha' \leftarrow \max\{\ell_{min}, (\alpha - s - \ell_{max} \cdot d)/P(u)\}$
9:     $\beta' \leftarrow \min\{\ell_{max}, (\beta - s - \ell_{min} \cdot d)/P(u)\}$
10:     $e \leftarrow$ EXPECTI-ALPHA-BETA(u, α', β')
11:     $s \leftarrow s + P(u) \cdot e$
12:     **if** $e \leq \alpha$ **then**
13:       **return** $s + \ell_{max} \cdot d$
14:     **end if**
15:     **if** $\beta \leq e$ **then**
16:       **return** $s + \ell_{min} \cdot d$
17:     **end if**
18:   **end for**
19:   **return** s
20: **else if** $label(v) =$ MIN **then**   ▷ v is a MIN node.
21:   $e \leftarrow +\infty$
22:   **for all** $u \in children(v)$ **do**
23:     **if** $e < \beta$ **then** $\beta \leftarrow e$ **end if**
24:     $t \leftarrow$ EXPECTI-ALPHA-BETA(u, α, β)
25:     **if** $t < e$ **then** $e \leftarrow t$ **end if**
26:     **if** $e \leq \alpha$ **then return** e **end if**
27:   **end for**
28:   **return** e
29: **else**   ▷ v is a MAX node.
30:   $e \leftarrow -\infty$
31:   **for all** $u \in children(v)$ **do**
32:     **if** $\alpha < e$ **then** $\alpha \leftarrow e$ **end if**
33:     $t \leftarrow$ EXPECTI-ALPHA-BETA(u, α, β)
34:     **if** $e < t$ **then** $e \leftarrow t$ **end if**
35:     **if** $\beta \leq e$ **then return** e **end if**
36:   **end for**
37:   **return** e
38: **end if**

reduce its size by either limiting the search depth or cutting the branches. In a partial game tree, the depth is reduced artificially by making the internal nodes as leaves. This can be done using a heuristic to estimate their outcome, which of course can lead to suboptimal results. The branching factor can be reduced with alpha-beta pruning, which cuts off nodes that cannot provide a better outcome than the current best result. If we set tighter limits for the pruning (like in PVS), we can improve the running even further. The game tree can include probabilistic elements, which can be accounted by modelling them as chance nodes.

Game trees can be used in many classical board games, and they have been studied widely. There are many game-specific improvements that allow, for example, to choose the opening and closing moves from a set of pre-calculated alternatives. Nevertheless, in the middle of the game play where the number of possible situations is much greater, the methods revert back to building game trees to find out the best move for the next round.

Exercises

4-1 The most famous non-zero sum game is Prisoner's Dilemma, where two prisoners (i.e. players), accused of the same crime, have two possible moves:

- Cooperate with the other prisoner and keep silent during the interrogation.
- Defect and rat on the other prisoner.

The moves have the following pay-offs:

	You cooperate.	*You defect.*
I cooperate.	6 months imprisonment	10 years imprisonment
I defect.	Freedom	5 years imprisonment

Not knowing the opponent's move, each prisoner must now select a move and face the consequences.

In Iterated Prisoner's Dilemma, these encounters are repeated, and the players try to minimize the sum of the prison sentences. The players have a memory of all the previous encounters. Devise a strategy for the Iterated Prisoner's Dilemma. Try out both egoistic and altruistic approaches.

4-2 Assume that we have the game trees of Figure 4.8 and Figure 4.9, where player MAX has the first move. Show how to solve for the winner of the games using the minimax method. Illustrate how the algorithm operates with the given game trees.

4-3 In practice we are interested in not only the evaluation value of the root node but also the best move from it. Devise a simple method that extends the game tree algorithms presented to support this aspect.

4-4 In the game tree algorithms presented, the moves are generated implicitly by the statement $u \in children(v)$. Concretize these algorithms by introducing a primitive routine $child(v)$ that iterates all the nodes in $children(v)$ one by one and returns NIL when they are exhausted.

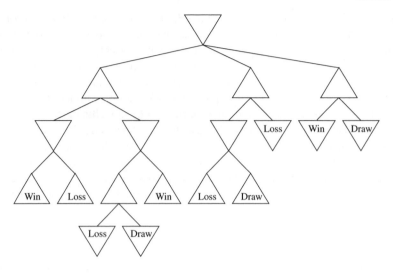

Figure 4.8 A game tree with three possible outcomes (from the perspective of MAX): win, draw, loss.

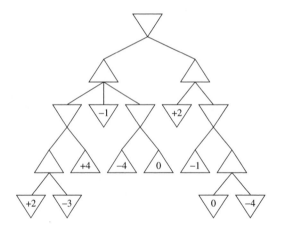

Figure 4.9 A game tree with outcomes from the range $[-4, +4]$.

4-5 In Exercise 4-4, we concretize the game tree algorithms with an iterator abstraction. In this exercise use the following state changing functions instead:

move(v)	Iterates all the possible moves from node v of player *label*(v) and returns NIL when they are exhausted.
apply(v, m)	Returns the successor node of v for move m.
cancel(u, m)	Yields the parent node of u when move m is taken back.

You can assume that a move is reversible (i.e. $v = cancel(apply(v, m), m)$).

4-6 Draw a complete game tree for Division Nim with eight matches. Analyse the outcome using minimax.

4-7 In Division Nim, the heap cannot be divided into equal halves. Factor Division Nim relaxes this constraint by allowing a heap of $2n$ matches to be divided into two heaps of n matches if n has a common prime factor with the player's turn number. The turns are numbered consecutively starting from zero. Give a complete game tree for Factor Division Nim with seven matches and assign the values 'win', 'loss', and 'draw' to the nodes.

4-8 One-Two-Three Nim is another simplification of Nim. It starts with a heap of n matches and on each turn a player removes one, two, or three matches from the heap. The player to pick the last match wins. Draw a complete game tree and analyse the outcome using minimax for this variant of Nim when $n = 6$ (see Figure 4.10).

4-9 Extend the game tree of Exercise 4-8 for $n = 9$. Observe how wins and losses behave in MAX and MIN nodes. Can you design an evaluation function that gives for each node a perfect estimate of the utility function? If so, how does this affect playing One-Two-Three Nim?

4-10 In Nim proper, there are initially several heaps of matches. On each turn, a player selects one heap and removes at least one match from that heap. The player to pick the last match wins. Draw a complete game tree and analyse the outcome using minimax for Nim with three heaps having 1, 2 and 3 matches (see Figure 4.11).

4-11 Poker is an imperfect information game. Why cannot the minimax method be used to solve it?

4-12 Minimax assumes that the players are rational and try to win. If this is not true, does the method still work?

4-13 When searching a game tree, which would be a preferable situation: having a large d or a large b (i.e. having a deep game tree or a wide game tree)?

4-14 Minimax can expand $(b^{d+1} - 1)/(b - 1)$ nodes in a game tree with a branching factor b and depth d. Obviously, the branching factor depends on the game: In Draughts

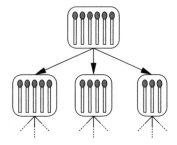

Figure 4.10 Partial game tree for One-Two-Three Nim.

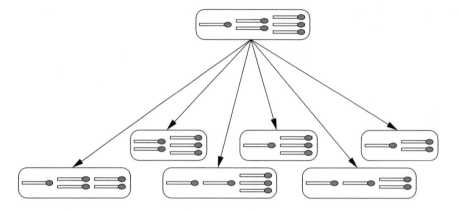

Figure 4.11 Partial game tree for Nim with heaps of size 1, 2 and 3.

each position has on average three possible moves, in Chess about thirty, and in Go there are hundreds of possible move candidates. Assume that expanding a node takes 1 ms of computation time. How long does it take to evaluate a game tree when $b \in \{3, 30, 300\}$ and $d \in \{2, 4, 8, 16\}$?

4-15 Equation (4.1) defines the minimax value for a node as a recursive function. Give a similar definition for negamax.

4-16 Assume that in Noughts and Crosses MIN (playing noughts) is using 1-move look-ahead heuristic with the evaluation function of Figure 4.4. Player MAX has made the first move by putting a cross in a corner (see the left subtree in Figure 4.1), and MIN has to select one of the five possible moves by estimating the outcome of the next ply. What move does MIN select and why?

If on the next turn MAX puts a cross to the opposite corner, what is MIN's next move? How does the game end and why?

4-17 A compact transposition table does not include redundant game state information. Design an algorithm that normalizes the game states of Noughts and Crosses so that rotations and mirror images are represented only by one game state as in Figure 4.1.

4-18 Some turn-based games allow the same state (e.g. the same board situation) to occur many times. How would you make them unique so that they can be differentiated in the game tree algorithms.

4-19 Show how alpha-beta pruning works on the game tree of Figure 4.9. Does the expanding order of nodes in the first ply from the root affect the overall number of pruned nodes?

4-20 The two-player game n^2-Pile Flipflop is played on an $n \times n$ board. Initially, each square of the board has a token with the value NEUTRAL. Player flip has $5n$ FLIP tokens and $\lceil \sqrt{n} \rceil$ fixed FLIP tokens, and player flop has $5n$ FLOP tokens and $\lceil \sqrt{n} \rceil$

fixed FLOP tokens. Player flip starts the game. On each turn, a player can put one token
on top of any pile that does not yet have a fixed token. The topmost token of a pile
is said to control the pile. When a token is added, all piles on the two horizontal, two
vertical, and four diagonal lines starting from the added token are reversed (i.e. the
undermost token is turned up to be the topmost and controls the pile). The reversing
line ends to the player's other control token, the opponent's fixed token, or at the end
of the board (see Figure 4.12). The game ends when either of the players has run out
of tokens or cannot add a token to the board. The player controlling more piles at the
end is the winner.

Write a program that plays n^2-Pile Flipflop. If $n = 1$, player flip wins. Is there a
winning strategy for other n values?

4-21 Simplify Algorithm 4.6 by assuming that the event probabilities in a chance node are
uniform. In other words, each chance node c has n children u_i for which $P(u_i) = 1/n$.

4-22 In Copper Noughts and Crosses all the chance moves are marked and fixed before
the coin is tossed for both of them. Let us change this rule: The player marks the first
empty square and then the coin is used for resolving the capture. Then the second
mark is handled in the same way. Draw a simple game tree for this variant.

Figure 4.12   An example of n^2-Pile Flipflop, where $n = 6$. Round pieces represent the
tokens for FLIP, FLOP or empty pieces for NEUTRAL; square pieces represent the fixed
tokens. When a token FLOP is added to a pile, all the piles along the marked lines are
reversed. The reversing line ends to another FLOP token, to a fixed FLIP token or at the end
of the board.

5

Path Finding

As in the real world, finding a path from one place to another is a common – if not the most common – algorithmic problem in computer games. Although the problem can seem fairly simple to us humans (most of the time), a surprising amount of the total computation time in many commercial computer games is spent in solving path-finding problems. The reasons for this are the ever-increasing complexity of game world environments and the number of entities that must be calculated. Moreover, if the environment changes dynamically (e.g. old paths become blocked and new ones are opened), routes cannot be solved beforehand but only reactively on the spot as the game progresses. Real-time interaction puts even further constraints, because the feedback to the human player should be almost instant and the path must be found before he gets too impatient to wait any longer.

The problem statement of path finding is simple: Given a start point s and a goal point r, find a path from s to r minimizing a given criterion. Usually this cost function is travelling time, which can depend on the distance, the type of terrain, or the mode of travel. We can think of path finding either as a search problem – find a path that minimizes the cost – or as an optimization problem – minimize the cost subject to the constraint of the path. Consequently, graph search methods can be seen as optimization methods, where the constraints are given implicitly in the form and weights of the graph. Although we can use general optimization methods such as simplex, they lose the graph-like qualities of the path-finding problem, which is why we focus mainly on the search problem throughout this chapter.

In an ideal case, we would do path finding in a continuous game world and solve for the route from s to r straightforwardly. Unfortunately, this is rarely a realistic option, since the search space gets too complex. Instead, we discretize the search space by restricting the possible *waypoints* into a finite set and reducing the paths to *connections* between them. In other words, we form a graph in which the vertices are the waypoints and the edges are the connections. We have thus reduced the original problem to that of finding a path in a graph (see Figure 5.1). The idea resembles travelling in the real world: Move to the closest waypoint (airport, bus stop, underground station, harbour etc.), go through waypoints until closest to the destination, exit the final waypoint, and proceed to the destination.

Algorithms and Networking for Computer Games   Jouni Smed and Harri Hakonen
© 2006 John Wiley & Sons, Ltd

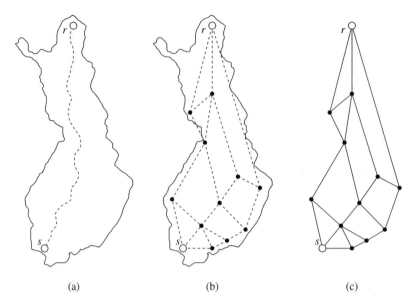

Figure 5.1 Real-world path finding is reduced into a graph problem by discretizing the search space into waypoints. The waypoints are the vertices and the connections between them are the edges of the graph.

This approach gives us a three-step method: First, we show how the game world can be discretized. On the basis of the discretization, we can form a graph, and the path-finding problem is transformed into that of finding the minimum path in the graph. Although there are several algorithms to solve this problem, we concentrate on A* algorithm, which uses a heuristic estimate function to enhance the search. Finally, when the minimum path in the graph has been found, it has to be realized as movements in the game world considering how realistic the movements look for the human observing them.

5.1 Discretization of the Game World

The first step in solving the path-finding problem in a continuous world is to discretize it. The type of the game world usually gives an indication on how this discretization ought to be done. We can immediately come up with intuitive choices for waypoints: doorways, centres of the room, along the walls, corners, and around the obstacles (Tozour 2003). Once the waypoints have been selected, we establish whether there is a connection between them based on the geometry of the game world. The connection can be associated with cost based on the distance or type of the environment, and this cost is set to be the weight of the edge.

Although the waypoints can be laid down manually during the level design, preferably it should be an automatic process. Two common approaches to achieve this are to super-impose a grid over the game world, or use a navigation mesh that observes the underlying geometry.

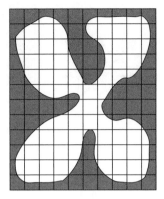 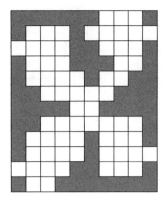

Figure 5.2   A square grid is laid over the game world. If the majority of the world inside a tile is open, the tile is included in the waypoints.

5.1.1   Grid

We can place a grid, which is a tiling of polygons (i.e. tessellation), over the game world. To simplify, we consider only grids in which each tile shares at most one edge with a neighbouring tile (see Figure 5.2). Now, the centre of a tile represents a waypoint, and its neighbourhood, composed of the adjacent tiles, forms the possible connections to other waypoints. The world inside the tile defines whether it is included in the waypoints and what are its connections to other waypoints.

Grids usually support random-access lookup, because each tile should be accessible in a constant time. The drawback of this approach is that a grid does not pay attention to the actual geometry of the game world. For instance, some parts of the world may get unconnected if the granularity of the grid is not fine enough. Also, storing the grid requires memory, but we can reduce this requirement, for example, by using hierarchical lookup tables (van der Sterren 2003).

There are exactly three regular tessellations composed of equilateral triangles, squares, or regular hexagons (see Figure 5.3). When we are defining a neighbourhood for triangular

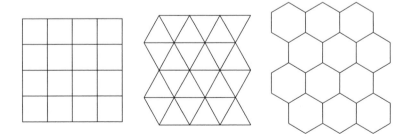

Figure 5.3   Square grid, triangular grid, and hexagonal grid are the only regular two-dimensional tessellations.

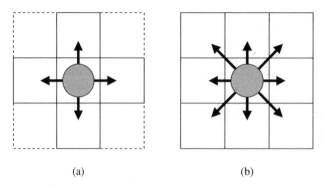

Figure 5.4 A square grid allows (a) four-connectivity and (b) eight-connectivity.

and square grids, we must first decide whether we consider only the tiles adjacent to the edges of a tile or also the tiles that share a corner point with the tile. Figure 5.4 illustrates the situation in a square grid: In the former case we have a four-connectivity (i.e. a tile has at most four neighbours), and in the latter case eight-connectivity. An obvious problem with eight-connectivity is that diagonal moves are longer than vertical or horizontal ones, which should be taken into account in calculations of distances. Because hexagonal grids allow only six-connectivity and the neighbours are equidistant, they are often used in strategy and role-playing games.

Instead of assigning the waypoints to the centre of the tiles, we can use the corners of the tiles. Now, the neighbourhood is determined along the edges and not over them. However, these two waypoint assignments are the dual of each other, since they can be converted to both directions. For the regular tessellations, the conversion is simple, because we can consider the centre of a tile as a corner point of the dual grid and vice versa, and – as we can see in Figure 5.3 – the square grid is the dual shape of itself and the triangular and hexagonal grids are the dual shapes of each other.

5.1.2 Navigation mesh

A navigation mesh is a convex partitioning of the game world geometry. In other words, it is a set of convex polygons that covers the game world, where all adjacent polygons share only two points and one edge, and no polygon overlaps another polygon. Each polygon (or shared edge) represents a waypoint that is connected to the adjacent polygons (see Figure 5.5). Convexity guarantees that we can move in a straight line inside a polygon (e.g. from the current position to the first waypoint, and from the final waypoint to the destination) and from one polygon to another.

By using dynamic programming, we can solve the convex partition problem (i.e. min-imize the number of convex polygons needed to cover the original polygon) optimally in the time $O(r^2 n \log n)$, where n is the number of points (i.e. vertices) and r is the

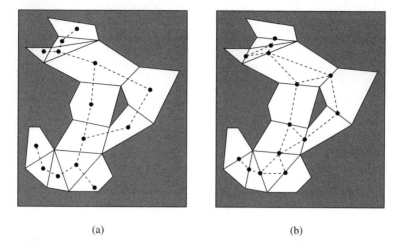

(a)   (b)

Figure 5.5 Navigation mesh is a convex partitioning of the game world geometry. (a) The waypoints have been placed in the middle of each polygon. (b) The centre of each shared edge is a waypoint.

Algorithm 5.1 Hertel–Mehlhorn method for convex partition.

CONVEX-PARTITION(P)
  in: polygon P
  out: convex partition R
  1: $R \leftarrow$ TRIANGULATE(P)
  2: **for all** $e \in E(R) \setminus E(P)$ **do**   ▷ Edges added by triangulation.
  3:   **if not** e divides a concave angle in R **then**
  4:      $E(R) \leftarrow E(R) \setminus \{e\}$
  5:   **end if**
  6: **end for**
  7: **return** R

---

number of notches (i.e. points whose interior angle is concave; $r \leq n - 3$) (Keil 1985). Hertel–Mehlhorn heuristic finds a convex partition in the time $O(n + r \log r)$, and the resulting partition has at most four times the number of polygons of the optimum solution (Hertel and Mehlhorn 1985). The method, described in Algorithm 5.1, first triangulates the original polygon. Although a simple polygon can be triangulated in the time $O(n)$ (Chazelle 1991), Seidel's algorithm provides a simpler randomized algorithm with expected running time of $O(n \log^* n)$ (Seidel 1991). After triangulation, the Hertel–Mehlhorn removes non-essential edges between convex polygons (see Figure 5.6).

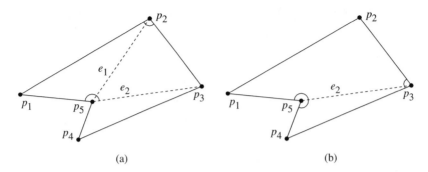

Figure 5.6 After triangulation, Hertel–Mehlhorn method begins to remove non-essential edges to form a convex partition. (a) Edge e_1 is non-essential, because it divides only convex angles at points p_2 and p_5. If it is removed, the resulting polygon $\langle p_1, p_2, p_3, p_5 \rangle$ will be convex. (b) When e_1 is removed, edge e_2 becomes essential and cannot be removed, because it divides a concave angle at point p_5.

5.2   Finding the Minimum Path

After the game world have been discretized, the problem of path finding has been transposed into that of path finding in a finite graph. The waypoints are the vertices of the graph, the connections are the edges, and if each connection is associated with a cost (e.g. travelling time), this is assigned to the weight of the edge.

We have a set of well-known graph algorithms for solving the shortest path problem (let $|V|$ be the number of vertices and $|E|$ the number of edges); for details, see Cormen *et al.* (2001).

- *Breadth-first search*: Expand all vertices at distance k from the start vertex before proceeding to any vertices at distance $k + 1$. Once this frontier has reached the goal vertex, the shortest path has been found. The running time is $O(|V| + |E|)$.

- *Depth-first search*: Expand an undiscovered vertex in the neighbourhood of the most recently expanded vertex, until the goal vertex has been found. The running time is $\Theta(|V| + |E|)$.

- *Dijkstra's algorithm*: Find the shortest paths from a single start vertex to all other vertices in a directed graph with non-negative weights. A straightforward implementation yields a running time of $O(|V|^2)$, which can be improved to $O(|V| \log |V| + |E|)$ with a proper choice of data structure.

We can improve the methods by guiding the search heuristically so that as few vertices as possible are expanded during the search. For instance, *best-first search* orders the vertices in the neighbourhood of a vertex according to a heuristic estimate of their closeness to the goal. Despite the use of a heuristic, best-first search returns the optimal solution because no vertex is discarded. Naturally, we can decrease the running time if we give up optimality: *Beam search* is based on best-first search but it expands only the most promising candidates in the neighbourhood thus allowing suboptimal solutions (see Figure 5.7).

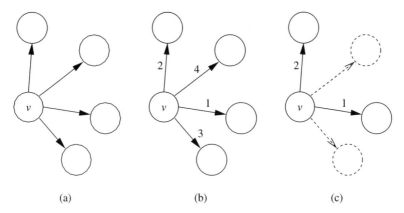

(a)   (b)   (c)

Figure 5.7 Expanding the vertices in the neighbourhood. (a) Breadth-first search does not consider in which order the neighbourhood of vertex v is expanded. (b) Best-first search uses a heuristic function to rank the neighbours but does not exclude any of them. (c) Beam search expands only a subset of the neighbourhood.

In the remainder of this section we consider the properties of a heuristic evaluation function used in guiding the search. Also, we describe and analyse A* algorithm, which is the *de facto* method for path finding in commercial computer games. The basic graph notations used in this section are introduced in Appendix A. The cost of moving (i.e. the sum of weights along a path) from vertex v to vertex u is stored in $g(v \rightsquigarrow u)$. Also, we need two distinguished vertices: a start vertex $s \in V$ and a goal vertex $r \in V$. Obviously, we are interested in the cases in which $s \neq r$, and we want to find a path minimizing $g(s \rightsquigarrow r)$.

5.2.1 Evaluation function

The vertex chosen for expansion is always the one minimizing the evaluation function

$$f(v) = g(s \rightsquigarrow v) + h(v \rightsquigarrow r), \qquad (5.1)$$

where $g(s \rightsquigarrow v)$ estimates the minimum cost from the start vertex s to vertex v, and $h(v \rightsquigarrow r)$ is a heuristic estimate of the cost from v to the goal vertex r. Hence, $f(v)$ estimates the minimal cost of the path from the start vertex to the goal vertex passing through vertex v.

Let $g^*(s \rightsquigarrow v)$ denote the exact cost of the shortest path from s to v, and $h^*(v \rightsquigarrow r)$ denote the exact cost of the shortest path from v to r. Now, $f^*(v) = g^*(s \rightsquigarrow v) + h^*(v \rightsquigarrow r)$ gives the exact cost of the optimal path from s to r through vertex v. Ideally, we would use the function f^* in our algorithm, because then we would not have to expand any unnecessary vertices. Unfortunately, for most search problems, such an oracle function h^* does not exist or it is too costly to compute.

The value of the cost function $g(s \rightsquigarrow v)$ is calculated as the actual cost from the start vertex s to vertex v along the cheapest path found so far. If the graph G is a tree, $g(s \rightsquigarrow v)$ will give the exact cost, because there is only one path leading from s to v. In general

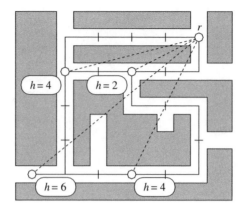

Figure 5.8 An example of a heuristic function. If the weight of an edge is the distance between the vertices using Manhattan metric, a heuristic function h can estimate them with truncated Euclidean distances.

graphs, the cost function $g(s \rightsquigarrow v)$ can err only in overestimating the minimal cost, and its value can be adjusted downwards if a cheaper path to v is found. If we let evaluation function $f(v) = g(s \rightsquigarrow v)$ and assume a cost of 1 unit for each move, we get breadth-first search, because shorter paths will be preferred over the longer ones; instead, if we let $f(v) = -g(s \rightsquigarrow v)$, we get depth-first search, since vertices deeper in the graph will now have a lower cost.

The heuristic function h carries information that is usually based on knowledge from outside the graph. It can be defined in any way appropriate to the problem domain (see Figure 5.8). Obviously, the closer the heuristic estimate is to the actual cost, the lesser our algorithm will expand the superfluous vertices. If we disregard h and our search is based solely on the value of g, we have cheapest-first search, where the algorithm will always choose the vertex nearest to the start vertex. Conversely, an algorithm using only the function h gives us the best-first search.

5.2.2 Properties

Let us define Algorithm A – a name due to tradition – as a best-first search using the evaluation function of Equation (5.1). A search algorithm is *admissible* if it is guaranteed to find a solution path of minimal cost if any solution path exists (e.g. breadth-first search is admissible). If Algorithm A uses the optimal evaluation function f^*, we can prove that it is admissible. In reality, however, the heuristic function h is an estimate. Let us define Algorithm A* as Algorithm A which uses such an estimate. It can be proven that Algorithm A* is admissible if it satisfies the following condition: The value of $h(v \rightsquigarrow r)$ must not overestimate the cost of getting from vertex v to the goal vertex r. In other words,

$$\forall v \in V : h(v \rightsquigarrow r) \leq h^*(v \rightsquigarrow r). \tag{5.2}$$

If the heuristic is locally admissible, it is said to be *monotonic*. In this case, when the search moves through the graph, the evaluation function f will never decrease, since the actual cost is not less than the heuristic cost. Obviously, any monotonic heuristic is also admissible. If Algorithm A* is monotonic, it finds the shortest path to any vertex the first time it is expanded. In other words, if the search rediscovers a vertex, we know that the new path will not be shorter than the one found previously. This allows us to make a significant simplification on the implementation of the algorithm, because we can omit the closed list employed by general search strategies.

Let us state an *optimality* result for Algorithm A*:

Theorem 5.2.1 *The first path from start vertex s to goal vertex r found by monotonic Algorithm A* is optimal.*

Proof. We use a proof by contradiction. Suppose we have an undiscovered vertex v for which $f(v) < g(s \rightsquigarrow r)$. Let u be a vertex lying along the shortest path from s to v. Owing to admissibility, we have $f(u) \leq f(v)$, and because u also must be undiscovered, $f(r) \leq f(u)$. In other words, $f(r) \leq f(u) \leq f(v)$. Because r is the goal vertex, we have $h(r \rightsquigarrow r) = 0$ and $f(r) = g(s \rightsquigarrow r)$. From this it follows that $g(s \rightsquigarrow r) \leq f(v)$, which is a contradiction. This means that there does not exist any undiscovered vertices that are closer to the start vertex s than the goal vertex r. ∎

Although h is sufficient to be a lower estimate on h^*, the more closely it approximates h^*, the better the search algorithm will perform. We can now compare two A* algorithms with respect to their *informedness*. Algorithm $\mathcal{A}_1$ using function h_1 is said to be more informed than algorithm $\mathcal{A}_2$ using function h_2 if

$$\forall v \in V \setminus \{r\} : h_1(v \rightsquigarrow r) \geq h_2(v \rightsquigarrow r). \tag{5.3}$$

This means that $\mathcal{A}_1$ will never expand more vertices than what are expanded by $\mathcal{A}_2$. Because of informedness, there is no better approach than Algorithm A* in the sense that no other search strategy with access to *the same amount of outside knowledge* can do any less work than A* and still be sure of finding the optimal solution.

5.2.3   Algorithm A*

Algorithm 5.2 describes an implementation of Algorithm A*. As mentioned earlier, monotonicity of the evaluation function means that we need only to update an open list of the candidate vertices (lines 15–20), and the algorithm can terminate when it has found the goal vertex (lines 10–12).

Figure 5.9 gives an example of how Algorithm A* works: (a) The weight of an edge describes the distance between its endpoints in Manhattan metric. (b) First, start vertex s gets selected, and its successors a and b are added to the set S (i.e. they are opened). The heuristic measure takes the maximum of the vertical and horizontal distance to the goal vertex. Because $f(b) < f(a)$, vertex b gets selected next. (c) Algorithm opens the successors of vertex b. Vertex e is the most promising candidate and gets selected. (d) Vertex e does not have undiscovered successors, because d was already opened by b. The remaining candidates have the same value, so algorithm selects c arbitrarily. Vertex f is opened. (e) Vertex a has the lowest value but has no undiscovered successors. Instead, vertex d gets selected and g is opened. (f) Of two remaining candidates, vertex g gets selected, and goal vertex r is found. The optimum path is $s \rightarrow b \rightarrow d \rightarrow g \rightarrow r$ and its cost is 12.

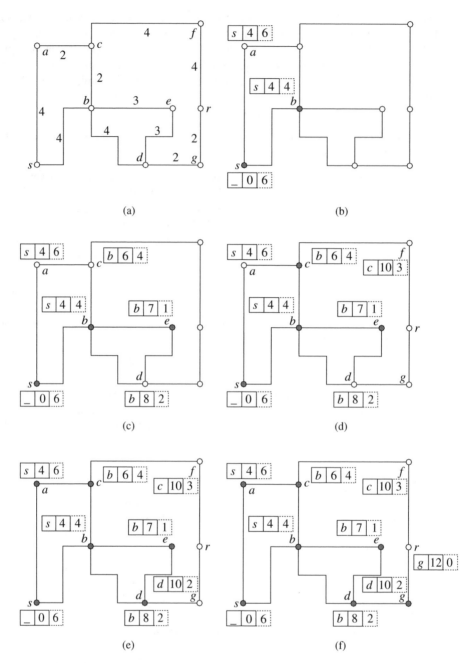

Figure 5.9   An example of Algorithm A*. The boxes next to a vertex v represent values $\pi(v)$, $g(s \leadsto v)$, and $h(v \leadsto r)$. Filled circles indicate the selected vertices.

Algorithm 5.2 Algorithm A* for a monotonic evaluation function.

A-STAR(G, s, r)
   in: graph $G = (V, E)$; start vertex s; goal vertex r
   out: mapping $\pi : V \to V$
   local: open list S; cost function $g(u \rightsquigarrow v)$; heuristic lower bound estimate $h(u \rightsquigarrow v)$
   1: **for all** $v \in V$ **do**   ▷ Initialization.
   2:    $g(s \rightsquigarrow v) \leftarrow \infty$
   3:    $\pi(v) \leftarrow$ NIL
   4: **end for**
   5: $g(s \rightsquigarrow s) \leftarrow 0$
   6: $S \leftarrow \{s\}$
   7: precalculate $h(s \rightsquigarrow r)$
   8: **while** $S \neq \emptyset$ **do**   ▷ Search.
   9:    $v \leftarrow$ vertex $v' \in S$ that minimizes $g(s \rightsquigarrow v) + h(v \rightsquigarrow r)$
  10:   **if** $v = r$ **then**   ▷ Is the goal reached?
  11:     **return** π
  12:   **end if**
  13:   $S \leftarrow S \setminus \{v\}$
  14:   **for all** $u \in successors(v)$ **do**
  15:     **if** $\pi(u) =$ NIL **or else** ($u \in S$ **and**
               $g(s \rightsquigarrow v) + weight(v, u) < g(s \rightsquigarrow u)$) **then**   ▷ Open u.
  16:       $S \leftarrow S \cup \{u\}$
  17:       $g(s \rightsquigarrow u) \leftarrow g(s \rightsquigarrow v) + weight(v, u)$
  18:       $\pi(u) \leftarrow v$
  19:       precalculate $h(u \rightsquigarrow r)$
  20:     **end if**
  21:   **end for**
  22: **end while**
  23: **error** no path from s to r exists

Apart from optimality, there may be practical considerations when implementing A*. First, the computational effort depends on the difficulty of computing the function h. If we use less informed – and computationally less intensive – heuristic, we may go through more vertices but, at the same time, the total computation requirement can be smaller. Second, we may content ourselves in finding a solution reasonably close to the optimum. In such a case, we can use a function that evaluates accurately in most cases but sometimes overestimates the cost to the goal, thus yielding an inadmissible algorithm. Third, we can weight (or even change) the heuristic function when the search has proceeded far from the source vertex s. For example, we can use a more precise heuristic for the nearby vertices and approximate the magnitude for the faraway ones. For dynamic graphs (i.e. the waypoints and their relationships can change in the game world), this can even be the best approach, because it is likely that we have to search new path after a while. To summarize, the choice of the function h and the resulting heuristic power of Algorithm A* depend on a compromise among these practical considerations.

5.3   Realizing the Movement

After the path has been solved in a graph, it must be realized in the game world. Although the solution may be optimal in the graph, it can be unrealistic or aesthetically displeasing in the game world (Patel 2003). For example, consider the situation illustrated in Figure 5.10, where a game character has to move from one room to another. Because the character goes through the waypoints, the resulting path has sharp turns instead of a smooth movement. This stems from the selection of the waypoints with respect to the intended movement: The more artificial or 'virtual' the waypoint is, the more unrealistic the movement through it looks. Of course, sharp turns at the wall extensions and beside the door frames can be realistic if the game character is under fire.

Naturally, we can use Bézier curves or B-splines (Watt 2000) instead of following the path in straight lines, but there are simpler approaches. One possibility is to use line-of-sight testing to reduce the number of waypoints the character has to visit (Snook 2000). Figure 5.11 illustrates the situation: Instead of heading to the next waypoint in the path, the character chooses the farthest waypoint it can see and heads there. This is repeated until the destination is reached. The path followed can be further reduced by changing the route to be always towards the farthest visible waypoint.

To avoid (possibly dynamic) obstacles, we can use the avoidance rule of flocking algorithm (see Section 6.3), and assign a repulsion vector to the obstacles (Johnson 2003). Figure 5.12 illustrates a situation in which an obstacle is blocking the direct path. To avoid it the character's velocity vector combines two components, the desired direction towards the destination and the repulsion away from the obstacle, which is enough to steer the character past the obstacle. In other words, force vectors (and vector fields) are a convenient balancing mechanism between local actualizations (i.e. reactive behaviour in the continuous world) and global intentions (i.e. planning in the discretization of the world).

Because path finding can be a time-consuming task, special care must be taken when it is accessed through a user interface. When players give orders to a game character, they expect it to respond immediately, even if the path finding required to comply with the order is not yet finished. One solution is to get the character moving towards the general direction

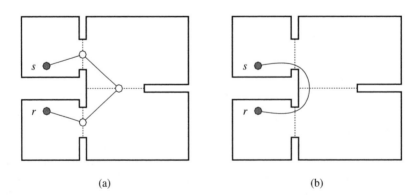

(a)   (b)

Figure 5.10   (a) The path through the waypoints can have sharp and unrealistic turns. (b) Sharp turns can be smoothed out when the movement is realized.

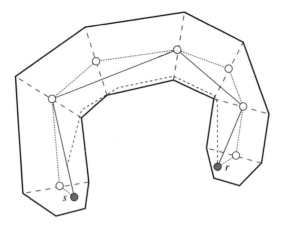

Figure 5.11   Line-of-sight testing allows to improve the original path (dotted line) by skipping waypoints (solid line). It is not necessary to visit the waypoints, but the heading can be changed immediately whenever a farther waypoint becomes visible (dashed line).

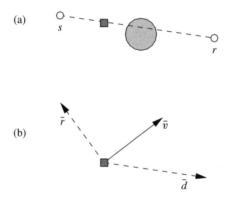

Figure 5.12   Avoiding dynamic obstacles. (a) The straight path from s to r is obstructed. (b) The desired direction $\bar{d}$ towards the destination and the repulsion direction $\bar{r}$ away the obstacle are combined to form the velocity vector $\bar{v}$.

of the destination (or animate that it is preparing to move), while the full path is still being calculated (Higgins 2002). When the path finding is ready, the character, which has moved somewhat, is redirected to the found path.

5.4   Summary

The future path for path finding is still unsolved. Many alternative methods have been proposed, but the three-stage approach presented in this chapter is still the standard approach in commercial computer games. Its main advantage is that we decompose the problem into more manageable sub-problems, each of which has set readily available, reliable, and reasonably fast solution methods.

Reactive agents from robotics have been proposed for solving the path-finding problem. They reduce the solution method to simple reactive rules akin to the flocking algorithm, and the emerging behaviour finds a path for the agent. At the moment the intelligence of these methods is at the level of insects, and, no matter however intelligent insects can be, designing a usable method for computer games seems a difficult task.

Analytical approaches take the opposite view and say that the more data we have the better. They try to solve path finding straightforwardly by modelling all related factors – which may sound good in theory, but in practice some relevant details can escape precise mathematical formulation.

A third approach suggested to solve path finding is artificial intelligence (AI) processors. The idea is that the usual methods for solving AI problems – including path finding – can be made into a hardware component much like 3D display cards, which would take away many time-consuming tasks from the software. Unfortunately, at the time of writing this book, this seems to be still some time ahead in the future. Also, the method used in the AI processor has to be based on some existing software solution – possibly the one presented here.

Exercises

5-1 Imagine that you would have to describe a route to a blindfolded person and describe how to get

(a) from the kitchen to the living room.

(b) from home to work/school.

(c) from home to Rome.

Be as accurate as necessary in your description.

5-2 A monkey is in a cage formed by a square grid (see Figure 5.13). He is hungry but cannot reach the banana dangling from the ceiling. There is a box inside the cage,

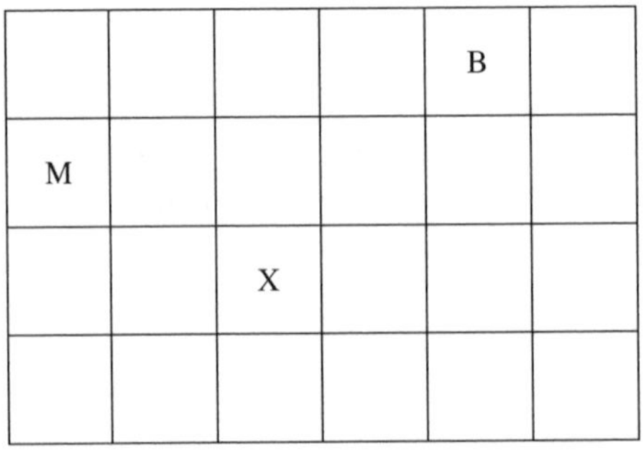

Figure 5.13 Monkey (M), box (X) and banana (B) in a cage formed by a square grid.

and the monkey can reach the banana if the box is underneath the banana. If the monkey is beside the box, he can lift it to one of the neighbouring tiles. The problem is to find a sequence of moves through which the monkey can get the banana from any given initial situation. The monkey sees the whole situation and can select the following operations: move to a tile in the grid, lift the box to a neighbouring tile, get on the box, get down from the box, and reach for the banana.

Form this monkey-in-a-cage problem as a path-finding problem and design an algorithm to solve it.

5-3 Waypoints can be laid down manually by the game world designer. What benefits and drawbacks does this have over the automated waypoint assigning process?

5-4 Prove that there are only three regular two-dimensional edge-sharing tessellations.

5-5 To have random-access lookup, a grid should have a scheme for numbering the tiles. For example, a square grid has rows and columns, which give a natural numbering for the tiles. Devise schemes for triangular and hexagonal grids. Use the numbering scheme to define a rule for determining the neighbourhood (i.e. adjacent tiles) of a given tile in the grid. For example, if we have a four-connected square grid, where the indices are i for rows and j for columns, the neighbourhood of tile $\langle i, j \rangle$ can be defined as

$$neighbourhood(\langle i, j \rangle) = \{\langle i \pm 1, j \rangle, \langle i, j \pm 1 \rangle\}.$$

5-6 A hexagonal grid is not straightforward enough to be represented on the screen (i.e. using square pixels). Devise an algorithm for displaying it.

5-7 Let us connect Exercise 5-5 and Exercise 5-6 and define a mapping τ from a position in a continuous game world to its corresponding tile number. For example, if we are using a square grid with edge length ℓ, we can define $\tau : \mathbb{R}^2 \rightarrow \langle \mathbb{N}, \mathbb{N} \rangle$ straightforwardly as

$$\tau : (x, y) \mapsto \langle \lfloor x/\ell \rfloor, \lfloor y/\ell \rfloor \rangle.$$

Write algorithms that calculate τ for triangular and hexagonal grids.

5-8 Triangulate the game world of Figure 5.14. Then apply the Hertel–Mehlhorn method and remove excess edges.

5-9 For what kind of search problems does breadth-first and depth-first suit best?

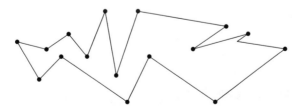

Figure 5.14   A game world as a polygon.

Figure 5.15 One possible solution to the 8 queens problem.

5-10 In *n* queens problem, *n* queens should be placed on an $n \times n$ chessboard so that they do not threaten each other. Figure 5.15 gives one solution to the 8 queens problem, which has in total – omitting rotations and mirror images – 12 different solutions. Formulate the *n* queens problem as a search problem.

5-11 If we had an oracle function $h^*(v \rightsquigarrow r)$, which gives the exact cost of getting from v to r, how could we solve the minimum path search problem? Why is such a function so hard to form?

5-12 Although A* algorithm works better with a more informed heuristic function, the overall computing time can be smaller with a less informed heuristic. How can that be possible?

5-13 What happens to the paths if we use an inadmissible search algorithm?

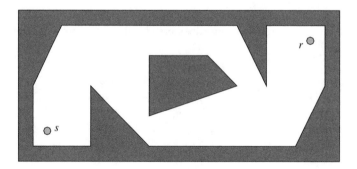

Figure 5.16 Two-dimensional game world, where white area represents open space.

5-14 What other aesthetic considerations are there in movement realization besides smooth movements and obstacle avoidance?

5-15 Assume we have the game world of Figure 5.16. The player wants to move from the point s to the point r using only the white area (i.e. the path cannot go to the grey area). How would you solve this path-finding problem? Describe the three phases of the approach in general terms. Select a method for each phase and apply them to the given problem instance to find a path from s to r.

6

Decision-making

The border between the game world and the entities inhabiting it is often muddy. In Chapter 1, we separated them conceptually and called the computer-controlled entities as synthetic players. At the implementation level, the limited computing resources often force us to accept some merger between the game world and the computer-generated entities inhabiting it. However, this is not necessarily a problem, since the human player is mainly interested in the other human players and the synthetic players with a recognizable identity. Moreover, the action and interaction in a computer game – like in any other form of storytelling – do not require so many participants to be compelling.

Naturally, if we are to have synthetic players in a game, they must be able to make appropriate decisions when the game progresses. Decision-making covers various topics – even path finding, game trees and tournaments, which we discussed in the previous chapters, can be seen as making a decision on what to do. In fact, almost any algorithmic method can be used in decision-making (e.g. sorting can be used to when deciding an attack against the opponent with the smallest army). For this reason, we can cover only a limited number of approaches and methods here.

We begin by taking a broader look on decision-making in computer games, which helps us to understand where different methods suit the best. This general discussion is then followed by a review on finite state machines (FSMs), and we analyse their role in decision-making. After that, we present two alternative approaches for decision-making in a dynamic game world. Flocking algorithms take an entity-centred view, where force vectors model the urges affecting the game characters' decisions. Influence maps model the game world and its attributes as force fields, which then guide the decision-making process.

6.1 Background

The artificial intelligence (AI) system of a computer game comprises two parts: *pattern recognition* and *decision-making system* (Kaukoranta *et al.* 2003). In Figure 6.1, the world, which can be real or simulated, consists of primitive events and states (phenomena) that are

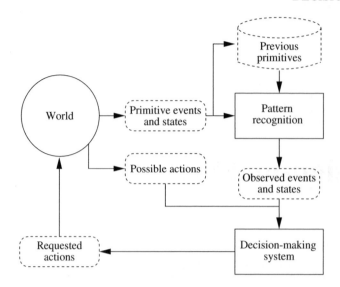

Figure 6.1 The primitive events and states originating from the world are used in pattern recognition and stored for later use. The decision-making system uses the observations made in pattern recognition to choose an appropriate action among the possibilities allowed by the world.

passed to the pattern recognition. The information abstracted from the current (and possibly the previous) phenomena is then forwarded to the decision-making system. The world allows a set of possible actions, and the decision-making system chooses the ones to carry out.

Because game worlds exist only virtually, computer games differ from the usual pattern recognition applications. We can omit certain problems that affect real-world pattern recognition (e.g. coping with noisy sensor data or unreliable actuators). This does not mean that the game world is wholly deterministic – if it were, we would hardly need a decision-making system. The two sources of indeterminism, as we saw in Chapter 1, are the built-in randomness and the human players' actions in the game world.

The synthetic player can act in different roles (e.g. reading the game in an ice hockey match, identifying threats during a campaign, or recognizing Proppian fairy-tale patterns in storytelling). Apart from the design considerations presented in Section 1.2, the role affects the level of decision-making, the use of the modelled knowledge, and the chosen method. These attributes set boundaries for the computational complexity and the quality required from the decision-making.

6.1.1 Levels of decision-making

Decision-making problems are classically divided into three levels:

- Strategic

- Tactical

- Operational.

On the *strategic level*, decisions are made for a long period of time and they are based on a large amount of data. The nature of the decisions is usually speculative (e.g. what-if scenarios), and the cost of a wrong decision is high. For example, a strategy for a war remains stable and should be based on all available information. Instead of considering the interactions of the soldiers in the field, the terrain is analysed to sort out regions that provide an advantage (e.g. hills provide an upper hand for defence, whereas narrow passages are suitable for ambushes). This information is then used in planning the manoeuvres to minimize the risks and to maximize the effect. A poor decision at this level dooms every soldier. Clearly, some details must be left out in the process, and this quantization always includes a possibility that some vital information is lost. To avoid quantization problems, the results of pattern recognition should have as high a quality as possible. This is not an unreasonable demand, because strategic decisions are infrequent and the computing can be done off-line or in the background.

The *tactical level* acts as an intermediary between strategic and operational levels. Tactical decisions usually consider a group of entities and their cooperation. For example, the decisions in a battle concentrate only on the engaging battalions and the conditions in the battleground. They weigh and predict events in the current focus points and dominated areas and, on the basis of the advantages gained on the strategic level, resolve the conflicts as they occur. Ultimately, the aim of tactical decisions is to follow through the plan made on the strategic level. Although tactical decisions directly affect a limited set of entities, a poor decision can escalate to ruin the chosen strategy. Because tactical decisions are made more frequently than strategic decisions, decision-making has less time available. The results must be delivered in real time and their quality cannot be as high as on the strategic level.

Operational level is concrete and closely connected with the properties of the game world. Although the number of decision-making entities at this level is high, the decisions consist of choosing short-term actions among a given set of alternatives. For example, a soldier must decide whether to shoot, dodge, or charge. Because the computational power must be divided among numerous atomic entities, the decision-making method must be reactive and run in real time.

Let us consider football as an example of the levels of decision-making. On the strategic level, there are the choices of how to win the game (e.g. whether to play offensively or defensively). On the tactical level, the choices concern carrying out the strategy the best possible way (e.g. whether to use man-marking defence or space-marking defence). On the operational level, the choices are simple and concrete (e.g. where should the player position himself and if he has the ball, whether to dribble it, kick it to the goal or pass it to another player). The problem is how to choose what to do (i.e. decision-making) and on what grounds (i.e. pattern recognition). It is fairly simple on the operational level – dribble if you have an opening, and pass if you can do it safely – but it gets harder and harder as the level of abstraction rises.

6.1.2   Modelled knowledge

On the basis of the information provided by pattern recognition, the decision-making system forms a model about the world. Because models are always simplifications, they are subject to uncertainty (see Chapter 7). Nevertheless, they are useful because the modelled knowledge can be seen as a mechanism that is used in conceptualizing and concretizing the important phenomena and in predicting events as well as producing them.

The model does not have to confine only to the opponent and the game world but it can cover the actions and reactions of the synthetic player itself. Whenever the synthetic player makes a decision, the outcome produces feedback – positive or negative, direct or indirect – which can be used in learning (Evans 2002). For example, in *Black & White*, the computer-controlled pet creature learns from other entities' reactions, from feedback from the human player, or from its own experiences. Hence, the rule 'Do not eat trees' can be derived either from the villagers' disapproval for wasting resources, from a sharp slap by the owner, or from the resulting stomach ache.

The complexity of the world can be simplified with *generators*, which label the events and states with symbols. For example, the punches in a boxing game can go through a generator that produces the symbols 'jab', 'uppercut', 'cross', and 'hook'. Now, we can construct a model for the behaviour of the generator from the generated symbol sequence. Modelling recognizes the underlying dependencies between symbols, which are typically stronger between symbols that are close to each other. Often a short-term history is sufficient, but the model gets more accurate if we increase the length of the modelling context at the cost of run time.

The decision-making system can use the modelled knowledge in two ways to do temporal reasoning (see Figure 6.2):

- Prediction

- Production.

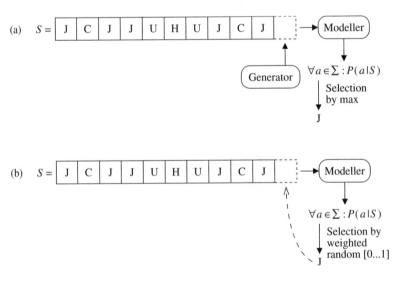

Figure 6.2 The model over a sequence S of symbols from the alphabet $\Sigma = \{J, U, C, H\}$ can be used in (a) prediction and (b) production.

In *prediction*, we want to know what symbol the generator will produce next. By storing the previous primitives we can use pattern recognition to take into account not only spatial but also temporal properties. The observation passed to the decision-making system can be a probability distribution of the occurred symbols rather than a single symbol. For example, if we have constructed a model of the opponent's punch series, we can compute what is the most likely punch the opponent will throw next, and use this prediction to calculate an effective counteraction.

In *production*, we use the model of a generator to produce symbols. This is no longer pattern recognition but decision-making in the form of pattern generation. For example, we can use the model to imitate the actions of a human player (Alexander 2002). Returning to our boxing example, we can model the punch series of a real-world boxer, and use the model when selecting the next punch for a computer-controlled boxer. Of course, we could construct the model simply by observing the human opponent's moves and start mimicking them.

6.1.3 Methods

As computer games become ever more complex, the methods of conventional 'hard' computing are becoming less effective. Whereas hard computing is founded on precision and categorizing, *soft computing*, a term coined by L.A. Zadeh, stresses the tolerance for approximation, partial truth, imprecision, and uncertainty. It describes methodologies that try to solve problems arising from the complexity of the natural world, which include probabilistic reasoning (e.g. Bayesian networks), genetic algorithms, neural networks, and fuzzy logic. We do not strictly adhere to Zadeh's classification but discuss soft computing methods related to *optimization* and *adaptation*. One can readily see that these methods have their counterparts in the human mind: Imagination does optimization and memory learns by adaptation.

Optimization

The term 'optimization' literally means making the best of something. Mathematically speaking, optimization problems comprise three elements: an objective function that we want to minimize or maximize, a set of variables that affect the value of the objective function, and a set of constraints that limits the set of feasible variable values (see Figure 6.3). The goal is to find, among the feasible solutions, the one that gives an optimum value of the objective function.

A decision-making problem can be formed as an optimization problem provided we have a (preferably non-complex) objective function to rank the solution candidates. Since optimization algorithms work iteratively, they are usually time consuming and are therefore used off-line or during pre-processing. For example, to balance civilizations and units in *Age of Empires II*, battles with different troop combinations were tested by using a combat comparison simulator (Street *et al.* 2001). Here, the attributes (such as armour, hit points, damage, and range) are the variables, which are constrained by the range of permitted values. The objective function is used to minimize the difference in the number of victories in the simulator battles, and the attributes are changed to even out discrepancies.

The use of optimization techniques assumes an inherent knowledge of the problem domain. Usually we can make good use of this knowledge by implementing heuristic rules

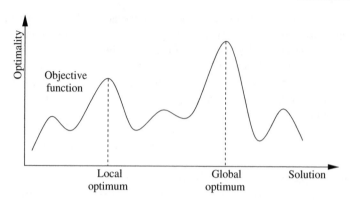

Figure 6.3 An objective function gives the optimality of a solution. The goal is to find the global optimum but the search space is usually scattered with local optima.

to guide the search for more promising variable values. In other words, effective heuristics attack the dominating variables. For example, if archers seem to have an upper hand in the combat simulator, a heuristic rule can increase the damage done by their counter-unit. The problem with this type of hill-climbing heuristic, which iteratively tries to find a better solution among the neighbouring solution candidates, is that the search can get stuck in a local optimum before finding the global optimum (see Figure 6.3). For example, instead of increasing the damage by the counter-unit, a better balance could be achieved by increasing the range of their weapons. To escape the lure of local optima, a gamut of approaches have been developed with the likes of tabu search (Glover 1989) and simulated annealing (Kirkpatrick *et al.* 1983).

Local optima can be avoided by having multiple search traces instead of one. Genetic algorithms have a population of candidate solutions, which go through stages resembling natural selection (Goldberg 1989). The objective function is used to weed out the weak candidates, thus allowing the best ones breed a new population. The variable values of the solution are encoded in the genes. Genetic algorithms work well when the variables are independent of each other, because the genetic operations like crossover and mutation are more likely to produce feasible solutions. In the worst case, the variables have strong dependencies (e.g. they form a sequence), and most of the offspring would not represent a feasible solution.

Swarm algorithms, which are based on flocking algorithms (see Section 6.3), present another approach with multiple search traces (Kennedy *et al.* 2001). Whereas in genetic algorithms the solution is encoded in the population, in swarm algorithms the members of the population 'fly' in the search space. Because of avoidance, they keep a minimum distance from each other and cover a larger area than a single search trace, and because they fly as a swarm, they tend to progress as a unit towards better solutions. As a way to escape local optima, the members can never slow down under a minimum velocity, which can allow them to fly past and free from local optimum, especially if it is crowded.

The suitability of optimization methods depends mainly on the level of decision-making. When making strategic analysis, we have to scrutinize a vast amount of data. Consequently, there are many variables and (combinatorial) interdependencies between them. In their natural state, the problems are computationally hard to tackle but if we weaken our criterion for optimality by, for example, reducing interdependencies, genetic algorithms become a viable option. Although the problem setting in the tactical level is somewhat easier – there are less interdependent variables and simpler combinatorial problems – the method must be more responsive. Owing to the computational demand inherent in making the method more responsive, multiple search traces are not useful and we should devise heuristic search rules. The reactivity of the operational level dictates that we can only solve problems with a few variables or a simple objective function.

Adaptation

Adaptation can be defined as an ability to make appropriate responses to changed or changing circumstances. In a sense, adaptation resembles learning a skill in the real world: When we learn to ride a bike, we do not receive, for example, the physical formulae describing the motions and forces involved. Instead, we get simple – and possibly painful – feedback of success or failure. On the basis of this, we adapt our behaviour and try again until we get it right.

Generally speaking, the difference between adaptation and optimization is that optimization searches for a solution for a given function, whereas adaptation searches for a function behind given solutions (see Figure 6.4). The assumption behind this is that the more the function adapts to the solution domain, the better it corresponds to the originator of the modelled data. Adaptation is useful when the affecting factors or mechanisms behind the phenomena are unknown or dynamic. The downside is that we have to sample the search space to cover it sufficiently, and the more dimensions (i.e. measured attributes) it has, the sparser our sample gets owing to combinatorial explosion.

Since the task of pattern recognition is to abstract significant observations and rules from the given data, it can be usually formed as an adaptation problem. In other words, a pattern recognition method is initially a blank slate, which then begins to adapt to the characteristics of the world. This learning process involves self-modification according to the response from the environment. For example, influence maps (see Section 6.4) are

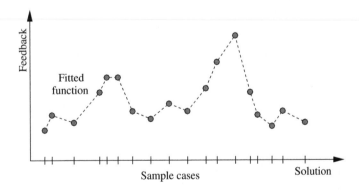

Figure 6.4 To model the underlying generator, the function is fitted to the solution samples according to the feedback.

a simple and statistical way to implement adaptive pattern recognition. On the basis of experience, we change the values in the map: If we get casualties at some point, we decrease its value to avoid it in the future; otherwise, if it has turned out to be safe, we increase its value.

Neural networks provide us a method to adapt in situations where we do not have background knowledge of dependencies (Freeman and Skapura 1991). They work in two different operation modes: training and execution. These are separate phases in supervised learning, where a trainer provides feedback for all sample cases, and the neural network constructs an input–output mapping accordingly. In unsupervised learning, the neural network – for example, a self-organizing map (Kohonen 1995) – adapts to the structure inherent in the input without any *a priori* classification of observations. If the input is a time series, hidden Markov models (Rabiner and Juang 1986) turn out to be useful because they can adapt to recurring multidimensional structures.

We can use supervised or unsupervised learning chiefly in the strategic level owing to their computational demands. The tactical level, however, is more dynamic and the results of pattern recognition are less thorough. Here, we should use methods such as hidden Markov models that yield results whose credibility can be evaluated. On the operational level, there are two possibilities: we have stochastic interpretation for input data or we use a ready-adapted neural network. One feature is common to all levels: Even after we have learned a skill, we can still try to hone it to perfection.

6.2   Finite State Machines

A finite state machine (FSM) is an algorithm described as a mechanism of a finite number of discrete *states* and directed *transitions* between them. The control flow of the FSM algorithm pauses in a state, and the outgoing transitions from this current state determine the next possible states. Each transition is labelled with an *event* name (e.g. referring to some actual event in the game world). When the event occurs, the corresponding transition from the current state is triggered and the succeeding state becomes the current state. In other words, the FSM algorithm moves from state to state in discrete steps. The set of all possible events is the input set of the FSM. Although the events can be asynchronous, the FSM handles them one at a time through a queue.

An FSM can be depicted as a statechart, which is a directed graph in which vertices denote the states and edges denote the transitions. Furthermore, each state must be reachable from the start state by following the transitions. Figure 6.5 illustrates possible high-level states for a patrol robot. The states could flow as follows: In the beginning, the robot is at the state 'Homing', and when it is fully operational, it moves to 'Patrolling'. The robot follows its patrol route, until it encounters an enemy. Depending on the encountered resistance, the robot initiates 'Attacking', 'Defending', or 'Retreating' manoeuvre. The robot's *raison d'être* is patrolling, and it can deviate from this behaviour only when it desperately needs repairing. Because we do not want to give the enemy a chance to find the route to the robot's home base, the robot heads back home only after it has shaken off any trailing enemies. If the robot is on the verge of destruction, it tries to follow a delaying engagement by swapping between 'Defending' and 'Retreating'.

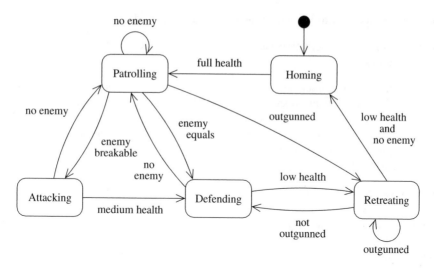

Figure 6.5 A statechart diagram for a finite state machine of a simple patrol robot. The start state is 'Homing' and there is no final state, because the robot remains operational until it is destroyed.

An FSM is an established way to describe and implement AI for synthetic players, because it

- gives a visual overall view of the behaviour (as in Figure 6.5);

- decomposes the control flow of the FSM algorithm spatially and temporally into discrete parts;

- introduces terminology by naming the states, input events, and transitions of the FSM algorithm;

- defines what are the valid relationships between the sequential and concurrent events and possibly their corresponding actions;

- is a perspicuous and concrete model for synchronizing internal and external events (i.e. defining interaction);

- can be formulated in different ways, which have an equal expressive power as any other computation model;

- provides a formalism that can be used in certain cases for automatic FSM simplification, verification, or validation;

- can be used as a subpart inside other methods (e.g. in decision-making);

- can be combined with other concepts (e.g. state and event stacking), probabilities, and fuzziness;

- is straightforward to implement and trace once devised;

- has various implementation variants that allow to find a balance between efficiency and compactness.

FSMs originate from mathematics, to be precise, from the theory of computability and complexity. The theoretical concepts behind FSMs include deterministic finite automata (DFA) and non-deterministic finite automata (NFA), finite transducers (FTs), pushdown automata (PDA), pushdown transducers (PDTs), extended finite state machines (EFSMs), and Turing machines (TMs) with variants. These concepts introduce the following utility properties that an FSM can include (see Figure 6.6).

(i) An FSM can act as an *acceptor* or a recognizer that maps the input sequence to a Boolean value. In this role, the FSM has a set of final states that return true to indicate that the input sequence has the property defined by the FSM. For example, Figure 6.6(a) defines the states for a merchandise in an auction.

(ii) An FSM can be used as a *transducer* or an interpreter that transforms the input sequence to an output sequence (i.e. it generates a symbol response for each input event). Now, the design question is what data sequence corresponds to the input sequence. For example, the FSM in Figure 6.6(b) converts a binary input sequence to a binary

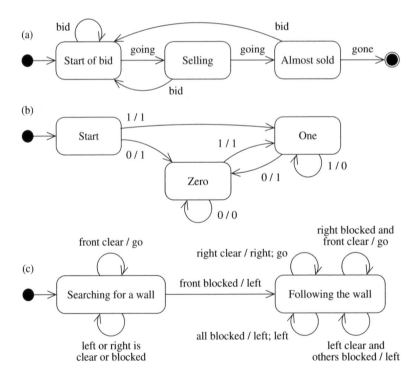

Figure 6.6 Three independent properties that an FSM can include: (a) an acceptor, (b) a transducer, and (c) a computator.

sequence that indicates the starts of the bit-runs. The conversion is denoted by the transition label i/o, where i is the next input bit and o is the output bit. Hence, sequence 001110000101 outputs sequence 101001000111.

(iii) A transition can include an action or procedure that is executed when the transition gets triggered. This property makes an FSM a *computator* that maps the input sequence to an action sequence (or behaviour). The computational nature of the actions allows the FSM to interact with its surroundings. The action (or a sequence of actions) is appended to the event trigger of the transition label with the notation *event/action*. Figure 6.6(c) illustrates a well-known traversal strategy for closed acyclic mazes: 'Keep your right hand on the wall and you will go through every wall once and arrive back at the starting location'. To simplify the problem, assume that the maze is laid on a square grid and the walls are four-connected. Our walk is also four-connected and we can go forward ('go') or make 90° turns (i.e. 'left' or 'right'). These actions are selected according to our sensor events: the neighbouring left, front, or right squares can be clear or blocked by a wall.

6.2.1 Computational FSM

Mathematical models for FSMs differ considerably from the computational software models for FSMs. A computational FSM has numerous definitions, but perhaps the most widespread agreement is the FSM model of *Unified Modeling Language* (UML) notation (Object Management Group 2005). In this section, we use the following fundamental parts from UML:

Action: An atomic (i.e. conceptually instantaneous) transaction that consists of computation (e.g. function calls or sending of signals). The action cannot be interrupted by an event but runs to completion.

Guard: A Boolean expression that expresses a condition (enclosed in square brackets) that must be fulfilled before any action can be executed.

State: An identifiable status or condition in which the FSM algorithm can pause and persist for a period of time. A state is depicted as a rectangle with rounded corners, and the state's name is placed inside the state's border.

The state can have entry action (executed when the state becomes the current state) and exit action (executed before the triggered transition is handled), which are noted with keywords 'entry' and 'exit':

entry / *action(arguments)*
exit / *action(arguments)*

In addition to actions, a state can run a non-atomic activity, which can be any kind of computation that continues until the FSM is interrupted by an event. This activity is specified by the keyword 'do':

do / *computable activity*

Current state: The state where the FSM resides and waits for an event to occur. When a state becomes a current state, it is *entered* and when a transition triggers the state is *exited*. A deterministic FSM has only one current state at a time.

Initial state: The default start of an FSM. Owing to determinism, an FSM has only one initial state, which is a pseudo-state because it cannot ever become the current state. The initial state is denoted by a black, filled circle with one outgoing triggerless transition, an *initial transition*, to the actual start state.

Start state: The target of the initial transition. Thus, it is the default initialization for the current state indicator.

Final state: A pseudo-state indicating that the FSM is terminated. An FSM can have zero or more final states, which are illustrated with a black, filled circle surrounded by an unfilled circle.

Event: An occurrence of phenomena that is given an identity. The event can trigger (or fire) a transition. In general, an event can be

- a signal that can be dispatched asynchronously (i.e. it does not block the control flow of the invocator),
- a method call that is invoked synchronously (i.e. it blocks the control flow of the caller),
- a time period, or
- a change in the situation.

Because signal and call events differ at the software client end only, they are illustrated similarly: the event and its content is denoted by a name and a list of arguments. The time event includes the keyword 'after' and expression for the time period. The change event is described simply by a Boolean condition.

Transition: A quaternary relationship between two states (called the *source* and the *target*), a specified event, and an action. When the source state is the current state and the event occurs, the action gets executed and the target state becomes the current state. In a *self-transition* the source and target are the same, but the entry and exit actions get executed similarly to ordinary transitions. A transition is illustrated as a directed edge from the source state to the target state. The edge label can be of the form

   event(arguments) [*guard*] / *action(arguments)*

where the action is executed only when the event has occurred and the supplementing guard evaluates to true.

A transition that lacks event and guard is called a *triggerless transition* (or completion transition or epsilon transition). It is fired and followed immediately after the source state becomes the current state and the possible state actions are finished. If a transition connects the initial state directly to the final state, it can include a guard and an action but not an event.

Local variable: A reference to shared data structures that the FSM can use in calculation. Local variables are often used for gathering information about the input instance.

To support step-wise refinement and modularity, the states of an FSM can be hierarchical, which means that a single state can contain one or more FSMs. Hierarchical structure makes it possible to hide irrelevant details and to support reuse. Typically, a state is refined to substates if its 'do' activity is complex but has discrete phases for event handling.

A state without any subparts is called a *simple state*. If a state contains concurrent sub-FSMs, it is called a *composite state* and the current state is defined as a combination of the current states of the nested FSMs. A state that is assigned to nest one FSM is called a *submachine state* and the current state is defined for each nesting level at the same time. Owing to hierarchical decomposition of the states, there are the *level preserving transitions* and the *level crossing transitions*. The incoming transitions of these types to a non-simple state s poses the question, what are the states of the nested FSMs when s becomes the current state. Because s defines the environment for its sub-FSMs, we can consider that any sub-FSM M is instantiated when s is entered. In this case, the start state of M is indicated by its initial state.

In addition to modularity, hierarchical states provide a way to denote many-to-one communication: A transition from a non-simple state can be triggered by any of its substates. In other words, if an FSM does not have a proper transition for an event in the current state level, the event is delegated upwards to the enclosing FSM. A many-to-one transition can be an outgoing transition (i.e. the consequent state is not in the source sub-FSM) or an incoming transition (i.e. the resulting state is back in the sub-FSM). In both cases, the exit and entry actions are executed.

Sometimes it is convenient to store the current states of the sub-FSMs of s, where the execution continues when s is re-entered. For this purpose, we can define two pseudo-states, a shallow history state and a deep history state. A *shallow history state* of a sub-FSM M represents the most recent current state c of M and the incoming transitions to this history state are directed to c. A *deep history state* resembles the shallow history state but it is applied recursively to every nested level. The shallow history node is illustrated with a circled H node and the deep history node with a circled H* node.

Figure 6.7 gives an example of an FSM for a generic pull-down menu logic, in which each menu item can be attached by a help document and related to advertisement animations. The menu is constructed and its n items are indexed uniquely from $[0, n-1]$ when the FSM is instantiated. Local variable 'e' is used for referring to the entry index of the current item; naturally, the actual implementation can use other methods to access the menu item behaviour. The menu logic relies on the events 'next' and 'previous', which are guarded by the conditions on the current entry index. The current entry index wraps over from the last menu item to the first one (or from the first entry to the last one) by consuming an extra 'next' (or 'previous') event without any actions.

In addition to the traversing logic, the FSM models the activation of a menu item with 'Execution' state. When the control flow returns, event 'done' activates the transition to the history state, which forces the menu to the same state where the execution got triggered. Composite state 'Guide' has concurrent substates 'Document' and 'Animation' and it is instantiated for one menu item at a time by the event 'help'. When 'Guide' becomes active, both of its sub-FSMs are run simultaneously. 'Guide' has a local variable 'gui' that refers to an object that can set up a help text for a given menu item, scroll the text at given speed, and run advertisement animations on the background. The scrolling text can be affected by events 'ahead' and 'back', and the cumulative scrolling speed (negative for scrolling backwards) is stored into the local variable 's'. It is worth noting that scrolling back the text when it is in the beginning depends solely on the object referred through

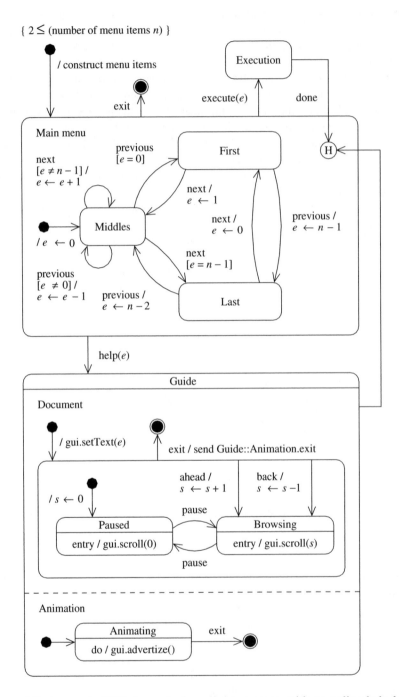

Figure 6.7 A generic FSM for a single pull-down menu with an online help logic.

'gui' and not the FSM itself. Scrolling can be paused at any time and restored by toggling 'pause'. When state 'Guide::Document' receives the event 'exit', it sends 'exit' signal to its co-FSM 'Guide::Animation' to finish the advertisement animation. When the sub-FSMs reach their final states, the triggerless transition (i.e. the right-most transition in the diagram) gets triggered.

The FSM presented does not describe how it should be implemented, how the menu is laid out on the screen, or how the user input is conveyed to the FSM. From the perspective of the FSM, these issues are irrelevant because it only defines the operation logic for the menu. In other words, the FSM notation – like pseudo-code used elsewhere in this book – is a convention to describe algorithmic behaviour.

6.2.2 Mealy and Moore machines

The UML description for FSMs allows an action to be attached to both a state and a transition. This approach is a mix of Mealy machine and Moore machine models. In a Mealy machine, an action can be located only into a transition and thus the next action is derived from both the current state and an input event. In a Moore machine, an action can only be as an entry action of a state, which means that the next action is derived solely from the target state. Figure 6.8 illustrates the difference between these two types of machines. Let us call a state that has an entry action a *Moore state*; otherwise, we call the state a *Mealy state*.

The two types of machines have an equal expressive power, but in practice the Mealy formulation tends to yield a smaller number of states – which is also the reason they are sometimes much harder to understand. If the Mealy and Moore models are equivalent, why does UML include them both? The rationale is that the models have different benefits

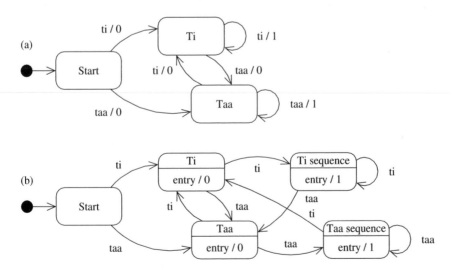

Figure 6.8   Detecting breaks in the repeating rhythm of 'ti' and 'taa' with (a) a Mealy machine, and (b) a Moore machine. The irregular beat outputs value 1.

and drawbacks with respect to the problem that is solved by the FSM. When a notation supports both the models, an experienced and careful designer can determine the proper balance between the models and have a combination of the best properties. Although the structure of the FSM of mixed machine models depends strongly on the application, some guidelines should be followed in the design (see Figure 6.7):

- The Mealy and Moore machine models do not include exit actions. Both the theory and the widely accepted FSM design practices indicate that the behaviour of an FSM should not be built on the exit actions. The only acceptable use for exit actions is to end something critical such as freeing resources, cancelling timers, or finishing synchronization blocks. Otherwise, the exit action should be independent from the FSM logic.

- The triggerless transitions should be avoided, because they blur the concept of current state. The alias name of the transition – a completion transition – expresses its adequate context of use: When the task is finished, we want to end up to the completion state.

- In a Moore state, the triggering of a self-transition or a level crossing transition also runs the exit and entry actions. If this behaviour is not wanted, the state should be converted to a Mealy state. This gives us a method for testing the 'Mooreness' of a state: If some (imaginary) self-transition or level crossing transition can cause problems with the entry and exit actions, the actions are too loosely connected to the state and should be relocated. In other words, if an action is attached to a state, the action must be an inherent property of that state without exceptions.

- Apart from the many-to-one transitions, the level crossing transitions should be avoided because they break the encapsulation between the FSM hierarchy levels. Also, the execution sequence for the 'entry', 'do', and 'exit' actions becomes too tedious to follow. Strict information hiding and encapsulation result in a more understandable form of modularity.

- If an application allows many alternative structures for the FSM, some transitions tend to become similar to one another and they seem to emulate the role of a non-existent state. However, a transition cannot be used as a state (i.e. the FSM cannot be in-between states). Documenting the rationale behind the chosen FSM design (e.g. why and how the structure gives the solution) helps to keep the Mealy and Moore approaches in balance.

6.2.3 Implementation

Up to now we have described FSMs mainly from the perspective of the supplier who implements the software component. In software development, we must also take into account the client who gives the technical and intentional environment to the component by using it. This line of thinking leads to various module realization techniques – such as design by contract principle (Meyer 1997) – that bring these two conceptual participants together. This discussion is a part of a larger philosophy of software development, which – regrettably! – falls outside the scope of this book. Nevertheless, let us discern the main software components of an FSM:

- a set of relationships between the states, the transitions, the events, and the actions;

- control logic that handles the instantiation and termination, implements the event dispatching mechanisms, keeps track of state changes, and invokes the action execu-tions;

- local data structures that can be accessed by the actions and activities of a state, by the guards and actions of a transition, and by the possible sub-FSMs;

- software client interface that describes the responsibilities of the FSM and how it is connected to the use environment (e.g. the application).

Figure 6.9 illustrates how these elements can be grouped according to their roles. The *structure* objects describe the FSM as static data, the *context* objects manage the dynamics of the FSM, and the *environment* models a software client that uses the FSM through a designed interface. Discerning the three roles makes it easier to transfer an FSM to a pseudo-code algorithm (and back). Moreover, it guides the direct implementation of an FSM (especially hierarchical states). For instance, we can deduce that if a state can have a sub-FSM, the interface part of Figure 6.9 must inherit the same properties that the states have. This is because in this case the state also fulfils the environment role for its sub-FSM.

The context role is important when we are defining an FSM. Context realizes the inter-face for the software clients (and possibly for other users through middleware interfaces) and describes how the dynamic memory is used for controlling the FSM implementa-tion. This means that the FSM context gives us some freedom for designing FSMs in an object-oriented software system. Especially, local variables make it possible to transfer re-sponsibilities from the FSM to the data object structures. In other words, we can simplify, for example, FSM communication by using object sharing and collapse combinatorial FSM

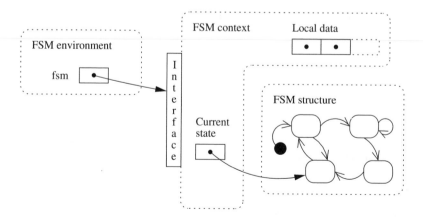

Figure 6.9 FSM as a software object has a static structure, a dynamic context, a fixed interface, and a use environment.

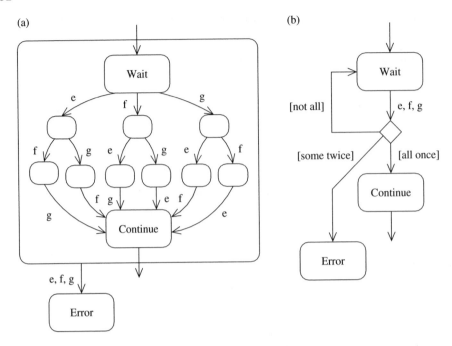

Figure 6.10 A combinatorial FSM that waits for signals 'e', 'f', and 'g' before proceeding. (a) Many-to-one signalling for detecting all erroneous situations is managed by a composite state. (b) The same FSM is collapsed by using a choice point and three Boolean guards.

substructures to member functions. We have already used member functions in Figure 6.7, where the properties of 'gui' are defined to support the FSM logic of the menu.

To sum up, there are two kinds of freedom for managing complexity in an FSM: nested states and local variables. Let us take an example and assume that we have to wait for three different signals 'e', 'f' and 'g' (in any order) before we can proceed in the transition sequence. Figure 6.10(a) models this behaviour between the states 'Wait' and 'Continue'. State 'Error' and nesting are used to collect invalid signalling. As we can see, the FSM has repetitive substructures, which usually indicate that with proper indirection constructs we could have designed a simpler solution. If we introduce three Boolean variables for the signals, we can check that each of them has occurred exactly once. Figure 6.10(b) illustrates the resulting FSM. The diamond square represents a multi-selection choice point of the disjointly guarded branches. Because Boolean flags and other mode variables rapidly ruin understandability, a better alternative is to introduce an object with two member routines that hide the accounting logic. Now, we use a procedure to keep a record of the encountered signals, and call a three-valued query function in the choice point to select the suitable transition branch.

6.2.4 Discussion

Computer games often use FSMs to control the behaviour of synthetic players. In other words, the FSM describes the 'main loop' of a synthetic player and the necessary activities are hooked into the states and transitions as actions (e.g. Figure 6.6(c) gives a complete decision-making logic for a friendly minotaur). However, this kind of approach suits only synthetic players whose behaviour can be defined and described directly in discrete terms. When considering FSM as an implementation, one must heed the following principles:

- The structure of an FSM is essentially static and defies modifications to its configuration. The purpose of an FSM is to define sequential and parallel relationships to achieve the intended behaviour for every possible input sequence. Since it gets harder to preserve the integrity of a complex FSM for all input instances, automatic modifications become troublesome to implement. In other words, the behaviour of an FSM is not very parametric at the FSM structure level.

- An FSM introduces a sequential control memory of reactive behaviours, which are triggered by an event. The current state is a memoryless representation of every possible transition chain leaving from the start state. Because the set of succeeding actions is determined solely by the current state, responding to (possibly numerous) exceptional situations that have not been taken into account beforehand is an onerous task.

- The states of an FSM are mutually exclusive at the same hierarchy level, and each deterministic FSM is exactly in one certain state. Since there is no 'in-between states' condition, a normal FSM is not well suited in situations where states should be continuous or have multiple levels of degrees. Although states can describe proposition logic, operations more suitable for predicate logic (e.g. comparing game situations) are difficult to model with FSMs.

- If one state machine is used for modelling independent properties, it can easily cause a combinatorial explosion in the number of states or transitions. For example, if we model a ranger in a role-playing game so that she can wander in the wilderness, eat when hungry, and illuminate her surroundings with a torch, the all-in-one FSM solution resembles the one given in Figure 6.11. By using this approach, the number

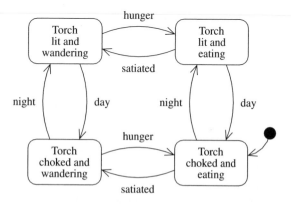

Figure 6.11   An FSM that joins two independent properties together.

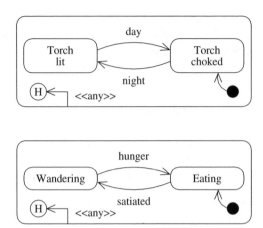

Figure 6.12   Two concurrent FSMs where the properties are disjoint. The FSMs discard every unknown event by the transition labelled as <<any>>.

of states and transitions multiply for each new property the ranger has. This seems to imply that the independent features should be modelled with separate FSMs, and they must be managed by some higher level context, which controls what FSMs are informed when an event occurs. Alternatively, all the separated FSMs can be constructed to discard unknown events as in Figure 6.12.

- FSMs tend to raise the risk of 'total rewriting' in the iterative software development processes. This problem stems from that the software gets built up gradually: It is possible that the required set of states is not known when the first FSMs are sketched and their dominant structures are fixed. Because the FSMs are often highly cohesive, they are rarely patchable and, instead, they should be restructured – with enthusiastic effort.

On the basis of these observations, it looks quite obvious that FSMs are not at their best in controlling the synthetic player directly but only in keeping up the state of the entity. If we take a closer look at the decision-making component of a synthetical player (see Figure 6.1), the synthetic player's decision-making is based on a sense of self, the others, the world, and the causality of the actions and events. When the decision-making system compares the appropriate actions, it tries to manage time-related issues as follows: The history repository models the past, the present is upheld by defining what the current state means, and the future is understood through the dynamic models of information and rules. FSMs have properties that are needed when we are implementing any of these supportive tasks: First, a state in an FSM represents all possible transition walks from the initial state (i.e. a state is a compressed image of the past). Second, the FSM maintains the current state that is recursively defined according to its nesting structure. Third, the outgoing transitions from the current state determine the set of possible actions in the future. On the other hand, FSMs lack many capabilities that are useful in realizing intelligent behaviour.

By limiting the scope of FSMs to that of supporting components for decision-making (e.g. pattern recognition) rather than decision-making itself, the purpose of FSMs becomes clearer and their implementation more manageable. For each specific sequential or concurrent task, we can design an own FSM that is relatively independent from the other FSMs. This leads to better software modularity because it adheres to the principle of 'low coupling and high cohesion'. Owing to modularity, the decision-making subsystem becomes more adaptable. As AI programmers know, this property is essential because general decision-making methods must be adjusted, tuned, and made robust until they become practical in the application.

6.3 Flocking

Whenever we see a flock of birds flying, the whole flock seems to react as an autonomous entity rather than as a collection of separate individual birds. Still, we can be quite sure that each bird in the flock reacts individually to the changes in the flockmates and the surroundings. Flocking algorithm, introduced by C.W. Reynolds (1987), tries to emulate this phenomenon in a computer program. The resulting behaviour resembles various natural group movements like schools of fish, herds of sheep, swarms of bees, or – most interestingly – crowds of humans.

The core of the flocking algorithm is four *steering behaviour rules*, which give a group of autonomous agents (or *boids*) a realistic form of group behaviour (see Figure 6.13):

(i) *Separation*: Steer to avoid crowding local flockmates. A boid should maintain a certain distance from the nearby boids to avoid collisions with them.

(ii) *Alignment*: Steer towards the average heading of local flockmates. A boid should move in the same direction as the nearby boids and match its velocity accordingly.

(iii) *Cohesion*: Steer to move towards the average position of local flockmates. A boid should stay close to the nearby flockmates.

(iv) *Avoidance*: Steer to avoid running into local obstacles or enemies. A boid should escape dangers when they occur.

As we can see, separation and alignment are complementary rules, which ensure that the boids are free to move inside the flock without collision. Separation is based on the relative position of the flockmates ignoring their velocity. Conversely, alignment is based only on the velocity of the flockmates ignoring their position. Alignment sustains the separation between the boids, and it can be thought of as a predictive separation: If the boid manages to match its velocity with that of the neighbours, it is unlikely that it will collide with any of them in the near future. Simply put, separation serves to establish the minimum separation distance, and alignment tends to maintain it.

Cohesion keeps a group of boids together, because it urges each boid to get to the centre of the flock. If the boids have a limited perception, the centre implies the centre of the nearby flockmates – but, cumulatively, this still keeps the whole flock cohesive. When a boid is inside the flock (i.e. the density of the surrounding population is the same in all directions), it does not have to adjust its heading or velocity due to the cohesion rule. However, when a boid is in the boundary of the flock, the centre resides on one side forcing the boid towards the flock.

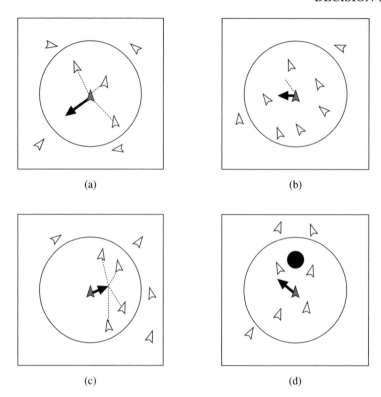

Figure 6.13 Steering behaviour rules: (a) Separation: Do not crowd flockmates. (b) Alignment: Move in the same direction as flockmates. (c) Cohesion: Stay close to flockmates. (d) Avoidance: Avoid obstacles and enemies.

Avoidance lets the boids avoid collisions with entities not belonging to the flock. Although cohesion keeps the flock together, sometimes it has to split apart to go around an obstacle or to evade a hunter. When a flock splits, the resulting smaller flocks are drawn together again by cohesion. Later on, when the obstacle has been passed or the hunter has withdrawn, the bifurcated flock can reunite.

Flocking is a stateless algorithm, because no history information needs to be maintained from update to update. Each boid re-evaluates its environment at every update cycle. There is no centralized control among the boids, but each acts individually allowing the emergent behaviour built in the system to unfold.

Algorithm 6.1 gives an implementation for flocking. The four steering behaviour rules are described in Algorithm 6.2, which use the following auxiliary function:

UNIT-VECTOR($\bar{v}$)

    1: **if** $\bar{v} = \bar{0}$ **then return** a random unit vector

    2: **else return** $\bar{v}/|\bar{v}|$ **end if**

The function returns a unit vector in the direction of $\bar{v}$, or a unit vector pointing at a random direction if $\bar{v}$ is a zero vector.

Algorithm 6.1 Flocking algorithm.

FLOCK(B, A)

    in: set B of boids in a flock; set A of avoidable elements

    out: updated set of boids R

    constant: separation weight w_s; alignment weight w_a; cohesion weight w_c; avoidance weight w_v; maximum velocity v_m

    local: set F of boids to be updated; boid f; updated boid b; acceleration vector $\bar{a}$; set $V = visible(S, x)$ of elements from S visible to x

1: $F \leftarrow$ **copy** B

2: $R \leftarrow \emptyset$

3: **while** $F \neq \emptyset$ **do**   ▷ Update each boid once.

4:   $f \leftarrow$ a boid from F

5:   $F \leftarrow F \setminus f$

6:   $V \leftarrow visible(F \cup R, f)$

7:   $\bar{a} \leftarrow \bar{0}$

8:   **if** $V = \emptyset$ **or** $leader(B) = f$ **then**

9:     realize an individual movement

10:   **else**   ▷ There are visible flockmates.

11:     $\bar{a} \leftarrow \bar{a} + w_s \cdot$ SEPARATION(V, f)

12:     $\bar{a} \leftarrow \bar{a} + w_a \cdot$ ALIGNMENT(V, f)

13:     $\bar{a} \leftarrow \bar{a} + w_c \cdot$ COHESION(V, f)

14:   **end if**

15:   $\bar{a} \leftarrow \bar{a} + w_v \cdot$ AVOIDANCE($visible(A, f)$, f)

16:   $b \leftarrow$ **copy** f ▷ The boid is updated.

17:   $velocity(b) \leftarrow velocity(b) + \bar{a}$

18:   **if** $|velocity(b)| > v_m$ **then**   ▷ Is velocity too high?

19:     $velocity(b) \leftarrow v_m \cdot$ UNIT-VECTOR($velocity(b)$)

20:   **end if**

21:   $position(b) \leftarrow position(b) + velocity(b)$

22:   $R \leftarrow R \cup \{b\}$

23: **end while**

24: **return** R

This is a sequential method to update a set of boids to their next position. Another possibility is to have a concurrent method, where each boid is moved simultaneously before the position updates are committed. Both require a time of $O(n)$ given that the visibility test runs in constant time, but the concurrent method consumes twice the space. However, because flocking is a reactive process, the sequential method provides sufficient results.

After release, boids that see one another begin to flock together. Owing to cohesion, they will stay near one another but always maintaining separation from their flockmates. When the flock is forming, the boids begin to align themselves in approximately the same direction and to move approximately at the same speed with the flock leader. Individual boids and smaller flocks join to become larger flocks, but an obstacle can split flocks into smaller ones.

Algorithm 6.2 Steering behaviour rules.

SEPARATION(M, f)
    in: set M of flockmates; boid f
    out: normalized correction vector
    constant: ideal flockmate separation distance d_s
    1: $m \leftarrow$ the flockmate in M nearest to f
    2: $\bar{v} \leftarrow position(m) - position(f)$
    3: $r \leftarrow 1 - 2 \cdot d_s/(|\bar{v}| + d_s)$ $\triangleright$ $\lim_{|\bar{v}| \to 0} r = -1, \lim_{|\bar{v}| \to \infty} r = 1,$
                                          and $r = 0$ if $|\bar{v}| = d_s$.
    4: **return** $r \cdot$ UNIT-VECTOR($\bar{v}$)

ALIGNMENT(M, f)
    in: set M of flockmates; boid f
    out: unit vector of the heading of the nearest flockmate
    1: $m \leftarrow$ the flockmate in M nearest to f
    2: **return** UNIT-VECTOR($velocity(m)$)

COHESION(M, f)
    in: set M of flockmates; boid f
    out: unit vector towards the centre, or zero vector if already there
    1: $\bar{v} \leftarrow \bar{0}$
    2: **for all** $m \in M$ **do** $\triangleright$ Iterate over the flockmates.
    3:   $\bar{v} \leftarrow \bar{v} + position(m)$
    4: **end for**
    5: $\bar{v} \leftarrow \bar{v}/|M|$
    6: $\bar{v} \leftarrow position(v) - position(f)$
    7: **if** $\bar{v} \neq \bar{0}$ **then return** UNIT-VECTOR($\bar{v}$) $\triangleright$ Not at the centre.
    8: **else return** $\bar{0}$ **end if**

AVOIDANCE(A, f)
    in: set A of objects to be avoided; boid f
    out: unit vector indicating avoidance, or zero vector if nothing to avoid
    constant: avoidance distance d_a
    1: $a \leftarrow$ the object in A nearest to f
    2: $\bar{v} \leftarrow position(f) - position(a)$
    3: **if** $|\bar{v}| < d_a$ **then return** UNIT-VECTOR($\bar{v}$) $\triangleright$ Is the object close enough?
    4: **else return** $\bar{0}$ **end if**

    The behavioural urges provide the boid with suggestions regarding which way to steer. These urges can be viewed as acceleration requests, which can conflict with each other. The requests are collected, prioritized, and aggregated to form the acceleration to be realized. Prioritization can be implemented, for example, by associating the requests with weights describing their importance. For instance, avoidance can have a large weight for a prey, because it represents a critical situation that must be handled promptly, whereas predators need to avoid (almost) nothing.

6.4   Influence Maps

An influence map is a discrete representation of the synthetic player's knowledge of the world. In a sense, grids and navigation meshes, which are discussed in Section 5.1, are influence maps representing the cost of travelling. However, an influence map can also provide the decision-making system with other kinds of strategic and tactical information. The idea of using influence maps (or spheres of influence) in the game of Go was introduced by A.L. Zobrist (1969). Because of its simplicity, the method is widely used, especially in RTS games such as *Age of Empires II* (Pottinger 2000).

Each influence map collects information about a certain type of effect in the game world (e.g. strengths and positions of military troops or deposits of natural resources). Influence is a twofold function, because it can indicate *repulsiveness* or *alluringness*: Enemy troops should be avoided (i.e. their influence is repulsive), and untapped resources should be capitalized (i.e. their influence is alluring). Influence maps also allow to make inferences about the characteristics of different locations in the game world (e.g. finding strategic control points and pointing out weaknesses in the enemy's defence). For a discussion of different strategic dispositions for outmanoeuvring the opponent, see Woodcock (2002).

Although an influence map overlays the game world, it does not have to follow its geography. However, for the sake of argument, we assume that the map is divided into tiles with a regular grid. As in path finding, the granularity of the grid is a trade-off between accuracy and computational demand. Each tile in the grid holds numeric information of the corresponding area of the game world. The tile can represent alluringness with positive values and repulsiveness with negative values.

Influence map is constructed in two phases (see Figure 6.14). Initially, the tiles where the given influence exists are assigned to a corresponding value. After that, the influence is propagated over the map by spreading their effect to the neighbouring tiles. The influence has a fall-off which diminishes (usually linearly or exponentially) its effect when it is spread. Moreover, if the influence map includes floating point values, there should be some cut-off point so that minuscule influence values, which have little or no effect at all, do not get spread all over the map.

Influence maps based on terrain or other static features of the game world can be created beforehand. Unfortunately, most of the influences have a dynamic nature and the maps need to be updated periodically. As a remedy, we can categorize the maps on the basis of the rate of changes so that the more animate ones are updated more frequently. Also, lazy evaluation, where the values are updated only when the influence map is accessed, may improve the overall performance.

It is possible to generalize influence maps as graphs. For example, consider the game *Hunt the Wumpus* (Yob 1975), which has become a classic in AI research. Although the game world is usually simplified into a grid, G. Yob, the game creator, was bored with grid-based games, and the squashed dodecahedron depicted in Figure 6.15 was his original design for the game world. The subsequent versions of the game included a diverse set

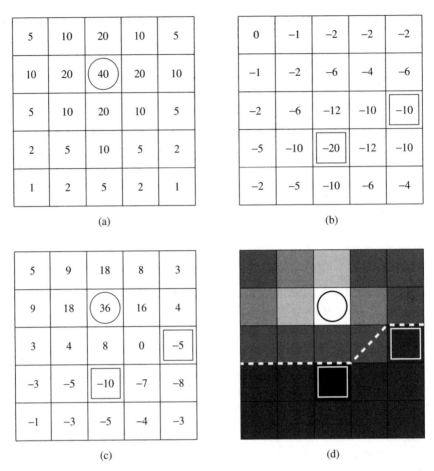

5	10	20	10	5
10	20	(40)	20	10
5	10	20	10	5
2	5	10	5	2
1	2	5	2	1

(a)

0	−1	−2	−2	−2
−1	−2	−6	−4	−6
−2	−6	−12	−10	[−10]
−5	−10	[−20]	−12	−10
−2	−5	−10	−6	−4

(b)

5	9	18	8	3
9	18	(36)	16	4
3	4	8	0	[−5]
−3	−5	[−10]	−7	−8
−1	−3	−5	−4	−3

(c)

(d)

Figure 6.14 Let the circled tile represent the strength and position of own troops and squared tiles represent enemy's troops. (a) After the initial influence values have been assigned, their effect is propagated over the map. The fall-off halves the influence in the neighbouring tiles. (b) The same is done to the influence map based on the enemy's troops. (c) By aggregating the two influence maps, we get a new influence map that combines the troops' information. (d) The resulting map demarcates, for example, the frontier between the players.

of game worlds based on, for example, torus surfaces and Möbius strips. Fundamentally, the game world comprises a graph, where the vertices represent the rooms and the edges are the tunnels between two rooms (see Figure 6.15). The somewhat simplified rules of the game are as follows: A hunter roams inside this world, equipped with a limited supply of arrows, in search of a wumpus. In each turn, the hunter must decide from two actions: Move through a tunnel into a new room, or shoot an arrow through the tunnel into a neighbouring room. If the hunter moves to the same room as the wumpus, it eats him and

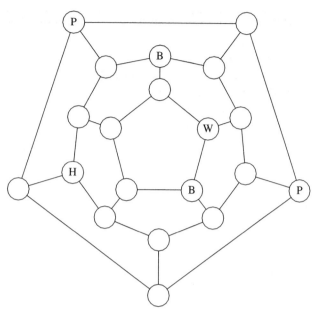

Figure 6.15 The game world of *Hunt the Wumpus* is a graph, where the vertices are the rooms and the edges are the tunnels connecting them. The hunter (H) moves from room to room avoiding bats (B) and pits (P), and is ready to shoot the wumpus (W).

the game is lost; if the hunter shoots an arrow into the room where the wumpus is lurking, he kills it and wins the game. There are also other hazards hidden in the game world: If the hunter encounters bats, they will carry him into a randomly selected room. If there is a pit in the room, the hunter will fall into it and the game is over. Luckily, the hunter can sense if there is a danger in any of the neighbouring rooms (although he does not know in which one): He can smell the wumpus, hear the noise of the bats, and feel the draft from the pit.

Algorithm 6.3 describes a simple decision-making system for the hunter, which is based on influence maps. The hunter maintains four influence maps – bats, pits, wumpus, and visited rooms – which are updated on the basis of the sense data and discoveries. Here, a large value means repulsion. All maps are initialized to the value 1. When the hunter enters a room and nothing happens, we know that there are no bats or pits, nor is the wumpus there, and the associated map positions are set to the value 0. The visited map, which encourages the hunter to choose undiscovered rooms, is updated so that the value of the current room is doubled. If the hunter perceives any sensory information in the neighbourhood, all neighbouring rooms are updated by doubling the current values in the relevant influence map. The hunter makes a decision based on two rules: If the value of any of the neighbouring rooms exceeds a given threshold value in the wumpus map, the hunter will shoot an arrow into that room. Otherwise, he will move to the room for which the sum of influence map values is the smallest. Hence, the hunter tries to avoid possible dangers and the already visited rooms.

Algorithm 6.3 Decision-making for a wumpus hunter using influence maps.

WUMPUS-HUNTER-REACT(v)
    in: current room $v \in V$
    out: action $\langle a \in \{\text{SHOOT, MOVE}\}, u \in neighbourhood(v)\rangle$
    constant: threshold t_s for shooting an arrow
    local: influence maps *bats*, *pit*, *wumpus*, and *visited* (initially
               $\forall u \in V : bats(u) = pit(u) = wumpus(u) = visited(u) = 1$)
1: $bats(v) \leftarrow pit(v) \leftarrow wumpus(v) \leftarrow 0$
2: $visited(v) \leftarrow 2 \cdot visited(v)$
3: **for all** $u \in neighbourhood(v)$ **do**
4:   **if** $noise(v)$ **then**
5:     $bats(u) \leftarrow 2 \cdot bats(u)$
6:   **else**
7:     $bats(u) \leftarrow 0$
8:   **end if**
9:   **if** $draft(v)$ **then**
10:    $pit(u) \leftarrow 2 \cdot pit(u)$
11:   **else**
12:    $pit(u) \leftarrow 0$
13:   **end if**
14:   **if** $smell(v)$ **then**
15:    $wumpus(u) \leftarrow 2 \cdot wumpus(u)$
16:   **else**
17:    $wumpus(u) \leftarrow 0$
18:   **end if**
19: **end for**
20: $w \leftarrow$ vertex $w' \in neighbourhood(v)$ that maximizes $wumpus(w')$
21: **if** $wumpus(w) \geq t_s$ **and** arrows left **then**
22:   $wumpus(w) \leftarrow 0$
23:   **return** $\langle \text{SHOOT}, u \rangle$
24: **end if**
25: $u \leftarrow u' \in neighbourhood(v)$ which minimizes $bats(u') + pit(u') + wumpus(u') + visited(u')$
26: **return** $\langle \text{MOVE}, u \rangle$

6.5 Summary

The technical requirements and expectations on synthetic players are constantly increasing. Whereas in the traditional turn-based games the computer opponent can think for (almost) as long as it requires, nowadays games mostly require real-time response. This puts a hard computational strain on the synthetic player, because it can no longer delve into finding an optimal strategy but should react promptly. Response is the keyword – even to such an extent that game developers tend to think that it is better to have hordes of mindless cannon fodder than to grant the synthetic players a shred of intelligence. In the past, the main reason for this was that decision-making was not slated a fair share of the overall processing resources. Surprisingly, even today AI in commercial computer games gets on average about 10% of the processor capacity (Dybsand 2004).

Distribution has become more important now that games using networking are more common. This may present a solution to the dilemma of achieving both real-time response and intelligence: Instead of running the synthetic players on one machine, they can be distributed so that the cumulative computational power of the networked nodes gets utilized. For example, *Homeworld* uses this technique and distributes the computer-controlled opponents among the participating computers.

Distribution naturally begs the question as to how autonomous the synthetic players should be. As long as we can rely on the network, there is no problem, but if nodes can drop out and join at any time, distributed synthetic players must display autonomy. This means two things: First, the synthetic player must be persistent, because it can be relocated to another node if the one where it is currently run gets cut off. Second, the synthetic player must be self-sufficient, because it cannot rely on outside processes but should be able to operate on its own. This is not necessarily a drawback, because autonomy can lead to a smaller and better design, and complex behaviour can emerge from seemingly simple autonomous agents.

A corollary from autonomy is that the synthetic players must have a way to communicate explicitly with each other. Because there is no central intelligence controlling them, they have to inform others on their decisions, indicate their plans, and negotiate with each other – just like we humans do in the real world. Of course, these communication skills may also come handy when interacting with the human players.

Exercises

6-1 Consider the process of doing the groceries. What strategic, tactical and operational decisions are involved in it?

6-2 Humans are predictable players. Verify this claim by implementing a modeller for Rock-Paper-Scissors, which analyses the sequence of human opponent's choices and predicts the next move. Analysis could be based on statistical data (i.e. it is likely that the human player favours a certain choice), or sequential data (i.e. it is likely that the human player repeats a certain sequence of choices).

6-3 Consider the following problems. Which of them should be solved with optimization and which of them with adaptation?

(a) Deciding which building to construct next in a RTS game

(b) Driving a jeep in a convoy

(c) Selecting the contents of the backpack in a role-playing game

(d) Casting a spell against a known enemy

(e) Casting a spell against an unknown enemy.

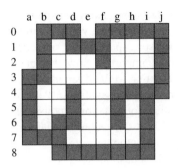

Figure 6.16 A closed acyclic maze on a square grid. The maze has walls (dark tiles) and an interior (white tiles), which are four-connected.

6-4 Execute the FSM illustrated in Figure 6.6(c) for the maze given in Figure 6.16. The starting location is at $(5, f)$ and the heading is to north.

6-5 Let us analyse the maze circulator of Exercise 6-4. Assume that a maze does not include unnecessary wall tiles. Given an $m \times n$ maze with w wall tiles, what is the maximum number of events keeping us in the state 'Searching for a wall'? How about remaining in the state 'Following the wall' for one walk cycle around the maze? Give at least two reasons why this kind of knowledge about an FSM is useful.

6-6 The right-hand rule modelled in the FSM of Figure 6.6(c) benefits left-handers (including the authors). Is it possible to define an equivalent rule for right-handers?

6-7 Figure 6.6(c) describes the FSM with a natural language, which is typical at the high-level design phase of a software development process. Refine the FSM so that it is closer to the implementation by incorporating a more formal handling of the sensory events $sensor(l, f, r)$. Boolean variables l, f, and r indicate whether there is a wall on the neighbouring left, front, or right tile. Also introduce a simple local variable interface for executing the actions 'go forward', 'turn left $90°$', and 'turn right $90°$'.

6-8 Inspired and amazed by the mazes, you decide to implement a stealth-based game Metal Hear Oil, in which the player secretly dwells in a maze-like world populated by hostile but nearsighted robots. Fortunately, each robot gives a visual feedback about its internal state through a row of lights etched on its occiput. By observing the robot, the player can learn how it reacts to the surroundings according to the sensory stimuli. You can even intensify the mood by including movable façade walls.

The robot's control logic is based on an FSM similar to the one in Exercise 6-7. Modify this FSM and its local variable interface so that the robot recognizes the following game world situations and flashes the back lights accordingly: 'in a convex corner', 'in a concave corner', 'in a corridor', 'in a dead end', 'beside the player', and 'facing the player'. In the last two cases, the robot also gives an intruder alert.

6-9 Assume that the game world is an infinite square grid. Figure 6.17 defines an acceptor FSM for events 'north', 'east', 'south', and 'west' that model the unit steps towards

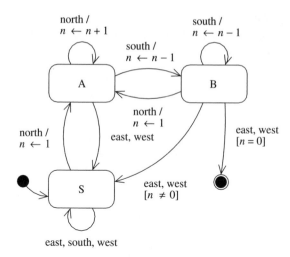

Figure 6.17 An acceptor FSM on a square grid.

the principal compass points. What is the general condition when the FSM terminates? Also give more descriptive names to the states.

6-10 At first glance, the menu FSM given in Figure 6.7 seems to serve only the user interface subsystem and have a little – if at all – to do with decision-making. To counter this, let us put aside the menu logic and just focus on the events, states, and transactions. Consider a bartender in a small, cosy bar serving drinks to customers, entertaining them with stories, managing the bar bookkeeping, and occasionally doing some maintenance work. Use the skeleton of the menu FSM to define a control logic for this simple but busy synthetic bartender.

You can use this alternative view in the exercises from 6-11 to 6-14.

6-11 Implement the state 'Guide::Document' of Figure 6.7 using the pseudo-code notation and the **case–of** control structure.

6-12 The state 'Main menu' in Figure 6.7 is a Mealy machine. Redesign it as a Moore machine.

6-13 The state 'Guide::Document' in Figure 6.7 has one anonymous state that contains a sub-FSM with states 'Paused' and 'Browsing'. This sub-FSM is a combination of Mealy and Moore machine models. Change it to a pure Mealy model that does not have any incoming transitions from the superstate.

6-14 Figure 6.7 describes an FSM for a simple but generic pull-down menu. Supplement it with the following features:

(a) In the original FSM, the help documentation of a menu item is accessed through the main menu. Change the FSM so that it is possible to go through all item documentations without leaving the 'Guide' state.

(b) The original FSM is designed to handle only one pull-down menu. Or is it? How would you proceed if your application requires multiple disjoint submenus with various nesting levels?

6-15 Figure 6.8 defines a Mealy machine and a Moore machine for detecting the rhythm breaks 'ti'–'ti' and 'taa'–'taa'. Device a Mealy machine and a Moore machine for detecting the subsequences of the form 'ti'–'taa'–'taa'–'ti' from any given input.

6-16 Study Figure 6.9 and give a condition for the situation when it is possible to share a FSM substructure among multiple FSM structures. The condition should be necessary and sufficient. Give at least two reasons why shared sub-FSMs are beneficial.

6-17 Model a simple pocket calculator with an FSM that uses floating point values and operators '+', '−', '∗', and '/'. To avoid parenthesis, the expressions are given using *reverse Polish notation* and they are evaluated using stack as a data structure. For example, $(3 + 1)/4$ can be given to the FSM as the input events '3', '1', '+', '4', '/', 'print'. The event 'print' outputs the topmost value of the stack without other side effects. Does the FSM notation suit this kind of problem? Would an algorithmic pseudo-code be easier to understand? Can you generalize your observation by considering only the FSM structure? If you can, what consequences does it have concerning decision-making methods?

6-18 The structure of the FSM of Exercise 6-9 can also be interpreted as a model for a specific walking pattern in a square grid. Supplement it by introducing suitable frequency counters so that it can be used for predicting the player's movements. What kind of a software client interface should the FSM have? How can it be used for producing randomized square grid walks with respect to the model?

6-19 Table 6.1 defines the states for a player on the move as a combination of the step and heading directions. How can you model this matrix with an FSM? Is it worth the effort?

Table 6.1   The states of a player on the move in terms of a step direction and a heading direction. The directions are absolute in the game world (i.e. they are not relative to the player). State 'Forward step' is denoted by 'F', 'Backward step' by 'B', 'Left sidestep' by 'L', and 'Right sidestep' by 'R'.

	Heading towards			
Step towards	north	east	south	west
north	F	L	B	R
east	R	F	L	B
south	B	R	F	L
west	L	B	R	F

6-20 In Section 6.2 we do not describe how the FSM context of Figure 6.9 actually receives the events. There are two opposite approaches for conveying signals, routine calls, time delays, and condition changes to an FSM: In a *pull approach*, the FSM is actively polling the events that can affect it. In a *push approach*, the FSM is passive, until it is given an indication about the events. Of course, each type of event can have its own delivering logic, and the approaches can be combined. What object-oriented design patterns – for example, from the catalogue by Gamma *et al.* (1995) – can be used when implementing these pull and push approaches?

6-21 Let us continue with Exercise 6-20. What object-oriented design patterns would you use when implementing the hierarchical FSMs? Note that *State* design pattern of Gamma *et al.* (1995) is not necessarily the best way to implement an FSM state.

6-22 Consider what would happen if we leave out one of the flocking behaviour rules? Are some rules more essential to flocking than others?

6-23 The steering behavioural urges SEPARATION and ALIGNMENT presented in Algorithm 6.2 consider only the nearest flockmate. Rewrite both routines so that the boid observes n nearest flockmates.

6-24 What happens if a flock does not have a leader? What happens if the leader drifts to the middle of the flock?

6-25 Flocking can be used to realize the solution of a path-finding problem for a group of entities so that the leader follows the path and the other members of the group follow the leader. Are there groups that this approach does not suit?

6-26 Influence maps – like any discretization – can lead to quantization problems, where relevant details get lost because of the coarseness of the model. How can this problem be tackled?

6-27 Influence maps are often closely connected to path finding. Explain why and how.

6-28 Influence maps are often used in path finding. In the game of Goldrush (see Figure 6.18), the game world is formed by a square grid, where each tile has a height. Piles of gold have been scattered randomly to the world, and a gold digger, starting from home, must find a path through all the piles and ending back home. The game world also includes towers, which can shoot arrows to the north, the south, the east, and the west. The accuracy of a tower depends on the distance d to the gold digger, and the probability of a hit is $1/2^d$. Going uphill or being shot reduces the gold-digger's vitality. Design a method that helps the gold digger to find a path that conserves his vitality as much as possible.

6-29 Trace the wumpus hunter's decisions using Algorithm 6.3 in the game world of Figure 6.15. What happens if you change the multiplier of the influence map *visited*(•) from 2 to $1\frac{1}{2}$ or $2\frac{1}{2}$?

6-30 Algorithm 6.3 does not always lead the hunter to the wumpus. Design a game world where the hunter can get stuck. Update the algorithm so that the hunter can escape these situations.

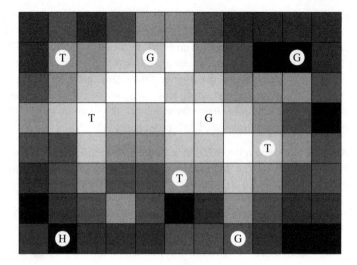

Figure 6.18 Game world for Goldrush. The gold digger starts from home (H) and must visit all gold piles (G) and return back to home. The towers (T) shoot arrows to the four principal compass points. The colour of a tile illustrates the height of the terrain (i.e. the lighter the colour, the higher the ground). To conserve his vitality the gold digger should avoid travelling uphill and getting too close to the towers.

6-31 If the game world of *Hunt the Wumpus* was a Möbius strip, what would that mean to the hunter's decision-making?

6-32 The bats and the wumpus in *Hunt the Wumpus* do not move. If they could also wander around in the cave (as in the original game), what would that mean to the hunter's decision-making?

7

Modelling Uncertainty

Because decision-making is based on a model of the world, it is often subject to uncertainties. The dictionary gives us two meanings for the word 'uncertainty': something that is uncertain and the state of being uncertain. In the first case, we usually talk about probability (like the outcome of a die), whereas in the latter case, the uncertainty concerns our own abilities or the possibility to classify objects. If you draw a circle freehand, there is uncertainty about whether it is a circle. However, that uncertainty has nothing to do with probability. This *possibilistic* uncertainty brings forth problems of classification, and we face them everyday. In the purest form, they present themselves as *sorites* paradoxes: When does a heap of sand cease to be a heap if we remove one grain of sand at a time from it?

In this chapter, we take a look at both probabilistic uncertainty and possibilistic uncertainty. Statistical reasoning models beliefs on the basis of the probability of events, whereas fuzzy sets help us in modelling the possibility of events by allowing partial membership in a set. Fuzziness can be embedded to 'classical' solution methods, and, as an example, we present how constraint satisfaction problems can be fuzzified.

7.1 Statistical Reasoning

Sometimes, we do not have enough evidence for a full certainty, and we have to make decisions based on beliefs. This situation can occur when we are facing random events (e.g. throwing dice or drawing cards from a shuffled deck) or when we have only statistical knowledge on the chain of events. In the latter case, the belief on the likelihood of an event can be based on the statistical data. In this section, we go through some techniques for modelling probabilistic or statistical knowledge.

7.1.1 Bayes' theorem

Bayes' theorem, introduced by T. Bayes in the eighteenth century, provides a method to calculate conditional probabilities. Suppose that we have a hypothesis H and evidence E,

Algorithms and Networking for Computer Games   Jouni Smed and Harri Hakonen
© 2006 John Wiley & Sons, Ltd

and we know a priori the probabilities for the hypothesis $P(H)$, the evidence $P(E)$, and the evidence assuming the hypothesis is true $P(E|H)$. Bayes' theorem gives us now the probability of the hypothesis based on the evidence:

$$P(H|E) = \frac{P(H \cap E)}{P(E)},$$ (7.1)

which we can rewrite as

$$P(H|E) = \frac{P(E|H) \cdot P(H)}{P(E)}.$$ (7.2)

More generally, if we have a set of n hypotheses $\{H_0, H_1, \ldots, H_{n-1}\}$, Bayes' theorem can be restated as

$$P(H_i|E) = \frac{P(E|H_i) \cdot P(H_i)}{\sum_{j=0}^{n-1}(P(E|H_j) \cdot P(H_j))},$$ (7.3)

provided that the whole event space equals $\bigcup_{i=0}^{n-1} H_i$, $H_i \cap H_j = \emptyset$ when $i \neq j$, and $P(E) > 0$.

Bayes' theorem has assumptions that restrict its usability: First, all the statistical data regarding the evidence with the various hypotheses is assumed to be known. Because Bayesian reasoning requires complete and up-to-date probabilities, we have to adjust them whenever we find a new connection between a hypothesis and an evidence. Second, the terms $P(E|H_i)$ must be independent of one another (i.e. the hypotheses are alternative explanations for the evidence). Both of these assumptions can be quite problematic to establish in the real world.

Let us take a simple (but instructive) example of Bayes' theorem. Suppose there is a 10% probability that an alpha-tested computer game has a bug in it. From past experience, we have observed that the likelihood of a detected bug to have resulted from an actual bug in the program is 90%. The likelihood of detecting a bug when it is not present (e.g. it is caused by the test arrangement) is 10%. Now, the components are as follows:

- H – there is a bug in the code;

- E – a bug is detected in the test;

- $E|H$ – a bug is detected in the test given that there is a bug in the code;

- $H|E$ – there is a bug in the code given that a bug is detected in the test.

The known probabilities are as follows:

$$P(H) = 0.10$$
$$P(E|H) = 0.90$$
$$P(E|\neg H) = 0.10.$$

By using the law of total probability, we can calculate for partitions H and $\neg H$

$$P(E) = P(E|H) \cdot P(H) + P(E|\neg H) \cdot P(\neg H) = 0.18.$$

To get the probability of detecting an actual bug in the code, we apply Equation (7.2) and get

$$P(H|E) = 0.5.$$

To conclude, even if 90% of the time we can detect the actual bugs, a detected bug has a fifty-fifty chance that it is not in the actual code – which is not a reassuring result for a programmer.

7.1.2 Bayesian networks

Bayesian network tries to solve the independence problem by modelling the knowledge modularly. Generally, propositions can affect each other in two alternative ways:

(i) observing a cause changes the probabilities of its effects, or

(ii) observing an effect changes the probabilities of its causes.

The idea of a Bayesian network is to make a clear distinction between these two cases by describing the cause-and-effect relationships with a directed acyclic graph. The vertices represent a proposition or variable. The edges represent the dependencies as probabilities, and the probability of a vertex is affected by the probabilities of its successors and predecessors.

Let us take an example in which a guard is observing the surroundings. If he hears a noise, its cause is either a sentry making the rounds or an intruder, who is likely to avoid the time when the sentry is doing the rounds. The situation can be formed as a graph illustrated in Figure 7.1. If we know the probabilities for the dependencies between the vertices, we assign them to the edges or list them as in Table 7.1.

We still need a mechanism to compute the propagation between the vertices. Suppose the guard hears a noise, what does it tell about the probability of the intruder? The propagation methods base on the idea that the vertices have local effects. Instead of trying to manage the complete graph, we can reduce the problem by focusing on one sub-graph at a time; for details, see Pearl (1986). Still, the problems of Bayesian reasoning – establishing the probabilities and updating them – remain, and Bayesian networks are usually too static for practical use.

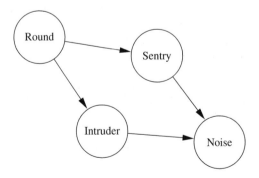

Figure 7.1 A Bayesian network as a directed acyclic graph.

Table 7.1   Probabilities for a Bayesian network.

$H\,|\,E$	$P(H\,|\,E)$
Noise | Sentry ∧ Intruder	0.95
Noise | Sentry ∧ ¬Intruder	0.9
Noise | ¬Sentry ∧ Intruder	0.8
Noise | ¬Sentry ∧ ¬Intruder	0.1
Sentry | Round	1.0
Sentry | ¬Round	0.0
Intruder | Round	0.1
Intruder | ¬Round	0.9
Round	0.3

7.1.3   Dempster–Shafer theory

To address the problems of Bayesian reasoning, Dempster–Shafer theory (Shafer 1990)
allows beliefs about propositions to be represented as intervals

$$[\text{belief, plausability}] \subseteq [0, 1].$$

Belief (Bel) gives the amount of belief that directly supports the proposition. Plausability
(Pl), which is defined as

$$\text{Pl}(A) = 1 - \text{Bel}(\neg A),$$

describes how much the belief supporting the contradicting proposition $\neg A$ reduces the
possibility of proposition A (i.e. $\text{Bel}(A) \le \text{Pl}(A)$). Especially, if $\text{Bel}(\neg A) = 1$ (i.e. the
contradicting proposition is a certain), then $\text{Pl}(A) = 0$ (i.e. A is not plausible) and the only
possible belief value is $\text{Bel}(A) = 0$ (i.e. A is not believable).

The belief–plausability interval indicates how much information we have about the
propositions (see Figure 7.2). For example, suppose that the proposition 'there is an intruder' has a belief of 0.3 and a plausibility of 0.8. This means that we have evidence
supporting that the proposition is true with probability 0.3. The evidence contrary to the
hypothesis (i.e. 'there is no intruder') has probability 0.2, which means that the hypothesis is possible up to the probability 0.8, since the remaining probability mass of 0.5 is
essentially 'indeterminate'. Additional evidence can reduce the interval – increase the belief or decrease the plausibility – unlike in Bayesian approach, where the probabilities of

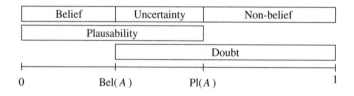

Figure 7.2   Belief and plausability.

the hypotheses are assigned beforehand. For instance, in the beginning when we have no information about hypothesis A, we let $\text{Bel}(A) = 0$ and $\text{Pl}(A) = 1$. Now, any evidence that supports A increases $\text{Bel}(A)$ and any evidence supporting the contradicting hypothesis decreases $\text{Pl}(A)$.

Let us take an example and see how we use the belief function with a set of alternative hypotheses. Suppose that we have four hypotheses, 'weather', 'animal', 'trap' and 'enemy', which form the set $\Theta = \{W, A, T, E\}$. Now, our task is to assign a belief value for each element of Θ. The evidence can affect one or more of the hypotheses. For example, evidence 'noise' supports hypotheses W, A, and E.

Whereas Bayesian reasoning requires that we assign a conditional probability for each combination of propositions, Dempster–Shafer theory operates with sets of hypotheses. A *mass function* (or basic probability assignment) $m(H)$, which is defined for all $H \in \wp(\Theta) \setminus \emptyset$, indicates the current belief to the set H of hypotheses. Although the amount of subsets is exponential and the sum of their probabilities should be one, most of the subsets will not be handled and their probability is zero.

Let us continue with our example: In the beginning we have no information at all, and we let $m(\Theta) = 1$ and all the subsets have the value zero. In other words, all hypotheses are plausible and we have no evidence supporting any of them. Next, we observe a noise and know this evidence points to the subset $\{W, A, E\}$ (i.e. we believe that the noise is caused by the weather, an animal, or an enemy) with the probability 0.6. The corresponding mass function m_n is

$$m_n(\{W, A, E\}) = 0.6, \quad m_n(\Theta) = 0.4.$$

Note that the 'excess' probability of 0.4 is not assigned to the complement of the subset but to the set of all hypotheses.

We can now define belief for a set X of hypotheses with respect to $m(\bullet)$ as

$$\text{Bel}(X) = \sum_{Y \subseteq X} m(Y) \tag{7.4}$$

and its plausability as

$$\text{Pl}(X) = \sum_{Y \cap X \neq \emptyset} m(Y). \tag{7.5}$$

To combine beliefs, we can use Dempster's rule: Let m_1 and m_2 be the mass functions and X and Y be the subsets of Θ for which m_1 and m_2 have non-zero values. The combined mass function m_3 is

$$m_3(Z) = \frac{\sum_{X \cap Y = Z} m_1(X) \cdot m_2(Y)}{1 - \sum_{X \cap Y = \emptyset} m_1(X) \cdot m_2(Y)}. \tag{7.6}$$

An implementation for this is given in Algorithm 7.1. Dempster's rule can be used in both chaining (e.g. $A \to B$ and $B \to C$) and conjoining (e.g. $A \to C$, $B \to C$) multiple propositions.

Reverting to our example, evidence 'footprints' (supporting the hypotheses 'animal', 'trap' and 'enemy') has the mass function m_f, which is defined as

$$m_f(\{A, T, E\}) = 0.8, \quad m_f(\Theta) = 0.2.$$

Algorithm 7.1 Combining two mass functions.

COMBINED-MASS-FUNCTION(m_1, m_2)

    in: mapping $m_1 : \wp(\Theta) \setminus \emptyset \to [0, 1]$ (the domain elements with non-zero range
                    value is denoted by $\mathcal{M}_1 \subseteq \wp(\Theta) \setminus \emptyset$); mapping m_2 is defined similarly as
                    m_1

    out: combined mapping m_3

    constant: set of hypothesis Θ

  1: **for all** $M \in (\wp(\Theta) \setminus \{\emptyset, \Theta\})$ **do**
  2:   $m_3(M) \leftarrow 0$
  3: **end for**
  4: $m_3(\Theta) \leftarrow 1$
  5: $\mathcal{M}_3 \leftarrow \Theta$
  6: $e \leftarrow 0$
  7: **for all** $M_1 \in \mathcal{M}_1$ **do**   ▷ For pairs of members between $\mathcal{M}_1$ and $\mathcal{M}_2$.
  8:   **for all** $M_2 \in \mathcal{M}_2$ **do**
  9:     $M_3 \leftarrow M_1 \cap M_2$
10:     $p \leftarrow m_1(M_1) \cdot m_2(M_2)$
11:     $m_3(\Theta) \leftarrow m_3(\Theta) - p$
12:     **if** $M_3 = \emptyset$ **then**   ▷ Excess for imaginary $m_3(\emptyset)$.
13:       $e \leftarrow e + p$
14:     **else**   ▷ M_3 contributes to $\mathcal{M}_3$.
15:       $m_3(M_3) \leftarrow m_3(M_3) + p$
16:       **if** $M_3 \notin \mathcal{M}_3$ **then**
17:         $\mathcal{M}_3 \leftarrow \mathcal{M}_3 \cup \{M_3\}$
18:       **end if**
19:     **end if**
20:   **end for**
21: **end for**
22: **if** $0 < e < 1$ **then**   ▷ Normalization.
23:   **for all** $M \in \mathcal{M}_3$ **do**
24:     $m_3(M) \leftarrow m_3(M)/(1 - e)$
25:   **end for**
26: **end if**
27: **return** m_3

Assuming that the intersections $X \cap Y$ are non-empty, we get the combination m_{nf} for the two evidences directly from the numerator of Equation (7.6):

$$m_{nf}(\{A, E\}) = 0.48, \qquad\qquad m_{nf}(\{A, T, E\}) = 0.32,$$

$$m_{nf}(\{W, A, E\}) = 0.12, \qquad\qquad m_{nf}(\Theta) = 0.08.$$

It is possible that we get the same intersection set Z more than once, but in that case we just add the mass functions together.

    The situation gets a bit more complicated if the intersection of subsets is empty. The numerator in Equation (7.6) ensures that the sum of different probabilities is one (provided that this holds also for m_1 and m_2). If some intersections are empty, the amount given to the empty sets must be distributed to all non-empty sets, which is handled by the denominator of Equation (7.6).

Let us add m_c to the mass functions, which describes the evidence 'candy wrapper':

$$m_c(\{E\}) = 0.6, \qquad\qquad m_c(\{T\}) = 0.3,$$

$$m_c(\Theta) = 0.1.$$

By combining functions m_{nf} and m_c, we get the following result from the numerator:

$$m_{nfc'}(\{E\}) = 0.6, \qquad\qquad m_{nfc'}(\{T\}) = 0.12,$$

$$m_{nfc'}(\{A, E\}) = 0.048, \qquad\qquad m_{nfc'}(\{A, T, E\}) = 0.032,$$

$$m_{nfc'}(\{W, A, E\}) = 0.012, \qquad\qquad m_{nfc'}(\Theta) = 0.008,$$

$$m_{nfc'}(\emptyset) = 0.18.$$

The denominator is $1 - m_{nfc'}(\emptyset) = 0.82$, and we use it to scale to get m_{nfc} (rounded to two decimals):

$$m_{nfc}(\{E\}) = 0.73, \qquad\qquad m_{nfc}(\{T\}) = 0.15,$$

$$m_{nfc}(\{A, E\}) = 0.06, \qquad\qquad m_{nfc}(\{A, T, E\}) = 0.04,$$

$$m_{nfc}(\{W, A, E\}) = 0.01, \qquad\qquad m_{nfc}(\Theta) = 0.01.$$

From this it follows that if we have evidences 'noise', 'footprints' and 'candy wrapper', Equation (7.4) gives the belief in the hypothesis 'enemy' $\text{Bel}(E) = 0.73$, and Equation (7.5) gives its plausability $\text{Pl}(E) = 0.85$. In comparison, the combined hypothesis 'trap or enemy' has belief $\text{Bel}(\{T, E\}) = 0.88$ and plausability $\text{Pl}(\{T, E\}) = 1$, which means that a human threat is a more likely explanation to the evidence than natural phenomenon.

7.2 Fuzzy Sets

Fuzzy sets acknowledge uncertainty by allowing elements to have a partial membership in a set. In contrast to classical sets with Boolean memberships, fuzzy sets admit that some information is better than no information. Although multi-valued logic was already developed in the 1920s by J. Łukasiewicz, the term 'fuzziness' was coined forty years later. In a seminal paper Zadeh (1965) applied Łukasiewicz's multi-valued logic to sets: Instead of belonging or not belonging to a set, in a fuzzy set an element belongs to a set to a certain degree.

One should always bear in mind that fuzzy sets depend on the context: There can be no universal agreement on a membership function, for example, on the adjective 'small' (cars, humans, nebulae), and, subjectively speaking, a small car can be something completely different for a basketball player than for a racehorse jockey. Furthermore, fuzziness is not a solution method in itself but we can use it in modelling to cope with uncertainty. For example, we can describe the objective function using an aggregation of fuzzy sets (see Figure 7.3). In effect, fuzziness allows us to do more fine-grained evaluations.

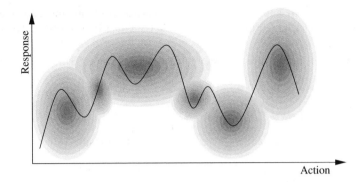

Figure 7.3 Uncertain or complex dependencies can be modelled with fuzzy sets that cover the solution space.

7.2.1 Membership function

In classical (or 'crisp') set theory, the elements of set S are defined using a two-valued characteristic function

$$\chi_S(x) = \begin{cases} 1 & \Longleftrightarrow x \in S \\ 0 & \Longleftrightarrow x \notin S \end{cases}$$

In other words, all the elements x in the universe U either belong to S or not (and there is nothing in between).

Fuzzy set theory extends the characteristic function by allowing an element to have a degree with which it belongs to a set. This degree is called a *membership* in a set, and a fuzzy set is a class in which every element has a membership value.

Theorem 7.2.1 *Let U be a set (universe) and $\mathcal{L}$ be a lattice, $\mathcal{L} = \langle L, \vee, \wedge, \mathbf{1}, \mathbf{0} \rangle$. A fuzzy set A in the universe U is defined by a* membership function μ_A

$$\mu_A : U \to L. \tag{7.7}$$

Each element $x \in U$ has an associated membership function value $\mu_A(x) \in L$, which is the membership value of the element x. If $\mu_A(x) = \mathbf{0}$, x does not belong to the set A. If $\mu_A(x) = \mathbf{1}$, x belongs to the set A. Otherwise (i.e. if $\mu_A(x) \neq \mathbf{0}, \mathbf{1}$) x belongs partly to the set A.

This general definition of a fuzzy set is usually used in a limited form, where we let the lattice $\mathcal{L}$ to be $L = [0, 1] \subset \mathbb{R}$, $\mathbf{0} = 0$ and $\mathbf{1} = 1$. In other words, the membership function is defined on a real number range $[0, 1]$, and the fuzzy set A in universe U is defined by the membership function

$$\mu_A : U \to [0, 1],$$

which assigns for each element $x \in U$ a membership value $\mu_A(x)$ in the fuzzy set A. Another way to interpret the membership value is to think it as the truth value of the statement 'x is an element of set A'. For example, Figure 7.4 illustrates different fuzzy sets for a continuous U. Here, the universe is the distance d in metres, and the sets describe the accuracy of different weapons with respect to the distance to the target.

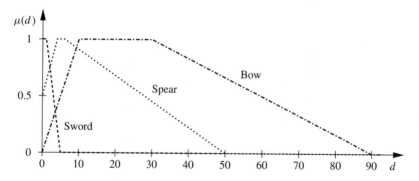

Figure 7.4 Membership functions μ_{sword}, μ_{spear} and μ_{bow} for the attribute 'accuracy' of weapons with respect to the distance (in metres) to the target.

When defining fuzzy sets, we inevitably face the question, how should one assign the membership functions. Suggested methods include the following:

- *Real-world data*: Sometimes we can apply physical measurements, and we can assign the membership function values to correspond to the real-world data. Also, if we have statistical data on the modelled attribute, it can be used to define the membership functions.

- *Subjective evaluation*: Because fuzzy sets often model human's cognitive knowledge, the definition of a membership function can be guided by human experts. They can draw or select, among pre-defined membership functions, the one corresponding to their knowledge. Even questionnaires or psychological tests can be used when defining more complex functions.

- *Adaptation*: The membership functions can be dynamic and evolve over time using the feedback from the input data. This kind of hybrid system can use, for example, neural networks or genetic algorithms for adaptation as the nature of the modelled attribute becomes clear.

The beauty (and agony) of fuzzy sets is that there are an infinite number of possible different membership functions for the same attribute. Although by tweaking the membership function we can get more accurate response, in practice even simple functions work surprisingly well as long as the general trend of the function reflects the modelled information. For example, if we are modelling the attribute 'young', it is sufficient that the membership value decreases as the age increases.

7.2.2 Fuzzy operations

The logical fuzzy operations $\vee$ (i.e. disjunction) and $\wedge$ (i.e. conjunction) are often defined using $\max\{\mu_A(\bullet), \mu_B(\bullet)\}$ and $\min\{\mu_A(\bullet), \mu_B(\bullet)\}$, although they can be defined in various alternative ways using t-norms and t-conorms (Yager and Filev 1994). Also, negation can be defined in many ways, but the usual choice is $1 - \mu_A(\bullet)$. All classical set operations have fuzzy counterparts.

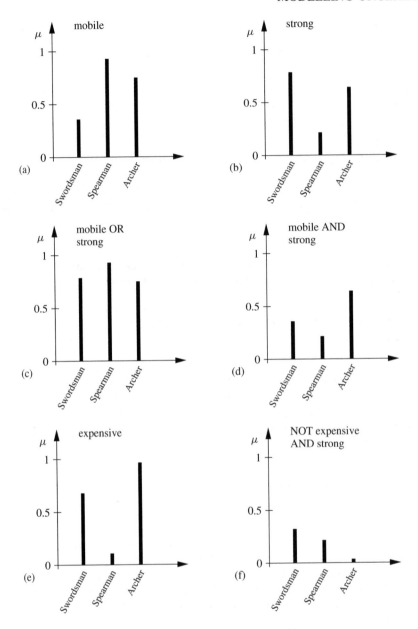

Figure 7.5 Fuzzy operations for different attributes. (a) The membership function for mobility. (b) The membership function for strength. (c) The membership function for the union of mobility and strength. (d) The membership function for the intersection of mobility and strength. (e) The membership function for expensiveness. (f) The membership function for the intersection of the complement of expensiveness and strength.

Theorem 7.2.2 *Let A, B, and C be fuzzy sets in the universe U. Further, assume that all operations have the value range* [0, 1]. *We can now define for each element* $x \in U$

Union	$C = A \cup B$	$\Longleftrightarrow$	$\mu_C(x) = \max\{\mu_A(x), \mu_B(x)\},$	(7.8)
Intersection	$C = A \cap B$	$\Longleftrightarrow$	$\mu_C(x) = \min\{\mu_A(x), \mu_B(x)\},$	(7.9)
Complement	$C = \bar{A}$	$\Longleftrightarrow$	$\mu_C(x) = 1 - \mu_A(x).$	(7.10)

Figure 7.5 illustrates the use of fuzzy set operations for a discrete U. The universe consists of three elements – swordsman, spearman, and archers – and they have three attributes – mobility, strength, and expensiveness. The union of mobility and strength describes the set of mobile or strong soldiers, whereas the intersection describes the set of mobile and strong soldiers. The intersection of the complement of expensiveness and strength gives the set of inexpensive and strong soldiers.

7.3 Fuzzy Constraint Satisfaction Problem

Fuzzy optimization originates from ideas proposed by Bellman and Zadeh (1970), who introduced the concepts of fuzzy constraints, fuzzy objective, and fuzzy decision. Fuzzy decision-making, in general, concerns deciding future actions on the basis of vague or uncertain knowledge (Fullér and Carlsson 1996; Herrera and Verdegay 1997). The problem in making decisions under uncertainty is that the bulk of the information we have about the possible outcomes, the value of new information, and the dynamically changing conditions is typically vague, ambiguous, or otherwise unclear. In this section, we focus on multiple criteria decision-making, which refers to making decisions in the presence of multiple and possibly conflicting criteria.

In a constraint satisfaction problem (CSP), one must find states or objects in a system that satisfy a number of constraints or criteria. A CSP consists of

- a set of n variables X,

- a domain D_i (i.e. a finite set of possible values) for each variable x_i in X, and

- a set of constraints restricting the feasibility of the tuples $(x_0, x_1, \ldots, x_{n-1}) \in D_0 \times \cdots \times D_{n-1}$.

A solution is an assignment of a value in D_i to each variable x_i such that every constraint is satisfied. Because a CSP lacks an objective function, it is not an optimization problem. As an example of a CSP, Figure 7.6 illustrates a monkey puzzle problem (Harel 1987, pp. 153–155). The $3 \cdot 4 = 12$ tile positions identify the variables, the tiles define the domain set, and the requirement that all the monkey halves must match defines $(3 - 1) \cdot 4 + 3 \cdot (4 - 1) = 17$ constraints.

Unfortunately, the modelled problems are not always as discrete and easy to form. Fuzzy sets have also been proposed for extending CSPs so that partial satisfaction of the constraints is possible. The constraints can be more or less relaxable or subject to preferences. These flexible constraints are either soft constraints, which express preferences among solutions, or prioritized constraints that can be violated if they conflict with constraints with a higher priority (Dubois *et al.* 1996).

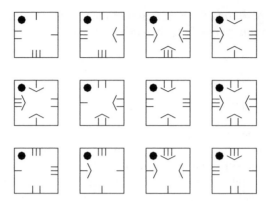

Figure 7.6 A monkey puzzle with 3×4 tiles. The monkey is depicted as an arrow with separated tail and head ends. The solution is an arrangement of the tiles so that tiles are not rotated (i.e. a black circle stays at the upper left corner of a tile) and all the tails and heads match (i.e. form a one-directed arrow) inside the 3×4 rectangle.

In the *fuzzy constraint satisfaction problem* (FCSP) both types of flexible constraints are regarded as local criteria that give (possibly partial) rank orderings to instantiations and can be represented by means of fuzzy relations (Guesgen 1994; Slany 1995). A fuzzy constraint represents the constraints as well as the criteria by the fuzzy subsets C_i of the set S of possible decisions: If C_i is a fuzzy constraint and the corresponding membership function μ_{C_i} for some decision $s \in S$ yields $\mu_{C_i}(s) = 1$, then decision s totally satisfies the constraint C_i, while $\mu_{C_i}(s) = 0$ means that it totally violates C_i (i.e. s is infeasible). If $0 < \mu_{C_i}(s) < 1$, s satisfies C_i only partially. Hence, a fuzzy constraint gives a rank ordering for the feasible decisions much like an objective function.

More formally, FCSP is a five-tuple

$$P = \langle V, C_\mu, W, T, U \rangle,$$

which comprises the following elements:

- a set of variables V;

- a set U of universes (domains) for each variable in V;

- a set C_μ of constraints in which each constraint is a membership function μ from the value assignments to the range $[0, 1]$ and has an associated weight w_c representing its importance or priority;

- a weighting scheme W (i.e. a function that combines a constraint satisfaction degree $\mu(c)$ with w to yield the weighted constraint satisfaction degree $\mu^w(c)$);

- an aggregation function T that produces a single partial order on value assignments.

Let us go through the stages of FCSP using the game Dog Eat Dog as an example (see Figure 7.7): Players are moving inside a closed two-dimensional play field. Each player

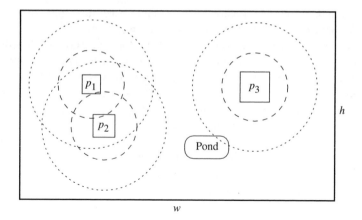

Figure 7.7 The set-up of Dog Eat Dog for three players. Player p_1 has the enemy p_2 and the prey p_3, player p_2 has the enemy p_3 and the prey p_1, and player p_3 has the enemy p_1 and the prey p_2. The dashed circles represent the limit of the players' visual range and the dotted circles represent their olfactory range. Players p_1 and p_2 can see one another but cannot smell the pond. Player p_3 does not see the other players but can smell the pond. The game world is a rectangle of size $w \times h$.

has one prey, which is to be hunted, and one enemy, which is to be avoided. The play field includes also a pond, which restores the player's health. Initially, the players and the pond are placed at random positions inside the play field. The players have two senses: They can see other players or smell the pond. However, the senses have limitations: The farther away an object is, the noisier the player's sensory data gets, until after a cut-off distance the player receives no sensory input from the object. The players have no control over their velocities, but they get set randomly for each turn. Instead, the player's only decision at every turn is to choose a direction where to move.

7.3.1 Modelling the criteria as fuzzy sets

Each criterion associated to the problem can be fuzzified by defining a membership function that corresponds to the intuitive 'rule' behind the criterion. In our example, we need membership functions to describe different attributes. Intuitively, the rules are simple:

- If the visual observation of the enemy is reliable, then avoid the enemy.

- If the visual observation of the prey is reliable, then chase the prey.

- If the olfactory observation of the pond is reliable, then go to the pond.

- If the visual observation of the enemy is reliable, then stay in the centre of the play field.

Although we have given the rules as if–then statements, the first (i.e. if) part defines the importance given to the second (i.e. then) part. For example, the first rule could be rewritten

'The more reliable the visual observation of the enemy is, the more important it is to avoid the enemy'. We return to this when we are discussing weighting.

First, let us define a membership function $\mu_a(\theta)$ for the 'attraction' of direction θ given in radians (see Figure 7.8). If $n \in \mathbb{Z}$, direction $\theta = 2n\pi - \pi$ is towards the target, for which $\mu_a(\theta) = 1$; direction $\theta = 2n\pi$ is away from the target, for which $\mu_a(\theta) = 0$. The rest of the function is defined linearly between these points. For 'avoidance' we do not have to define a new membership function but can use the complement of attraction, $1 - \mu_a(\theta)$.

Since the player's senses are unreliable, we can model them conveniently with fuzzy sets. Figure 7.9 gives a simple linear membership function $\mu_s(d)$ for reliability of visual input at distance d. The membership value starts with one and it decreases as the distance increases, until after the visual cut-off distance s the membership value is zero. The membership function $\mu_o(d)$ for reliability of olfactory input is defined in a similar fashion.

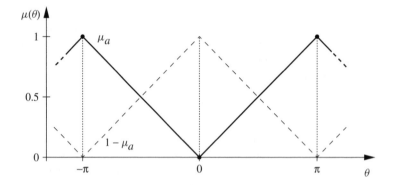

Figure 7.8 Membership function $\mu_a(\theta)$ for the attraction of the direction θ. The complement $1 - \mu_a(\theta)$ gives a membership value for avoidance.

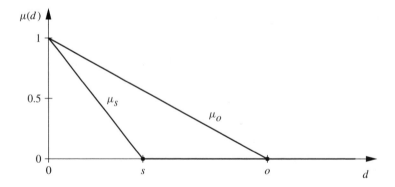

Figure 7.9 Membership functions for the reliability of sensory inputs: $\mu_s(d)$ for the reliability of visual input at the distance d, and $\mu_o(d)$ for the reliability of olfactory input at the distance d.

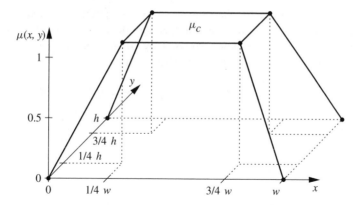

Figure 7.10 Membership function $\mu_c(x, y)$ for the centralness of position (x, y).

Getting trapped to the side or the corner of the play field is a lousy move, especially when the enemy is chasing. The closer the player is to the centre of the play field, the better it can manoeuvre away from the enemy. Figure 7.10 illustrates a two-parameter membership function $\mu_c(x, y)$ for the centralness of the position (x, y) in the play field.

7.3.2 Weighting the criteria importances

Our set of rules includes importances, which can be realized by weighting the corresponding fuzzy sets. Weights ensure that the important criteria have a greater effect on the decision than the less important ones. In our example, we want to weight the avoidance of the enemy and attraction of prey with the reliability of the visual observation. Similarly, the attraction of the pond is weighted with the reliability of the olfactory observation, and the attraction of the centre with the reliability of the visual observation of the enemy.

Weighting can be based on an interpretation of the fuzzy implication as a boundary, which guarantees that a criterion has at least a certain fulfilment value. If a fuzzy criterion C_i has a weight $w_i \in [0, 1]$, where a greater value w_i corresponds to a greater importance, the weighted value of a criterion is obtained from the implication $w_i \rightarrow C_i$. Weighting operation can be defined classically (i.e. $A \rightarrow B \iff \neg A \vee B$), which gives us the rule $\min\{(1 - w_i), C_i\}$.

We can also use the weighting scheme defined by Yager (1981), where the weighted membership value $\mu_C^w(x)$ of a criterion C is defined as

$$\mu_C^w(x) = \begin{cases} 1, & \text{if } \mu(x) = 0 \text{ and } w = 0, \\ (\mu_C(x))^w, & \text{otherwise.} \end{cases}$$

In the case $w = 0$, the criterion is 'turned off' because the corresponding weighted membership value always equals one (i.e. it does not affect the overall aggregated result).

7.3.3 Aggregating the criteria

To make the decision, the different criteria must be aggregated together. Although we can use any fuzzy conjunction operator, it is usually preferable that the aggregator has compensatory properties, because then the effect of one poorly satisfied criterion is not so drastic on the overall result. Mean-based operators have this property, and the *ordered weighted averaging* (OWA) operator, proposed by Yager (1988), is particularly useful, because the amount of compensation can be adjusted freely.

An OWA operator of dimension n is a mapping $F: \mathbb{R}^n \to \mathbb{R}$, which has an associated weight sequence $W = (w_0, w_1, \ldots, w_{n-1})^{\mathrm{T}}$ where each weight $w_i \in [0, 1]$, $0 \le i \le (n - 1)$, and $\sum_{i=0}^{n-1} w_i = 1$. Furthermore, $F(a_0, \ldots, a_{n-1}) = \sum_{j=0}^{n-1} w_j b_j$, where b_j is the $(j + 1)$th largest element of the sequence $A = \langle a_0, \ldots, a_{n-1} \rangle$. A fundamental aspect of this operator is the re-ordering step. An aggregate a_i is not associated with a particular weight w_i, but rather a weight is associated with a particular ordered position of the aggregate. Algorithm 7.2 gives an implementation for the OWA operator.

Algorithm 7.2 Ordered weighted aggregation.

OWA(M, W)
    in: sequence of membership values M; sequence of weights W
    out: aggregated result
   1: $V \leftarrow$ **copy** M
   2: sort V into non-increasing order
   3: $r \leftarrow 0$
   4: **for** $i \leftarrow 0 \ldots (|V| - 1)$ **do**
   5:    $r \leftarrow r + W_i \cdot V_i$
   6: **end for**
   7: **return** r

By setting the weight sequence W, we can get different aggregation operator ranging from conjunction $W = \{0, 0, \ldots, 1\} = \min\{A\}$ to disjunction $W = \{1, 0, 0, \ldots, 0\} = \max\{A\}$ and average $W = \{1/n, 1/n, \ldots, 1/n\}$. One possibility is to use the 'soft-and' operator (Slany 1994), where the weight sequence is

$$w_i = \frac{2i + 1}{n(n + 1)}.$$

This weight distribution yields a fair compensation, which in our Dog Eat Dog example is better than imposing strict rules on the evaluation of the optimality of the direction.

7.3.4 Making a decision

We are now ready for the actual decision-making (see Algorithm 7.3). The player decides the direction by first evaluating possible choices one by one and then choosing the best one. The evaluation follows the phases laid out in this section (and the routines WEIGHT-CRITERION and SOFT-AND-WEIGHTS are defined accordingly). First, we calculate the distances and directions to the enemy, the prey, and the pond. This information is used to weight the four criteria – avoid the enemy, chase the prey, go to the pond, and stay in the centre – which are finally aggregated together to form the evaluation value for the desirability of the given direction.

Algorithm 7.3 Fuzzy decision-making for Dog Eat Dog.

DECIDE-DIRECTION()

    out: best direction θ_b

    local: best evaluation e_b; direction candidate θ; evaluation e of the direction

    constant: number of directions s

  1: $\theta_b \leftarrow 0$; $e_b \leftarrow 0$

  2: $\theta \leftarrow -\pi$

  3: **for** $i \leftarrow 1 \ldots s$ **do**   ▷ Check each direction.

  4:    $e \leftarrow$ EVALUATE-DIRECTION(θ)

  5:    **if** $e > e_b$ **then**

  6:       $\theta_b \leftarrow \theta$

  7:       $e_b \leftarrow e$

  8:    **end if**

  9:    $\theta \leftarrow \theta + 2\pi/s$

10: **end for**

11: **return** θ_b

EVALUATE-DIRECTION(θ)

    in: direction candidate θ

    out: evaluation of the direction

    constant: enemy position E; prey position P; pond position W; own position O; attraction membership function μ_a; reliability of sight membership function μ_s; reliability of smell membership function μ_o; centralness membership function μ_c

  1: $d_x \leftarrow E_x - O_x$; $d_y \leftarrow E_y - O_y$

  2: $\delta_e \leftarrow \sqrt{d_x^2 + d_y^2}$ ▷ Distance to the enemy.

  3: $d_e \leftarrow \operatorname{sgn}(d_y) \cdot \arccos(d_x/\delta_e)$ ▷ Direction to the enemy.

  4: $d_x \leftarrow P_x - O_x$; $d_y \leftarrow P_y - O_y$

  5: $\delta_p \leftarrow \sqrt{d_x^2 + d_y^2}$ ▷ Distance to the prey.

  6: $d_p \leftarrow \operatorname{sgn}(d_y) \cdot \arccos(d_x/\delta_p)$ ▷ Direction to the prey.

  7: $d_x \leftarrow W_x - O_x$; $d_y \leftarrow W_y - O_y$

  8: $\delta_w \leftarrow \sqrt{d_x^2 + d_y^2}$ ▷ Distance to the pond.

  9: $d_w \leftarrow \operatorname{sgn}(d_y) \cdot \arccos(d_x/\delta_w)$ ▷ Direction to the pond.

10: $m_e \leftarrow$ WEIGHT-CRITERION($1 - \mu_a(d_e - \theta), \mu_s(\delta_e)$)

11: $m_p \leftarrow$ WEIGHT-CRITERION($\mu_a(d_p - \theta), \mu_s(\delta_p)$)

12: $m_w \leftarrow$ WEIGHT-CRITERION($\mu_a(d_w - \theta), \mu_o(\delta_w)$)

13: $m_c \leftarrow$ WEIGHT-CRITERION($\mu_c(O_x + \cos(\theta), O_y + \sin(\theta)), \mu_s(\delta_e)$)

14: **return** OWA($\langle m_e, m_p, m_w, m_c \rangle$, SOFT-AND-WEIGHTS(4))

Surprisingly, even a small number of direction choices leads to good results – of course, as long as they allow the player to move inside the two-dimensional play field. Also, if we increase the level of noise in the observations, the players can cope with it quite well without any modifications done on their decision-making. Naturally, if the environment gets too noisy (i.e. the observations get too random), it becomes almost impossible to form a coherent picture of what is going on.

7.4 Summary

As the complexity of the game world increases, it becomes more difficult to model it accurately. In fact, adhering to preciseness tends to make the model less usable, because modelling is not about collecting detailed information but is about abstracting (from Latin *abstrahere* 'to drag away') knowledge from the details. Therefore, the model should tolerate uncertainties – both probabilistic and possibilistic – rather than single them out.

The key to knowledge is conciseness: Having some information – albeit not perfect and complete – is better than having no information or having too much information. If we humans were to follow perfect and complete information all the time, we would hardly be able to make any decisions at all. Instead, we are capable and willing to base our actions on beliefs, conjectures, rules of thumb, hunches, and even sheer guesswork.

Exercises

7-1 Whenever we discretize an attribute, we get exposed to sorites paradoxes (deriving from the Greek word *soros*, 'heap'). Consider the case in which you first see a lone enemy soldier wandering to your area. Is that an invasion? What if another does the same, then another, and so forth. When does the invasion begin, and – more importantly – when should you make the decision and start ringing the alarm bells?

7-2 Consider following questions. Is the uncertainty probabilistic or possibilistic?

   (a) Is the vase broken?

   (b) Is the vase broken by a burglar?

   (c) Is there a burglar in the closet?

   (d) Is the burglar in the closet a man?

   (e) Is the man in the closet a burglar?

7-3 We can improve the software development practices of the example given in page 150 by investing in either the implementation or the testing phase. Which improvement yields a better result: catching an actual bug increases from 90 to 95% or bugs caused by the test arrangement decreases from 10 to 5%?

7-4 Let us extend the Bayesian network of Figure 7.1. The noise could be caused by a dog, which is likely to bark if a sentry or an intruder is on the move. Assume that the probability of barking because of a sentry is 0.3 and because of an intruder 0.6

(and sometimes the dog barks just because he is lonely). Add this information to the Bayesian network and recalculate the values of Table 7.1.

7-5 Explain (intuitively) how the terms 'plausability' and 'doubt' presented in Figure 7.2 relate to one another.

7-6 Model the situation of Exercise 7-4 using Dempster–Shafer theory.

7-7 Why is the empty set excluded from the mass function?

7-8 Let us add to the example given in page 153 a new evidence 'eaten leaves' with the mass function m_e:

$$m_e(\{A\}) = 0.85, \qquad\qquad m_e(\{E\}) = 0.1,$$

$$m_e(\Theta) = 0.05.$$

Replace the evidence 'candy wrapper' with this new evidence and determine a new combined mass function m_{nfe}. What are the belief and plausability of the hypotheses 'enemy' and 'animal'?

What are the beliefs and plausabilities if we observe all four evidences 'noise', 'footprints', 'candy wrapper' and 'eaten leaves'?

7-9 Figure 7.4 gives fuzzy sets for the accuracy of weapons and Figure 7.5 gives the attributes of infantry. Given that we know the distance to the enemy and the current economical situation, how can this information be combined for making the decision as to what kind of troops to train.

7-10 Model the criteria affecting the decision-making of a race driver as fuzzy sets.

7-11 Formulate the n queens problem of Exercise 5-10 as a CSP.

7-12 Write an algorithm that solves the monkey puzzle of Figure 7.6. How many solutions does it have? What is the time complexity of the program?

7-13 A tile of a monkey puzzle has four monkey halves that can be labelled as north (N), east (E), south (S), and west (W) half. In addition to the shape of the border rectangle, these halves determine which edges can be placed next one other. There is also another way to define how the tiles can be placed: Each tile corner (i.e. compass directions NE, SE, SW, and NW) has a monkey quarter. If we abstract this quarter, for example, with a letter, only the tiles with the same letter in their touching corners can be adjacent. Figure 7.11 illustrates one valid solution for this *quarter monkey puzzle*. Are the two monkey puzzle representations equivalent in the sense that if we have a pile of 'half monkey' tiles H, it is possible to define a pile of 'quarter monkey' tiles Q that gives exactly the same set of solutions for the puzzle (and vice versa)?

7-14 Is it possible to formulate the monkey puzzle problems of Exercises 7-12 and 7-13 as FCSPs?

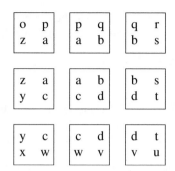

Figure 7.11 Monkey puzzle variant in which the tiles can be adjacent only when their corner letters match.

7-15 Let us denote the quarter monkeys of Exercise 7-13 with numbers. To evaluate the solution, we observe the difference in the corner numbers: The closer the numbers, the better the solution. Formulate this generalization of monkey puzzle as a FCSP.

7-16 Formulate the gold-digger's decision-making in Goldrush (see Exercise 6-28) as a FCSP.

Part II

Networking

8

Communication Layers

When multiple participants take part in the same activity such as a game, they interact through some *shared-space technology*. Figure 8.1 illustrates a broad classification of shared-space technologies by Benford *et al.* (1998). The transportation axis indicates the level to which the participants leave behind their local space (i.e. whether they remain in the physical world or leave their body behind), and the artificiality axis represents the level to which a space is computer generated or from the real world. By using these two dimensions, we can discern four main categories:

- Physical reality resides in the local, physical world where things are tangible and the participants are corporeal (e.g. children playing football in the yard).

- Telepresence allows the participants to be present at a real-world location but remote from their physical location (e.g. operating a rover on Mars from Earth).

- Augmented reality overlays synthetic objects on the local environment (e.g. a head-up display in a fighter plane indicating the whereabouts of selected targets).

- Virtual reality allows the participants to be immersed in a remote, synthetic world (e.g. adults playing football in a computer game).

Apart from physical reality, where interaction is immediate, other shared-space technologies require a distributed system – namely, computers and networks – so that the participants can interact with each other.

Networked computer games mainly belong to the virtual reality category, although location-based games, which use wireless networking and mobile platforms, have more in common with augmented reality. Nevertheless, what is universal to all networked computer games is that they must be able to manage network resources, cope with data loss and network failures, and maintain concurrency. In addition, networked games differ from many other distributed applications (e.g. databases) in that they are *interactive real-time applications*, where the players should experience and share the same game world as if it exists locally in their computers.

Algorithms and Networking for Computer Games   Jouni Smed and Harri Hakonen
© 2006 John Wiley & Sons, Ltd

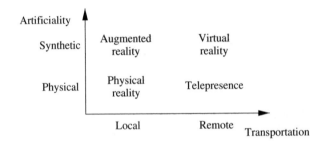

Figure 8.1 Classification of shared-space technologies according to transportation and artificiality.

To clarify conceptually how networked games work, we can discern three communication layers:

(i) The physical platform induces resource limitations (e.g. bandwidth and latency) that reflect the underlying infrastructure (e.g. cabling and hardware).

(ii) The logical platform builds upon the physical platform and provides architectures for communication, data, and control (e.g. mutually exclusive data locks and communication rerouting mechanisms).

(iii) The networked application adds context interpretation to the data (e.g. an integer value represents a position) and orchestrates separate control flows together (e.g. by managing synchronization and resolving deadlocks).

Operations on data – storing, processing, and transferring – have related concepts on each level, which are illustrated in Table 8.1. Normally, there is not much we can do to change the physical platform – except perhaps invest on new hardware. The logical platform is intended for system designers, since it provides programming language level abstractions like data entities and communication channels. The networked application is built upon the logical platform and is related to the end-users. Let us now go through each of these levels in more detail.

Table 8.1   Layers of networking with respect to data.

Level	Operation on data		
	Storing	Processing	Transferring
Physical platform	Memory	Processor	Network
Logical platform	Data entity	Control process	Communication channel
Networked application	State	Integrity control	Multi-source support

8.1 Physical Platform

Networking is subject to resource limitations (e.g. physical, technical, and computational), which set boundaries for what is possible. Once we have established a network of connections between a set of *nodes* (i.e. the computers in the network), we need a technique for transmitting the data from one node to another. The content and delivery of information are expressed using a protocol, which defines the form of the data transmission so that the nodes can understand it.

8.1.1 Resource limitations

Networked applications face three resource limitations (Singhal 1996):

- network bandwidth,

- network latency, and

- the nodes' processing power for handling the network traffic.

These resources refer to the technical attributes of the underlying network and they impose physical restrictions, which the networked application cannot overcome and which must be considered in its design.

Bandwidth refers to the transmission capacity of a communication line such as a network. Simply put, bandwidth is the proportion of the amount of data transmitted or received per time unit. In a wide area network (WAN), bandwidths can range from tens of kbps (bits per second) of dial-up modems up to 1.5 Mbps of T1 and 44.7 Mbps of T3. In a local area network (LAN), bandwidths are much larger, ranging from 10 Mbps to 10 Gbps. However, LANs have a limited size and they support a limited number of users, whereas WANs allow global connections. In addition to how often and how large are the messages that are sent, bandwidth requirements depend on the amount and distribution of users and the transmission technique, as we will see in Section 8.1.2.

Networking *latency* indicates the length of time (or delay) that results when a message gets from one designated node to another. In addition, the variance of latency over time (i.e. jitter) is another feature that affects networked applications. Latency cannot be totally eliminated. For example, speed-of-light propagation delays and the slowdown of electrical signal in a cable alone yield a latency of 25–30 ms for crossing the Atlantic. Moreover, routing, queuing, and packet handling delays add dozens of milliseconds to the overall latency – which is partly due to nodes processing the traffic. It should be noted that latency and bandwidth are not necessarily related: We can have a high-bandwidth network that has a low latency and vice versa.

For interactive real-time systems such as computer games, the rule of thumb is that latency between 0.1 and 1.0 s is acceptable. For instance, the Distributed Interactive Simulation (DIS) standard used in military simulations specifies that the network latency should be less than 100 ms (Neyland 1997). Latency affects the user's performance non-linearly: Continuous and fluid control is possible when the latency does not exceed 200 ms, after which the interaction becomes more observational and cognizant. Consequently, the threshold of when latency becomes inconvenient for the user depends on the type of computer game. In a real-time strategy game, a higher latency (even up to 500 ms) may be acceptable as long as it remains static, which means that jitter should be low (Bettner and Terrano 2001). Interestingly, experiments on collaborative virtual environments have yielded similar results (Park and Kenyon 1999; Shirmohammadi and Georganas 2001). On the other hand, games requiring a tight hand–eye motor control such as first-person shooters demand that the latency runs closer at 100 ms.

8.1.2   Transmission techniques and protocols

Transmission techniques can be divided into three types (see Figure 8.2):

- Unicasting is communication between a single sender and a single receiver, which allows to control and direct the traffic from point to point. If the same message is intended for multiple receivers, unicasting wastes bandwidth by sending redundant messages.

- Multicasting is communication between a single sender and multiple receivers, which allows receivers to subscribe to groups that interest them. The sender does not need to know all the subscribers but sends only one message, which is received by multiple receivers belonging to the group. Because no duplicate messages are sent down the same distribution path, multicasting provides an efficient way to transmit information among a large number of nodes.

- Broadcasting is communication between a single sender and all recipients, which means that every node has to receive and process every broadcast message. Obviously, this leads to problems as the number of participants grows, which is why broadcast transmissions are not guaranteed on the WANs.

Protocol is a set of rules that two applications can follow in order to communicate with each other. In networking, protocol includes definitions on the message format (i.e. understanding what the other endpoint is transmitting), message semantics (i.e. what the node can

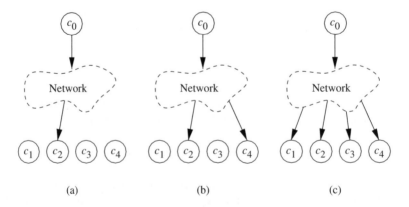

Figure 8.2   Transmission techniques: (a) In unicasting, the message is sent to a single receiver. (b) In multicasting, the message is sent to one or more receivers that have joined a multicast group. (c) In broadcasting, the message is sent to all nodes in the network.

assume and deduce when it receives a packet), and error behaviour (i.e. what the node can do if something goes wrong). For example, the Internet Protocol (IP) comprises low-level protocols that guide the messages from the source to the destination node hiding the actual transmission path (Defense Advanced Research Projects Agency 1981). Networked applications rarely use the IP directly but use the protocols that are written on top of IP. The most common among them are Transmission Control Protocol (TCP/IP) and User Datagram Protocol (UDP/IP):

- TCP/IP provides a reliable point-to-point connection by dividing the data into network packets. To extract the data, the receiver sorts the packets in the correct order, discards duplicates, and asks the sender to retransmit lost or corrupted packets. Naturally, this reliability results in processing time and larger packets. Also, because the transmission is sequential, it is hard to have a random access to the data.

- UDP/IP provides a connectionless best-effort delivery, which means that transmission and receiving is immediate. Because it does not guarantee that data is in order (or received at all) or that data is not corrupted, the transmission is unreliable. However, the packets contain minimal header information, they are easy to process, and they can be sent to multiple hosts, which means UDP/IP can be used also in broadcasting and multicasting.

8.2 Logical Platform

Whereas the physical platform sees the network as nodes that are connected together physically, logical platform defines how the messages flow in this network. The logical platform defines architectures for *communication*, *data*, and *control*.

8.2.1 Communication architecture

The communication architecture can be chosen from different models, which can be arranged as communication graphs according to their *degree of deployment* (see Figure 8.3). In a communication graph, the nodes represent the processes running on remote computers and the edges denote that the nodes can exchange messages. The simplest configuration has only a *single node* (i.e. one computer and no network). For example, two or more players can participate in the same game if the screen is split so that each of them has thier own view.

In a *peer-to-peer* architecture, we have a set of equal nodes connected by a network. Since no node is more special than the others, the nodes must be connected to each other (at least latently). There is no intermediary and each node can transmit its messages to every node in the network. Peer-to-peer architecture was widely used in the first networked computer games, because it is quite straightforward to realize and to expand from a single-player game. However, it does not scale up easily owing to the lack of hierarchical structure. It is useful when the number of participants is small or they communicate in a LAN.

In *client–server* architecture, one node is promoted to the role of a server. Now, all communication is handled through this server node, while the other nodes remain in the role of a client. Each client sends packets to the other clients through the server. Although

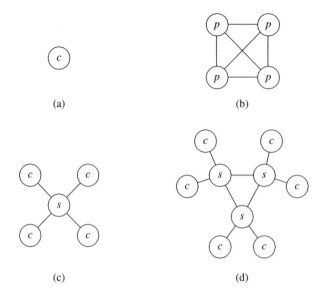

Figure 8.3 Communication architectures as degrees of deployment: (a) a single node, (b) a peer-to-peer architecture, (c) a client–server architecture, and (d) a server-network architecture.

the server slows down the message delivery, we get benefits because we can control the packet flow: We do not have to send all packets to all players (see Section 9.6), and we can aggregate multiple packets to a single packet and smooth out the packet flow (see Section 9.2). Moreover, the client–server architecture allows the implementation of administration features, because the server has a special message routing position.

In *server-network* (or server pool) architecture, there are several interconnected servers. Here, the communication graph can be thought of as a peer-to-peer network of servers over a set of client–server subnetworks. A client is connected to a local server, which is connected to the remote servers and, through them, to the remote clients. Of course, we can extend the server-network hierarchically so that servers themselves act as clients to higher-level servers. Server-network architecture reduces the capacity requirements imposed on a server. In consequence, this provides better scalability but increases the complexity of handling the network traffic.

8.2.2 Data and control architecture

Two attributes define the models for data and control architecture: *consistency* and *responsiveness* (see Section 9.1.1). To achieve a high consistency, the architecture must guarantee that processes running on remote nodes are tightly coupled. This usually requires high bandwidth, low latency, and a small number of remote nodes. To achieve high responsiveness (or timeliness), the queries made to the data must be responded to quickly, which leads to loosely coupled nodes. In this case, the nodes include more computation to reduce the bandwidth and latency requirements. In reality, an architecture cannot achieve both high

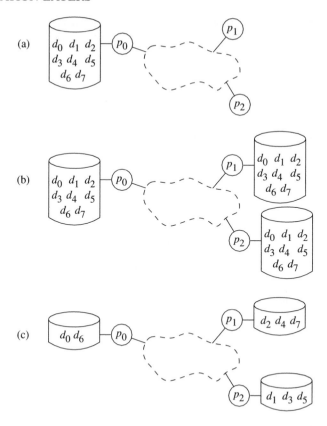

Figure 8.4   Data and control architectures: (a) In centralized data architecture, one (data server) node stores all data. (b) In replicated architecture, each node manages a replica of all data. (c) In distributed architecture, the data is partitioned among the nodes.

consistency and high responsiveness at the same time, and the choice of architecture is a trade-off between these two attributes.

Figure 8.4 illustrates three fundamental data and control architectures:

- In a centralized architecture, only one node holds all the data.

- In a replicated architecture, a copy of the same data exists in all the nodes.

- In a distributed architecture, each node holds a subset of the data.

Centralized architecture can be seen as a shared database that keeps the system consistent at all times. Obviously, it is likely to lack responsiveness, which is elemental for real-time networked applications like computer games. Distributed and replicated architectures suit better, because they allow higher responsiveness. The distinction between these architectures is that distributed architecture adapts more easily, for instance, player controlled entities, whose behaviour is unpredictable and for whom there can be only one source of commands (Chang 1996; Verna et al. 2000). Conversely, synthetic players are usually predictable and need not send frequent control messages, and a replicated architecture provides a better alternative (see Section 9.5). To put it briefly, indeterminism leads to distribution and determinism to replication.

8.3   Networked Application

The networked application is built upon the logical platform. Real-time, interactive networked applications have been researched in the fields of military simulations, virtual environments, and computer games; for further details, see Smed *et al.* (2002, 2003). The technical key issues in their design are

- scalability (i.e. the ability to adapt to resource changes),

- persistence (i.e. leaving and entering the game world), and

- collaboration between players (i.e. upholding integrity when sharing an object).

Scalability concerns how to construct an online application that dynamically adapts to varying number of players and how to allocate the computation of synthetic players among the nodes. This can be achieved only if we can utilize the network of nodes (i.e. hardware parallelism) for implementing asynchronous computation (i.e. software concurrency) of the networked application (see Section 9.1.2). Scaling up a networked application brings forth two complementary views: Each new participant naturally burdens the communication resources but, at the same time, it also offers additional computational power to the whole application.

Persistence concerns how a remote node can coexist with an application. Initially, the application has a state and the attaching node must be configured to conform to this state (e.g. when players join an online server, they receive the object data corresponding to the current situation). Throughout the game play, the node and application live in a symbiosis, which is supported by the underlying logical platform. For example, when a node leaves the application, the application must have a mechanism to uphold the game state by forwarding the node's responsibilities. On the other hand, if a node gets disconnected abruptly, the networked application loses the objects maintained by the node. To sum up, persistence must account for, among other things, configuration management, error detection and recovery, and administration on both the application and the node.

Collaboration usually means that there are team members that act together to achieve a shared goal (e.g. eliminate the other team or overcome some common obstacles). To support collaboration, the networked application has to provide a player with rich and accurate information about the other participants (Benford *et al.* 2001; Shirmohammadi and Georganas 2001). Technically, collaboration requires that the communication between players is prioritized: The closer the two entities are in the game world, the more they communicate with each other. However, the distance between team members does not have to be defined on spatial terms (e.g. they can have implicit knowledge about each other's status or they can share a dedicated communication channel). Clearly, team is an application-level concept. Because the concept of collaboration distance can be complex, cooperation consumes more resources than confrontation.

8.4 Summary

We presented communication as three layers – physical, logical, and application. This follows from the idea that some parts can be implemented as a software engine (e.g. graphics engines). Here, the logical layer acts as an engine, which provides the basic concepts and mechanisms for advanced distributed computing. We can think of the logical layer as a toolbox (derived from research and standards) that combines the networked application to the physical layer. In practice, to achieve this, we have to select and possibly hybridize the basic approaches.

Figure 8.5 gives an example of the three communication layers. It illustrates a networked application from the perspective of login management. The control of the access permissions and session log maintenance are centralized by using a server-network (i.e. nodes s_0, s_1, and s_2), to which the clients (i.e. nodes c_0, c_1 and c_2) subscribe. The servers s_1 and s_2 provide the application state, which is replicated in the other satellite servers over the Internet. For example, s_0 serves the clients in the local LAN (e.g. c_0) and possibly other geographically near clients (e.g. c_1). To supervise the game, the console clients (e.g. c_2)

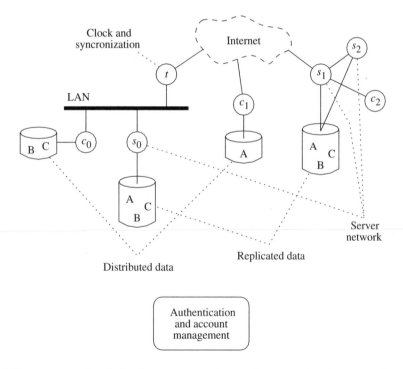

Figure 8.5 An example of the three communication layers to implement authentication and account management features. The physical platform consists of nodes (circles), data stores (cylinders), and cabling (lines). The logical platform includes a server-network (i.e. a communication architecture), distributed and replicated data (i.e. a data architecture), and timing functionality (i.e. a control architecture).

can connect directly to the server. The state data is distributed to the clients so that they are more responsive. Consequently, the networked application becomes more reliable, because we can tolerate a single point of server failure while having unreliable or high-latency connection to a server. Finally, the workload of the networked application is balanced by dedicating the node t for timing purposes only (e.g. sending clock signals and providing dispatching services).

To summarize, the physical layer, stemming from the underlying hardware, tells what we can do. The networked application layer, derived from the design specification of the game, tells what we should do. Most of the important decisions concerning resource utilization are then made on the logical layer. However, the compensatory techniques of the next chapter provide us with additional margin in design and implementation.

Exercises

8-1 Consider the children's game of tag. How would you implement it in different shared-space technologies?

8-2 Latency cannot be completely eliminated. What does this mean to the design of the networked application?

8-3 Multicasting and broadcasting can be simulated using unicasting. How can this be done? What are the problems that are encountered while doing this?

8-4 In a positive acknowledgement scheme, the receiver sends an acknowledgement message every time it receives a message, whereas in a negative acknowledgement scheme, an acknowledgment message is sent if the receiver has not received the message. What are the problems that are encountered in these schemes? How would you solve them?

8-5 Internet Protocol version 4 (IPv4) was deployed on 1 January 1983. The address format in IPv4 is a 32-bit numeric value often expressed with four octets from the interval [0, 255] separated by periods. At the time of writing this book, Internet Protocol version 6 (IPv6), with 128 bit-wide addresses, is slowly replacing IPv4. In theory, how many IP addresses can be assigned in IPv4 and IPv6?

8-6 Which protocol, TCP/IP or UDP/IP, suits better in the following situations:

  (a) Updating the player's current position

  (b) Informing that the player changed his weapon

  (c) Indicating that the player fired a weapon

  (d) Informing that the player got hit

  (e) Informing that a new player joined the game

  (f) Chatting with other players.

8-7 Compare the communication architectures (i.e. peer-to-peer, client-server, and server-network), and data and control architectures (i.e. centralized, distributed, and replicated). Analyse their usability together and explain in what kind of situations they are useful.

8-8 In *Amaze* (Berglund and Cheriton 1985) multiple players roam in a *Pac-Man*-like maze and try to shoot one another. You are updating this idea to meet the current twenty-first-century standard by designing an online *Amaze* game to be run over the Internet. The game would be ongoing and the players can form teams and participate from all over the world. Devise a design for this game and list the possible problems stemming from the physical and logical platforms.

8-9 Suppose that a networked application distributes autonomous synthetic players to the participating nodes to balance the workload. In other words, a synthetic player b resides only in one node c and participates in the game similarly to the human players. If node c gets abruptly cut off from the game, not only the human player but also the synthetic players assigned to that node disappear from the game world. What are the problems when we are implementing a single point (i.e. node) of failure capability for distributed synthetic players?

8-10 The game $2n$-Gong, where $2 \leq n$, takes place in a regular polygon of $2n$ sides (see Figure 8.6). The game consists of $2n$ players who have one side as a dedicated goal to defend. A player controls a paddle by moving it parallel to his own goal. The goal of the game is to score points by bouncing the ball to the other players' goal. All collisions are elastic and the ball follows its trajectory continuously (i.e. there is no kick-off after a goal). If a player makes an own goal, his score is reduced.

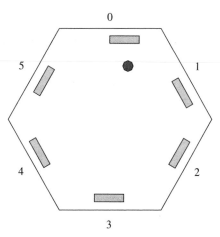

Figure 8.6 The game $2n$-Gong with $n = 3$ has six players, indicated by numbers [0, 5]. Each player controls a paddle (rectangle) that can be used to bounce the ball (circle).

Design and describe how 2n-Gong operates on the three communication layers. You can assume that the game runs on a LAN and the human players' nodes are connected using peer-to-peer architecture. By default, each paddle is controlled by a synthetic player. When a human player joins the game, he or she replaces a randomly selected synthetic player. When a human player leaves the game, a synthetic player takes over the control again. If there are no synthetic players left to be replaced, the joining player becomes an observer of the game until some other human player leaves the game.

8-11 The physical platforms can be organized in different ways. For example, we can have an Ethernet LAN that has a single coaxial cable shared by all nodes, or a hub connecting the nodes with twisted pair cables into a star-like network. Moreover, the number of nodes and their capabilities can also vary from LAN to LAN. If we want to run a massive networked application over a diverse set of physical platforms, we have to implement a workload balancing mechanism to the logical platform to make it more dynamic.

How can we make communication, data, and control architectures more dynamic in the following cases? Approach the problem from the point of view of roles, responsibilities, and functionalities and consider how they are interconnected.

(a) Dynamic communication: If we have a server-network on a LAN, how can we increase and decrease the number of servers on the fly without informing this change to the clients?

(b) Dynamic data: Suppose the data is distributed among the nodes on a WAN and we want to keep the overall delay of the data updates low. How can we realize handing over the data ownership (and its location site) to the node that is geographically nearer to the source of the update messages?

(c) Dynamic control: Suppose we have peer-to-peer nodes on a LAN. The most time consuming features of the networked application are implemented as autonomous components, which are runnable entities that implement some functionality with a fixed use interface. How can we transfer a component from a node with a high workload to a more idle one?

You can refer to the terminology of patterns presented by Buschmann *et al.* (1996), and enthusiastic readers might even want to acquaint themselves with Schmidt *et al.* (2000).

9

Compensating Resource Limitations

Because a networked application has limited resources at its disposal, we have to find ways to utilize them effectively. The amount of resources required in a networked application is directly related to how much information has to be sent and received by each participating computer and how quickly it has to be delivered by the network. Singhal and Zyda (1999) concretize this rule with the *information principle equation*

$$\text{Resources} = M \times H \times B \times T \times P, \qquad (9.1)$$

where M is the number of messages transmitted, H is the average number of destination nodes for each message, B is the average amount of network bandwidth required for a message to each destination, T is the timeliness with which the network must deliver messages to each destination (large values of T imply a need for a small delay and vice versa), and P is the number of processor cycles required to receive and process each message. These measures can be illustrated as a radar diagram as illustrated in Figure 9.1.

If the amount of resource requirements is fixed, we have a certain level of qualities (e.g. responsiveness or scalability) in the application. In this case, Equation (9.1) has many possible solutions for the given 'resources' and a system designer can use it as a tool to balance implementation requirements and restrictions. When we increase the expenditure on one resource, we have to compensate it by some means. This implies that the value of another variable in the equation decreases or the quality of experience of the game play becomes weaker (e.g. movements become jerkier). The choice of variables that are increased in value and variables that are used for compensating depends naturally on the application's requirements and resource bottlenecks. For example, if the number of players increases, the bandwidth (B) requirement also increases, because each additional player must receive the initial game state and the updates that other users are already receiving. Each new player introduces new interactions with the existing players and requires additional processing power from the existing players, which means that H and P increase. Also, if we want to

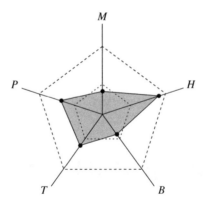

Figure 9.1 Information principle equation as a radar diagram.

keep Equation (9.1) in balance, we have to send fewer messages (M) or allow more delay (T) in our communication.

In this chapter, we present different compensation methods, which try to reduce resource requirements, usually by increasing processing. Processing power can be used, for example, to compress the outgoing messages or to filter out the recipients who are interested in receiving them. But before reviewing the compensation methods, we must take a look at two aspects affecting the choice of method: the balance between consistency and responsiveness and achieving scalability in computation and communication.

9.1 Aspects of Compensation

If we look at the terms of Equation (9.1), we can recognize two questions that resource compensation must address: how to achieve a balance between consistency and responsiveness (i.e. how to reduce T) and how to scale up to include more players in the game (i.e. how to reduce H). Since these two aspects form the basis for resource compensation, let us study both of them more closely.

9.1.1 Consistency and responsiveness

Consistency refers to the similarity of the view to the data in the nodes belonging to a network. Absolute consistency means that each node has uniform information, and to guarantee it we have to wait until everybody has received the information update before we can proceed. *Responsiveness* means the delay that it takes for an update event to be registered conceptually by the nodes, and to have high responsiveness we may have to proceed before everybody has physically received the information update. Consistency and responsiveness are not independent of each other. Traditionally, responsiveness has always been subjected to consistency requirements in database research. However, because of real-time interaction, responsiveness becomes a more important element in networked computer games and we may have to compromise consistency.

To achieve high consistency, the data and control architecture must guarantee that processes running on remote nodes are tightly coupled. This usually requires high bandwidth, low latency, and a small number of remote nodes. To achieve high responsiveness, the queries made to the data must be responded quickly, which requires loosely coupled nodes. In this case, the nodes must include more computation to reduce the bandwidth and latency requirements. In reality, a network architecture cannot achieve both high consistency and high responsiveness at the same time, and the choice of architecture is essentially a trade-off between these two attributes (Singhal and Zyda 1999). On the extremes, the game world is either consistent, where all nodes maintain identical information, or dynamic, where information changes rapidly.

To clarify, we can discern three parts in data and control architectures: the local node, the network, and the relay connecting them (Smed *et al.* 2002). Figure 9.2 illustrates the situation in which a networked application running in a local node sends control messages into a relay and receives data messages from it. In turn, the relay communicates with the relays of other nodes through a network. Here, a relay is a logical concept that illustrates how the control affects the data.

The relay acts as an intermediary between the local node and the network, and its structure defines how consistent and responsive the architecture can be. Obviously, the messages flow from i_{local} to o_{global}. Also a stream from i_{global} to o_{local} must exist. Let f and g be operations that the relay does on the messages upon sending and receiving (e.g. compression and decompression or encryption and decryption). This gives us the minimum form, a *two-way relay* (see Figure 9.3a), where $o_{\text{global}} = f(i_{\text{local}})$ and $o_{\text{local}} = g(i_{\text{global}})$. The two-way relay is the model used, for instance, in distributed databases and centralized systems. All new local messages are relayed to the network, and they do not appear in the local node until a message from the network is received. For example, a dumb terminal sends the characters typed on the keyboard to a mainframe, which sends back the characters to be displayed on the monitor. The two-way relay allows us to achieve high consistency, because all messages have to go through the network, where a centralized server or a group of peers can confirm and establish a consistent set of data. However, the two-way relay cannot guarantee high responsiveness, because it depends on the available networking resources.

To overcome this limitation, we can bridge the two flows with an operation h, which forms a *short-circuit relay* (see Figure 9.3b), where $o_{\text{global}} = f(i_{\text{local}})$ as before but $o_{\text{local}} = g(i_{\text{global}}) \times h(i_{\text{local}})$ The locally originated messages are now passed back into the local

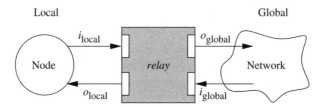

Figure 9.2 Data and control architecture defines how messages are relayed between local and remote nodes in a communication architecture.

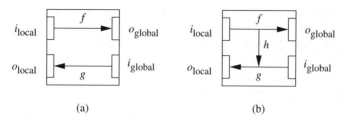

Figure 9.3 The relay has two basic alternatives for a structure: (a) A two-way relay sends the local control messages to the network, which sends back data messages to the node. (b) A short-circuit relay sends the local control messages to the network and passes them locally back to the node.

output inside the relay. We do not have to wait for the messages to pass through the network and return to us but we short-circuit them back locally. This short-circuiting can be realized with immediate feedback like in the DIS standard (Neyland 1997), acknowledgments (Frécon and Stenius 1998), or buckets delaying the arrival of local messages (Diot and Gautier 1999). Clearly, we can now achieve high responsiveness but it comes with a price: the local data can become inconsistent with the other nodes. This means that some kind of rollback or negotiation mechanism is required to solve the inconsistencies, when they become a problem.

It is important to differentiate between these two structures: A high consistency architecture requires a two-way relay, because all updates require confirmation from the other nodes. On the other hand, high responsiveness entails a short-circuit relay, because the local control messages must appear promptly in the local data. With this in mind, we can now look at the three data and control architectures: centralized, distributed, and replicated. In centralized architecture, the relay mostly conveys local control to the network and receives data from it, which is reversed in distributed architecture. In replicated architecture, the local input and output are a mixture of control and data messages. Also, each architecture has characteristic problems: in centralized architecture, access to the data may take time; in distributed architecture, the allocation of the data fragments between the nodes must be handled properly; in replicated architecture, updating the data in each replica can be tricky.

A networked application often has a hybrid architecture, where the system functionalities have their own implementation logic. For example, login authentication relies mostly on the client–server approach but configurations that affect the GUI representation are convenient to distribute to each node. By assigning designated relay types to each functionality, we can identify and manage this variety of architecture choices in one application. From this perspective, the relays can be seen as a part of the logical communication layer (see Section 8.2) and they define dedicated points for architecture realization and modification (e.g. in a form of interfaces). For example, the relays can be implemented so that they not only forward messages but also serve as a backbone for monitoring and administrating features of the whole networked application.

9.1.2 Scalability

Scalability is the ability to adapt to the *resource changes*. In computer games, this concerns, for example, how to construct an online server that dynamically adapts to the varying number of players, or how to allocate the computation of synthetic players among the nodes. To achieve this kind of scalability, there must be physical (i.e. hardware-based) parallelism that enables logical (i.e. software) concurrency of computation.

Serial and parallel execution

The potential speedup obtained by applying multiple nodes is bounded by the system's inherently sequential computations. Pipelining is a typical way to optimize such consecutive operations. Now, the operations are chunked and allocated to a chain of nodes, and the data flow to a node gets processed and then forwarded to the next node. Because each node runs simultaneously, the theoretical speedup is not more than the number of nodes. In practice, pipelining requires that data is transmitted quickly between nodes and is available when needed, which means that it does not go well with interaction or remote nodes. Thus, the time required by the serially executed parts of a networked application cannot be reduced by parallel computation.

The theoretical speedup S is achieved by non-centralized control and it can be measured by

$$S(n) = \frac{T(1)}{T(n)} \leq \frac{T(1)}{T(1)/n} = n, \tag{9.2}$$

where $T(1)$ is the time to execute with one node and $T(n)$ is the time with n nodes. The execution time can be divided into a serial part T_s and a parallel part T_p. Let $T_s + T_p = 1$ and $\alpha = T_s/(T_s + T_p)$. If the system is parallelized optimally, the equation can be rewritten as

$$S(n) = \frac{T_s + T_p}{T_s + T_p/n} = \frac{1}{\alpha + (1 - \alpha)/n} \leq \frac{1}{\alpha}. \tag{9.3}$$

This is called *Amdahl's law* for a fixed problem setting (Gustafson 1988). For example, if 5% of the program must be executed serially (i.e. $\alpha = 0.05$), the maximum speedup obtainable is 20.

Ideally, the serial part should be non-existent and, thus, everything would be computed in parallel. However, in that case, there cannot exist any coordination between the nodes. The only example of such multi-player computer games is a game that each player plays regardless of the others. The other extreme is that there is no parallel part with respect to the game state, which is the case in a round robin or a turn-based game. Between these extremes are the games that provide real-time interaction and which, consequently, comprise both parallel and serial computation (see Figure 9.4).

For the serial parts, the nodes must agree on the sequence of events. The simplest approach to realize this is to utilize a client–server architecture, where the server can control the communication by forwarding, filtering, and modifying the messages. It should be noted that even in a peer-to-peer architecture the network acts like a server (i.e. the peers share the same serializing communication channel), unless the nodes are connected to each other by a direct physical cable or they communicate by multicasting.

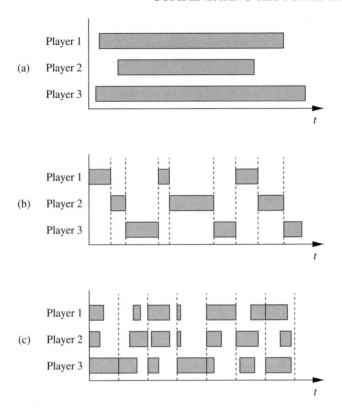

Figure 9.4 Serial and parallel execution in computer games. (a) Separate real-time games can run in parallel but without interaction. (b) A turn-based game is serialized and interactive but not real-time, unless the turns are very short. (c) An interactive real-time game runs both in serial and in parallel.

To concretize, let us calculate the communication capacity in a client–server architecture using unicast. Suppose that each client sends 5 packets per second using IPv6 communication protocol in a 10-Mbps Ethernet. Each packet takes at least a frame of size $68 \cdot 8 + 26 \cdot 8 = 752$ bits (or 94 bytes). Let d equal the number of bits in a message, f the transmission frequency, n the number of unicast connections and C the maximum capacity of the communication channel. Obviously, the following condition must hold:

$$d \cdot f \cdot n \leq C.$$

By using the values $d = 752 + 32$ (i.e. the payload comprises one 32-bit integer value), $f = 5$ and $C = 10^7$, we can solve the upper bound for the number of clients. Thus, if we are using a client–server architecture, one server can provide serializability for at most 2551 clients. In reality, the update frequency is higher and the payload much larger, and, consequently, the estimate on the number of clients is highly optimistic. Moreover, client communication requires computation power from the server.

Communication capacity

Because the coordination of serialized parts require communication, scalability is limited by the communication capacity requirements of the chosen deployment. Let us assume that clients are allowed to send messages freely at any moment (i.e. asynchronous messaging). In the worst case, all nodes try to communicate at the same time and the network architecture must handle this traffic without saturation.

Table 9.1 collects the magnitudes of communication capacity requirements for different deployment architectures (see Figure 8.3). Obviously, a single node needs no networking. In peer-to-peer, when all n nodes have direct connections to the other nodes or the communication is handled by multicasting, the magnitude of the communication capacity is $O(n)$; otherwise, the peers use unicasting, which yields $O(n^2)$. In client–server, the server-end requires a capacity of $O(n)$ because each client has a dedicated connection to it. In server-network, the server pool has m servers, and n clients are divided evenly among them. If the servers are connected as peer-to-peer architecture, the server communication requires $O(m)\dots O(m^2)$ in addition to $O(n/m)$ capacity for client communication. If the servers are connected hierarchically (e.g. as a tree), the server at the root is the bottleneck, requiring a capacity of $O(n)$.

In an earlier example, we calculated that a server can support up to 2551 clients. This demonstrates that, in practice, linear capacity requirement is too large. Therefore, the heart of scalability is to achieve *sub-linear communication*. In effect, this means that a client cannot be aware of all the other clients all the time.

To guarantee sub-linear communication in a hierarchical server-network, we must limit the communication between the servers. Suppose that the hierarchy is a k-ary tree. If we can now guarantee that a server sends to its parent $(1/k)$th part of its children's messages, we have a logarithmic capacity requirement (i.e. communication in the root is $O(\log n)$). Now, the problem is how to realize this reduction. This is where the compensatory techniques provide an answer: children's messages can be compressed and aggregated if we can guarantee that the size reduction is $1/k$ on each server level – which is quite unlikely. A more usable solution is, at each step, to first apply interest management (e.g. refrain from passing messages whose potential receivers are already inside the subtree, see Section 9.6), and then select one of the outgoing messages for the server to pass on. For each suppressed message, the nodes can approximate the information (e.g. by using dead reckoning, see Section 9.3).

Table 9.1   Communication capacity requirements for different deployment architectures when the network has n nodes and m servers.

Deployment architecture	Capacity requirement
Single node	0
Peer-to-peer	$O(n)\dots O(n^2)$
Client–server	$O(n)$
Peer-to-peer server network	$O(n/m + m)\dots O(n/m + m^2)$
Hierarchical server network	$O(n)$

9.2   Protocol Optimization

Since every message sent to the network incurs a processing penalty, we can improve the usage of the resource by reducing either the size of each message or the number of messages.

9.2.1   Message compression

The networked application can save bandwidth at the cost of computational power by compressing the messages. Since the purpose of compression is to reduce the number of bits needed to represent particular information, it provides us with an intuitive approach to minimize network traffic. With respect to Equation (9.1), we are reducing the average packet size (B) but because of encoding and decoding processes the computational work (P) increases.

Compression techniques can be classified according to their ability to preserve the information content (see Table 9.2). Lossless techniques preserve all the information, and the reconstructed data is exactly the same as the data before compression. To achieve a higher compression ratio, we can employ lossy compression techniques, where the idea is to leave out less relevant information so that the distortion in the reconstructed data remains unnoticeable. For further information on compression methods, see Witten *et al.* (1999).

On the basis of how compression operates on data in a sequence of messages, we can divide the techniques as internal and external. Internal compression concentrates on the information content of one message without references to other, previously transmitted messages, which is why it suits unreliable network transmission protocols (e.g. UDP). On the other hand, external compression can utilize information that has already been transmitted and can be assumed to be available to the receivers. For example, we can transmit delta (i.e. the amount of change) or transition information, which is likely to require lesser bits than the absolute information, or give reference pointers to the previously transmitted message if the same message occurs again. External compression can consider a large amount of data at a time, and, thus, it can observe redundancy in the information flow better and allow better compression ratios than internal compression. However, because of the references to the previous packets, external compression requires a reliable transmission protocol (e.g. TCP).

Table 9.2   Compression technique categories.

Compression	*Lossless*	*Lossy*
Internal	Encode the message in a more efficient format and eliminate redundancy within it.	Filter irrelevant information or reduce the detail of the transmitted information.
External	Avoid retransmitting information that is identical to that sent in the previous messages.	Avoid retransmitting information that is similar to that sent in the previous messages.

9.2.2 Message aggregation

Message aggregation reduces transmission frequency by merging information from multiple messages. Bundling up messages saves bandwidth because there is less header information but requires extra computation and weakens the responsiveness. To put the same in the terms of Equation (9.1), the number of messages (M) and timeliness (T) decrease, the average message size (B) increases, and the overall bandwidth consumption is reduced at a slight processing cost (P).

Message aggregation needs a criterion that indicates when we have collected enough messages to be sent as a single merged message. In *timeout-based approach*, all messages that are initiated before a fixed time period are merged. This approach guarantees an upper bound on the delay caused by aggregation. Now, bandwidth savings depend on the message initiation rate, and, in the worst case, no savings are gained because no messages (or only one) are initiated during the period. In *quorum-based approach*, a fixed number of messages are always merged. Because the transmission of the merged message is delayed until enough messages have been initiated, there is no guarantee for the transmission delay. Although bandwidth savings are predictable, long transmission delays can hinder the game play. The limitations of both approaches can be compensated for by combining them. In this hybrid approach, merging occurs whenever one of the conditions is fulfilled, either time period expires or there are enough messages to merge.

9.3   Dead Reckoning

Dead reckoning dates back to the navigational techniques used to estimate a ship's current position based on a known start position, travelling velocity, and elapsed time. In networked applications, dead reckoning is used to reduce bandwidth consumption by sending update messages less frequently and estimating the state information between the updates (see Figure 9.5). Apart from extrapolating the current state from the past states, the state update can include additional information for predicting how the state will change in the future. In terms of Equation (9.1), dead reckoning transmits update messages less frequently, which reduces M and T, but the nodes have to compensate for this by computing predictions, which increases P. When the next update message arrives, the predicted value can differ from the actual value, which can cause disruptive visual effects. To minimize this, the difference can be corrected by converging it, over time, closer to the true value.

9.3.1   Prediction

The most common prediction technique is to use derivative polynomials. If the state information represents a position p, the first two derivatives have natural interpretations as velocity v and acceleration a. State updates using zero-order derivative polynomials comprise only position information and no prediction information. In the case of first-order derivative polynomials, we transmit the velocity of an entity in addition to its position:

$$p(t) = p(0) + v(0)t \tag{9.4}$$

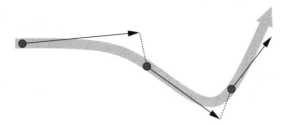

Figure 9.5 Dead reckoning is used to calculate the positions between the update messages. The actual movement (indicated by the grey arrow) differs from the movement predicted by dead reckoning (black arrows). The dotted lines indicate a position change caused by the update message, which has to be corrected using a convergence method.

Algorithm 9.1 Second-order prediction of a position.

PREDICTION-SECOND-ORDER(S, t)
  in: state information S; time stamp t
  out: predicted state value
  1: $d \leftarrow t - time(S)$
  2: $v \leftarrow velocity(prediction(S))$
  3: $a \leftarrow acceleration(prediction(S))$
  4: **return** $state(S) + vd + ad^2/2$

To improve the accuracy of the prediction, we can add acceleration to the transmitted information:

$$p(t) = p(0) + v(0)t + \frac{1}{2}a(0)t^2 \tag{9.5}$$

This second-order polynomial (see Algorithm 9.1) quite accurately models moving vehicles, but the first-order is better suited for less predictably moving entities such as human characters. The reason for this is that high-order polynomials are sensitive to errors, because the derivative information must be accurate. The prediction is more sensitive for high-order terms, and a small inaccuracy in these can result in significant deviations that might make the prediction worse. In other words, we must have a better model for high-order terms – but higher-order derivatives must be often estimated or tracked over time, because it is hard to get accurate instantaneous information. For example, although acceleration models how a car responds to the throttle, a third-order polynomial (i.e. jerk) would require some insight into the mind of the driver (i.e. his decision-making process). Also, with higher-order polynomials, more information has to be transmitted, which means that the computational complexity increases (i.e. each additional term requires few extra operations) and each additional term consumes the bandwidth resources.

    We can omit the derivative polynomials altogether and use the known history for extrapolating the data. The position history-based dead reckoning protocol transmits only the

---

Algorithm 9.2 Constructing dead reckoning messages.

DEAD-RECKONING-MESSAGE(s, t, P, Q)
   in: state value s; time stamp t; prediction information P; previously sent state
              Q
   out: new update message U or NIL if not necessary
   constant: difference threshold ℓ
   1: **if** $|s - \text{PREDICTION}(Q, t)| < \ell$ **then**
   2:   **return** NIL   ▷ Difference below the threshold.
   3: **end if**
   4: $state(U) \leftarrow s$
   5: $time(U) \leftarrow t$
   6: $prediction(U) \leftarrow P$
   7: **return** U

---

absolute positions, and the entity's instantaneous velocity and acceleration are approximated by using the update history (Singhal 1996). The method evaluates the motion over three most recent position updates and chooses dynamically between first-order and second-order polynomials: If acceleration is small or substantial, we use a first-order polynomial; otherwise, we use a second-order polynomial. The rationale behind this is to reduce the inaccuracies caused by the acceleration term. For example, if the entity's acceleration changes often, it is likely that a wrong value is going to applied to the prediction at some point and it might be safer to be content with first-order prediction at that time.

Naturally, prediction can be specialized to suit the entity in question. Derivative polynomials do not take into account what the entity is currently doing, what the entity is capable of doing, or who is controlling the entity. For instance, cars and aeroplanes – albeit obeying the same laws of physics – could have different prediction algorithms based on their overall behaviour. By including entity-specific information to the dead reckoning technique, we can achieve a more accurate and natural movement. However, this can be time consuming and maintaining several different algorithms requires special care.

The transmission frequency for updates need not be constant but the messages can be sent only when dead reckoning exceeds some error threshold (see Algorithm 9.2). By taking advantage of the knowledge about the computations at remote nodes, the source node can reduce the required state update rate. Because the source can use the same prediction algorithm as the remote nodes, it is enough to transmit updates only when the actual position and the predicted position differ significantly. This reduces the update rate if prediction algorithm is reasonably accurate. The source node can even dynamically balance its network transmission resources so that when bandwidth is limited, it increases the error threshold according to the distance between the objects (Cai *et al.* 1999) or the lifetime of an update packet (Yu and Choy 2001).

9.3.2 Convergence

When a node using a dead reckoning technique receives an update message, the predicted state of the entity is likely to differ from the state based on the just-arrived information.

In this case, the entity has to be updated to this new state using a convergence technique. The simplest technique is zero-order convergence (or snap), where the entity is changed immediately to a new state without any smoothing adjustments (e.g. visual corrections). However, this can cause annoyingly jerky or even impossible (e.g. through a wall) changes, which are known in many networked games as 'warping'.

A good convergence technique corrects errors quickly and as unnoticeably as possible. To do that, we must select a convergence period within which we want to correct the error. If the state represents a position of an entity, we can pick a convergence point along the new predicted path so that after the convergence period the displayed position coincides with the prediction. After that, we render the entity as if it travels between its current displayed position and the convergence point. When the entity has reached the convergence point, it begins to follow the new predicted path – until a new update is received and the convergence procedure gets repeated (see Algorithm 9.3).

Algorithm 9.4 gives an implementation for linear convergence, where the entity is moved along a direct path from the current position to the convergence point (see Figure 9.6). Although linear convergence is clearly better than zero-order convergence, it can still make unnatural turns when leaving the previously predicted path and entering the new predicted path. To smooth out these problems, more sophisticated curve-fitting techniques can be applied. The idea is to select, in addition to the current position and convergence point, a number of points along the previously predicted path and the new predicted path.

Algorithm 9.3 Using dead reckoning messages.

DEAD-RECKONING-VALUE(S, t)
    in: state information S; time stamp t
    out: state value
    constant: convergence period c
  1: $t' \leftarrow time(current(S))$
  2: $t'' \leftarrow t' + c$
  3: **if** $t > t''$ **then**
  4:    **return** PREDICTION($state(current(S)), t$)
  5: **else**
  6:    $s' \leftarrow$ PREDICTION($state(previous(S)), t'$)
  7:    $s'' \leftarrow$ PREDICTION($state(current(S)), t''$)
  8:    **return** CONVERGENCE(s', t', s'', t'', t)
  9: **end if**

Algorithm 9.4 Linear convergence.

CONVERGENCE-LINEAR(s', t', s'', t'', t)
    in: start state s'; start time t'; target state s''; target time t''; time stamp t ($t' \leq t \leq t''$)
    out: converged state value
  1: $d \leftarrow (t - t')/(t'' - t')$
  2: **return** $d \cdot (s'' - s') + s'$

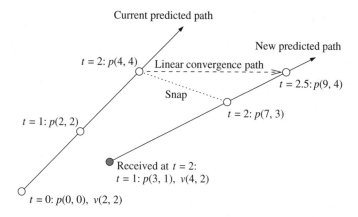

Figure 9.6 Dead reckoning comprises prediction and convergence. Open circles represent the predicted information about entity's position p at given time t. The closed circle represents entity's received position p and velocity v at given time t when the communication delay is 1 s. In zero-order convergence (or snap), the position is corrected immediately at $t = 2$ to the new predicted path. In linear convergence, the change is made smoothly along a linear convergence path during a convergence period of 0.5 s.

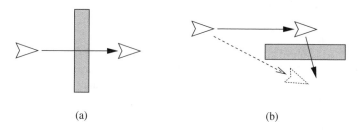

(a)   (b)

Figure 9.7 Locational problems caused by dead reckoning. (a) If prediction is not used with collision detection, the ship following its predicted path can fly through a wall. (b) If the predicted path has lead the ship to the wrong side of a wall, convergence has to correct the situation, possibly letting the ship fly through the wall.

The curve is fitted to go through all the selected points, and it is used as a path to shift the entity to its new predicted path. For example, in the case of a third-order curve, cubic spline, we pick one additional point on the previously predicted path before the current position and other additional points along the new predicted path after the convergence point. High-order curves provide smooth transition from the old path to the new path but they can be computationally intensive for some applications.

Although convergence helps to make errors less noticeable, there are situations in which dead reckoning causes locational problems that cannot be solved otherwise than by letting visual disruptions occur. These problems can stem both from prediction and convergence, as illustrated in Figure 9.7.

9.4   Local Perception Filters

Local perception filters (LPFs) hide the communication delays by exploiting the human perceptual limitations (Ryan and Sharkey 1999; Sharkey *et al.* 1998). Whereas in dead reckoning we try to maintain a consistent view by predicting the state, LPF allows temporal distortions in the view and entities can be rendered at slightly out-of-date locations based on the underlying communication delays. Naturally, we want to make these temporal distortions of the game world as unnoticeable as possible. Although we describe LPFs in visualization terms, the underlying idea is more general, because the application's control logic and proto-view (see Section 1.1) can also perceive the out-of-date state instance.

The entities of a game world can be separated into two classes:

(i) *Players* are indeterministic entities (e.g. controlled by human players), whose be- haviour cannot be predicted. On the basis of the communication delay, we divide the players as local players (e.g. sharing the same computer) and remote players (e.g. players connected by a network).

(ii) *Passive entities* are deterministic entities, whose behaviour follow, for example, the laws of physics (e.g. projectiles) or which are otherwise predictable (e.g. buildings).

Interaction means, theoretically speaking, that the interacting entities must communicate with each other to resolve the outcome. If the communication delay between entities is negligible (e.g. they reside in the same computer), the interaction seems credible. On the other hand, networking incurs communication delays, which can hinder the interaction between remote players.

LPFs address the problem of delays by discerning the actual situation from the rendered situation. The rendered situation, which is perceived by the player, need not coincide with the current actual situation but it can comprise some out-of-date information. The amount of this temporal distortion is easy to determine for players: Local players are rendered using up-to-date state information, while a remote player with a communication delay of d seconds is rendered using the known, d-seconds-old state information.

To preserve the causality, the temporal distortion of the passive entities changes dynam- ically. The nearer a passive entity is to a local player, the closer it has to be rendered to its current state, because it is possible that the player is going to interact with it. Conversely, a passive entity nearing on a remote player must be rendered closer to that remote player's time, because if there is an interaction between the remote player and the passive entity, the outcome is rendered after the communication delay. In other words, the rendered remote interactions, albeit occurring in real time, have happened in the past, and only when the local player itself participates in the interaction, it must happen in the present time.

Figure 9.8 gives an example in which the player controlling the white ship shoots a bullet (i.e. a passive entity) towards the grey ship controlled by a remote player. The players' views are not entirely consistent with each other: In the beginning, the white ship renders the bullet to the actual position but as it closes on the grey ship it begins to lag behind the actual position. Conversely, when the grey ship first learns about the bullet, it has already travelled some distance. For example, let us assume that the communication delay between the ships is 0.5 s and the bullet travels in 2.0 s from the white ship to the grey ship. When the white ship fires, it sees the bullet immediately but after that the rendered bullet starts

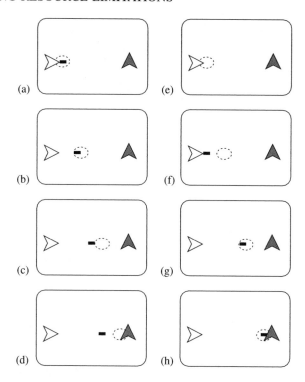

Figure 9.8 An example of local perception filters with two stationary players (the white ship and the grey ship) and one moving passive entity (a bullet shot by the white ship). (a)–(d) are the rendered views from the white ship's perspective; (e)–(h) are the corresponding views from the grey ship's perspective. Dashed ovals indicate the actual position of the bullet and black rectangles represent its rendered position. As the bullet closes on the grey ship, the white ship perceives it as slowing down, whilst the grey ship perceives it as gaining speed.

to drag behind the actual position. After 2.0 s, the bullet has arrived at the grey ship, but it is rendered as though it has travelled only 1.5 s. It takes 0.5 s for the grey ship's reaction to be conveyed to the white ship, and once that message arrives, after 2.5 s, the bullet is rendered near the grey ship and reaction occurs at an appropriate moment. From the grey ship's perspective, the chain of events is different: When it learns about the bullet, it has already travelled 0.5 s, but it is rendered as coming from the white ship. The rendered bullet must now catch up with the actual bullet so that in 2.0 s both the rendered bullet and the actual bullet arrive at the grey ship, which can then react and send the reaction to the white ship.

Each player has its own perception of the game world, where all entities, in addition to spatial coordinates (x, y, z), are associated with a time delay (t), thus forming a 3½-dimensional coordinate system. The local player is at the current time $t = 0$, and remote players are assigned t values according to their communication delays. Once we have assigned these values, we can define a *temporal contour* (or causal surface) over the game

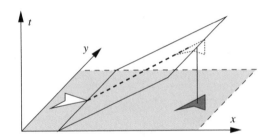

Figure 9.9 The 2½-dimensional temporal contour from the white ship's perspective. The bullet travels 'uphill' the contour until it reaches the t value of the grey ship.

world for each player. The temporal contour defines suitable t values for each spatial point. Figure 9.9 illustrates one possible temporal contour for the white ship of the previous example. When the bullet leaves the white ship, $t = 0$, but the t value increases as it closes on the grey ship, until they both have the same t value.

The changes in the movement of a passive entity caused by the temporal contour should be minimal and smooth. Moreover, all interactions between players and passive entities should appear to be realistic and consistent (e.g. preserve causality of events). The requirements for temporal contours can be summarized into three rules:

(i) The player should be able to interact in real time with the nearby entities.

(ii) The player should be able to view remote interactions in real time, although they can be out of date.

(iii) Temporal distortions in the player's perception should be as unnoticeable as possible.

The most important limitation of LPFs, which follows from the first rule, is that a player cannot interact *directly* with a remote player. The players can engage in an exchange of passive entities (e.g. bullets, arrows, missiles, or insults) but they cannot get into a mêlée with each other. In fact, the closer the players get to each other, the more noticeable the temporal distortion becomes, until they reach a critical proximity, when even interaction using passive entities becomes impossible.

The underlying assumption behind LPFs is that we know the exact communication delays between the players. In reality, latency and the amount of traffic in a network tend to vary over time, which means that the height of the peaks of the temporal contour must reflect these changes. If this jitter becomes too high, the passive entities begin to bounce back and forth in time instead of in smooth temporal transitions. Also, because remote players define the temporal contour, any sudden changes in their position or existence can cause drastic effects in the rendered view. For example, if a nearby remote player leaves the game world, it no longer affects the temporal contour and some passive entities may suddenly jump forward in time to match the updated temporal contour.

In the following subsections, we first study how to define linear temporal contours in the case of two players, and then extend the discussion to cover multiple players. After that, we discuss how LPFs can be used to realize the bullet time effect in a multi-player computer game.

9.4.1 Linear temporal contour

Let us first look at a case in which we have only two players, p and r, and one passive entity e. The players and the passive entity have a spatial location, and the players are associated with a communication delay, which is due to the network latency and cannot be reduced. If i and j are players or entities, let $\delta(i, j)$ denote the spatial distance between them and $d(i, j)$ denote the delay from the perspective of i. The communication delay between players does not have to be the same in both directions but we can allow $d(i, j) \neq d(j, i)$.

In the case of two players, the delay function d for the entity e must have the following properties:

$$d(p, e) = \begin{cases} 0, & \text{if } \delta(p, e) = 0, \\ d(p, r), & \text{if } \delta(r, e) = 0. \end{cases} \tag{9.6}$$

Simply put, if e and p are at the same position, the delay from p is zero, and if e and r are at the same position, the delay from p is the same as the communication delay from p to r.

The rest of the function can be defined, for example, linearly as

$$d(p, e) = d(p, r) \cdot \max\left\{1 - \frac{\delta(r, e)}{\delta(p, r)}, 0\right\}, \tag{9.7}$$

which is illustrated in Figure 9.10. The delay function now defines a symmetrical temporal contour around r, which the entities must follow when they are rendered. This is not the

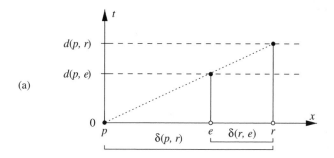

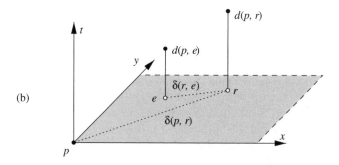

Figure 9.10 Examples of the linear delay function of Equation (9.7) defining the temporal contour in (a) one-dimensional game world and (b) two-dimensional game world.

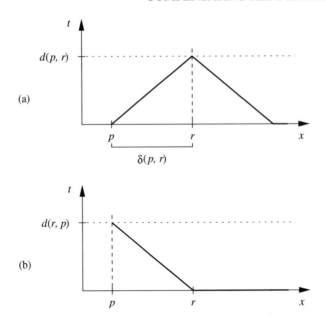

Figure 9.11 Player p shoots player r in a one-dimensional world. (a) The temporal contour from the perspective of player p. The corresponding values in t-axis illustrate the delay (i.e. the temporal difference) between the actual and rendered positions at each actual spatial point in x-axis. (b) The temporal contour from the perspective of player r.

only possibility, and the delay function can even be asymmetric (i.e. the slope does not have to be the same in all directions).

Let us take an example, which is illustrated in Figure 9.11, where player p shoots a bullet e towards player r. If we look at the situation from the perspective of player p, initially the distance to the bullet $\delta(p, e) = 0$ and the delay $d(p, e) = 0$. The delay increases as the bullet closes on r, until $d(p, e) = d(p, r)$ when $\delta(r, e) = 0$. Once the bullet has passed r, the delay reduces back to zero. Player p perceives the temporal contour so that the bullet moves slower when it is climbing 'uphill' and faster when it is going 'downhill'. From the perspective of player r, the bullet has an initial delay $d(r, e) = d(r, p)$, which reduces to $d(r, e) = 0$ when $\delta(r, e) = 0$. In other words, player r perceives the bullet as moving faster than its actual speed until it has passed the player.

If we define the temporal contour observing the constraints of Equation (9.6), we may notice a slight visual flaw in the rendered outcome. Assume player p shoots a bullet e towards a remote player r. The bullet slows down, and when $\delta(r, e) = 0$, the delay function has reached its maximum and $d(p, e) = d(p, r)$. However, when the actual bullet reaches r, the rendered bullet of p is still short of reaching r (see Figure 9.8(d)). Because the temporal contour is already at its peak value, the bullet begins to speed up before it is rendered at r. This can look disruptive, because the change happens before the bullet is rendered to interact with the remote player. Intuitively, acceleration should occur only after the bullet has passed the remote player. From the perspective of player r, the rendering has a similar problem: once r learns about the bullet, its rendered position is not next to p but some way forward along the trajectory. Simply put, the problem is that the delay function is defined using actual positions, whereas it should also observe the movement of the entity during the communication delay. This means that each individual entity requires a slight refinement of the temporal contour to reduce these perceptual disruptions.

To solve the problem, let us first introduce function $\delta_e(t)$, which represents the distance that the entity e travels in time t. Obviously, the function is based on the velocity and acceleration information, but the given generalization suffices for our current use. Let us now define a *shadow r'* of player r that has the following property:

$$\delta(r, r') = \delta_e(d(p, r)). \tag{9.8}$$

The shadow r' represents the position where the entity e actually resides when player p is rendering it at the position of the remote player r. Now, we can rewrite Equation (9.6) as

$$d(p, e) = \begin{cases} 0, & \text{if } \delta(p, e) = 0, \\ d(p, r), & \text{if } \delta(r', e) = 0. \end{cases} \tag{9.9}$$

Simply put, this means that we push the peak of temporal contour forwards through the distance $\delta_e(d(p, r))$ to r', which is illustrated in Figure 9.12. The reason why we want to

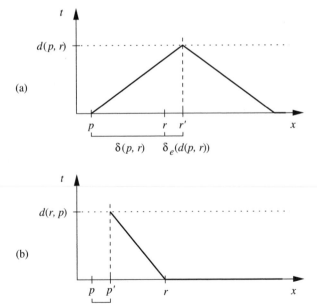

Figure 9.12 Temporal contours are adjusted by the distance the entity travels in the communication delay. (a) The corrected temporal contour of player p, where the peak is pushed forwards to r'. (b) The corrected temporal contour of player r, where the peak is pushed forwards to p'.

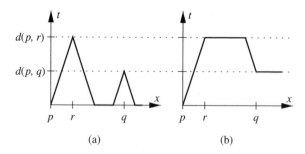

Figure 9.13 Two approaches to aggregate the temporal contour of player p when there are two remote players r and q. (a) Minimize the number of entities that are not in local time. (b) Minimize the number of delay changes.

use the actual spatial positions is that they, unlike the rendered positions, are consistent among all players.

When we have multiple remote players, they have their own delay functions, and to get the temporal contour we must aggregate them. To realize the aggregation, we can use the following approaches (see Figure 9.13):

- Try to minimize the number of entities that are not in the local time (i.e. whose delay is not zero). This means that once an entity has passed a remote player, its delay returns to zero. This approach aims at maintaining the situation as close to the actual situation as possible, and it suits best when there is a lot of interaction between the entities. The drawback is that an entity may bounce back and forth between the local and remote times, which can make its movements look jerky.

- Try to minimize the number of delay changes. Once an entity has reached some delay level, it remains unchanged unless it begins to approach a new remote player. This helps to reduce bouncing between different times, which is prominent especially if there are several remote players along the path of the entity. The drawback is that the rendered view, in its entirety, does not remain as close to the actual situation as in the first approach.

Once we have formed the temporal contour, it is used similarly as in the case of two players.

9.4.2 Adding bullet time to the delays

In the bullet time effect, a player can get more reaction time by slowing down the surrounding game world. Whereas the bullet time effect is quite easy to implement in a single-player game (e.g. *Max Payne*) simply by slowing down the rendering, in multi-player games the bullet time effect – if used at all – is implemented by speeding up the player rather than slowing down the environment. For instance, force speed in *Jedi Knight II* implements the bullet time effect differently in the single-player mode compared to the multi-player mode. The reason for this is obvious: if one player could slow down the time of the surroundings, it would be awkward for the other players within the influence area because, rather than enhancing the game play of the player using the bullet time, it would only hinder the game play of the other human players.

Since the player using bullet time has more time to react to the events of the surrounding game world, the delay between the bullet-timed player and the other players increases. This is quite straightforward to include into LPFs (Smed *et al.* 2005): In addition to the real-world communication delays, we have artificial, player-initiated delays – the bullet time – which are then used to form the temporal contours. The outcome is that entities approaching a bullet-timed player slow down and entities coming from a bullet-timed player speed up. Obviously, the game design should prevent the players from overusing bullet times by making it a limited resource that can be used only for a short period. Also, incorporating the temporal distortions as an integral part of the game could lead to new and intriguing game designs.

Let us denote the bullet time of player p with $b(p)$. As in the previous section, assume we have two players, p and r, and a bullet e shot by player p. Figure 9.14 illustrates the players' temporal contours when player p is using bullet time. From the perspective of player p, when the bullet reaches r, the delay is $d(p,r) - b(p)$. As before, the delay function represents the temporal difference between the actual entity and the rendered entity. However, whereas normally the delay values are positive (i.e. the actual position is ahead of the rendered position), bullet time can lead to negative delay values (i.e. the rendered position is ahead of the actual position). This becomes more obvious when we consider the same situation from the perspective of player r. When the bullet reaches player r, the

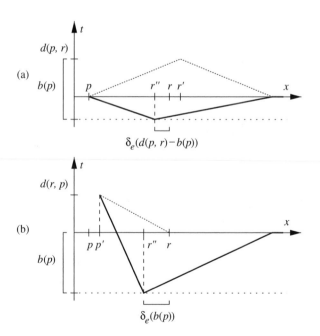

Figure 9.14 Player p shoots player r, and player p is using bullet time. (a) The temporal contour of player p. (b) The temporal contour of player r.

delay is $-b(p)$ because the bullet time, in effect, takes away time from player r. Naturally, collision detection and other reactions must be based on this rendered entity rather than the actual entity, which is still on the way to the target.

Like normal temporal contours, bullet-timed temporal contours also require refining to avoid visual disruptions. The *bullet time shadow* r'' of player r corrects the temporal contour based on the movement of e: For player p, r'' must have the property

$$\delta(r, r'') = \delta_e(d(p, r) - b(p)),$$

(9.10)

and for player r, r'' must have the property

$$\delta(r, r'') = \delta_e(b(p)).$$

(9.11)

In Figure 9.15, player r is using bullet time while being shot by player p. In this case, the bullet time $b(r)$ is added to the normal communication delay in the temporal contour of player p, which means that the delay is $d(p, r) + b(r)$ when the bullet reaches r. Conversely, player r has the delay $b(r)$ when the bullet reaches it. Again, to refine the temporal contours, we must calculate the bullet time shadow r''. For player p, r'' must have the property

$$\delta(r, r'') = \delta_e(d(p, r) + b(p)),$$

(9.12)

and for player r, r'' must have the property

$$\delta(r, r'') = \delta_e(b(r)).$$

(9.13)

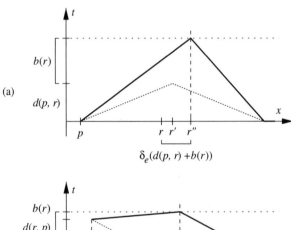

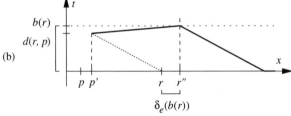

Figure 9.15 Player p shoots player r, and player r is using bullet time. (a) The temporal contour of player p. (b) The temporal contour of player r.

Bullet-timed temporal contours can be generalized to include multiple players in the same way as normal temporal contours.

9.5 Synchronized Simulation

In synchronized (or simultaneous) simulation, we have a replicated architecture with absolute consistency, where all players have their own copy of the game world and these replicas are always identical (i.e. synchronized) to one another. For example, *Age of Empires II* uses this approach to support up to eight players and 1600 controllable entities (Bettner and Terrano 2001).

To reduce the number of messages sent among the nodes, we try to keep the game states as synchronized as possible. The events in the game world can be divided into

(i) deterministic (events generated by the simulation) and

(ii) indeterministic (commands issued by a synthetic or a human player).

Because each simulation run can generate the same deterministic information, only indeterministic commands must be distributed among the participants. We reduce the communication even further if each node runs the same synthetic players. The only unpredictable event is what is generated by the human players, and such events are the only ones that need to be transmitted over the network.

To achieve indeterminism in the synthetic player's decision-making, we can use pseudo-random numbers. Now, the computer-issued commands – albeit deterministic – appear to be arbitrary enough. Ideally, the simultaneously run simulations agree on the seed value in the beginning and, after that, pass on only the commands issued by the human players. Of course, a real-world implementation also requires consistency checks and recovery mechanisms in case some input gets lost.

Consider a simple game, Guess a Number: In the beginning, each player chooses one number within a given interval. Next, the remaining players, one at a time, guess a number and all the other players who have chosen that number drop off from the game. In the end, there is only one player left, who is the winner. Algorithm 9.5 describes an implementation for this game, where the players can be controlled either by humans or the computer. Moreover, the algorithm can be run in a network, and the execution will be synchronized. The only information that must be distributed among the computers is the human players' input.

9.6 Area-of-Interest Filtering

The entities usually produce update packets that are relevant only for a minority of the nodes. Therefore, an obvious way to save bandwidth is to disseminate update packets only to those nodes that are interested in them. This interest management includes techniques that allow the nodes to express interest in only the subset of information that is relevant to them (Benford *et al.* 2001; Morse *et al.* 2000). With respect to Equation (9.1), interest management techniques aim to reduce the average number of messages (M) and bandwidth

---

Algorithm 9.5 Synchronized simulation for Guess a Number.

GUESS-NUMBER(H, C)

    in: set of human participants H; set of computer participants C

    out: winner w

    constant: minimum number $n_{\min}$; maximum number $n_{\max}$

    local: guessed number g

  1: agree on the seed value v with the participating nodes

  2: SET-SEED(v)

  3: **for all** $h \in H$ **do**

  4:    $number(h) \leftarrow$ the chosen number of the human participant h

  5: **end for**

  6: **for all** $c \in C$ **do**

  7:    $number(c) \leftarrow$ RANDOM-INTEGER($n_{\min}, n_{\max} + 1$)

  8: **end for**

  9: $P \leftarrow$ **copy** $H \cup C$

10: **repeat**

11:    **for all** $p \in P$ **do**

12:      **if** $p \in H$ **then**   ▷ Human guesses.

13:        $g \leftarrow$ guess from the human participant p

14:      **else**   ▷ Computer guesses.

15:        $g \leftarrow$ RANDOM-INTEGER($n_{\min}, n_{\max} + 1$)

16:      **end if**

17:      **for all** $q \in P \setminus \{p\}$

18:        **if** $number(q) = g$ **then**

19:          $P \leftarrow P \setminus \{q\}$

20:        **end if**

21:      **end for**

22:    **end for**

23: **until** $|P| = 1$

24: $w \leftarrow$ the single value in P

25: **return** w

(B) per message. This requires more organizing between the nodes, and, consequently, more processing (P).

An expression of data interest is called the *aura* (or area of interest), and it usually correlates with the sensing capabilities of the entity being modelled. Simply put, an aura is a sub-space where interaction occurs (see Figure 9.16). Thus, when two players' auras intersect, they can be aware of each others actions and should receive update messages from each other. Awareness can be based on senses like seeing or hearing, and we can have separate auras for different media (e.g. visual and aural awareness).

An aura does not have to follow the game world geometry or be of any regular shape. Figure 9.17 illustrates three different methods to define the aura. By using formulae, the aura can be expressed precisely, and in Figure 9.17(a) the circle around the grey ship indicates the observable range. However, the implementation can be complex and the required

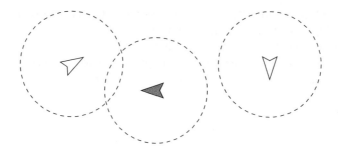

Figure 9.16 When two entities' auras intersect, they are aware of each other and receive update messages.

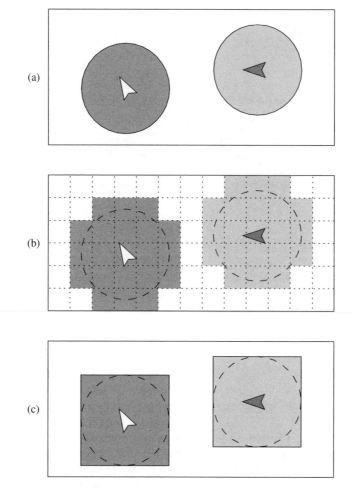

Figure 9.17 Auras (or areas of interest) can be expressed using (a) formulae, (b) cells, or (c) extents.

computation hard. In Figure 9.17(b) the game world is divided into static, discrete cells, and the grey ship is interested in the cells that intersect its aura. Cell-based filtering is easier to implement but it is less discriminating than formula-based filtering. Figure 9.17(c) show extents that approximate the actual aura with rectangles (i.e. bounding boxes). The computation is simpler than when using formulae and, in most cases, the filtering is better than when using large cells.

Filtering update messages with auras is always symmetric: if the auras intersect, both parties receive updates from each other. However, aura can be divided further into a *focus* and a *nimbus*, where focus represents an observing entity's interest and nimbus represents an observed entity's wish to be seen in a given medium (Benford *et al.* 1994; Greenhalgh 1998). Thus, the player's focus must intersect with another player's nimbus in order to be aware of him (see Figure 9.18). For example, in hide-and-seek, the nimbus of the hiding person could be smaller than the seeker's, and the seeker cannot interact with the hider. At the same time, the hider can observe the seeker if the seeker's nimbus is larger and intersects the hider's focus.

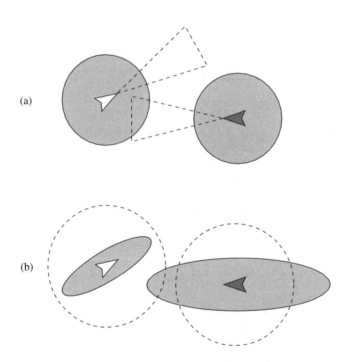

Figure 9.18 With focus (dashed areas) and nimbus (grey areas) the awareness needs not to be symmetric. (a) The grey ship's focus intersects the white ship's nimbus, which means that the grey ship receives update messages from the white ship. Because the white ship's focus does not intersect the grey ship's nimbus, it does not receive update messages from the grey ship. (b) Focus and nimbus can vary according to the medium (e.g. visual, aural, or textual).

Area-of-interest filters can be called *intrinsic filters* because they use application-specific data content of an update message to determine which nodes need to receive it. This filtering provides fine-grained information delivery but message processing may require a considerable amount of time. In contrast, *extrinsic filters* determine the receivers of a message merely on the basis of its network attributes (e.g. address). Extrinsic filters are faster to process than intrinsic filters, and the network itself can provide techniques such as multicasting to realize them. The challenge in the design of a multicast-based application is how to categorize all transmitted information into multicast groups. Each message sent to a multicast group should be relevant to all subscribers. In group-per-entity allocation strategy, each entity has its own multicast group to which the object transmits its updates. Assigned servers keep a record of the multicast addresses so that the nodes can subscribe to the relevant groups. In group-per-region allocation strategy, the game world is divided into regions that have their own multicast groups. All entities within the region transmit updates to the corresponding multicast address. Typically, entities subscribe to groups corresponding to their own region and the neighbouring regions.

9.7 Summary

The basic idea of compensation techniques is to replace communication with computation. If we want to reduce network traffic, we can do it at the cost of processing power: In dead reckoning, we compute predictions and correct them; in synchronized simulation, we recreate the deterministic events; and in area-of-interest filtering, we select to whom to send the updates.

The compensation techniques address two aspects: the consistency–responsiveness dichotomy and scalability. To balance consistency and responsiveness, we must choose which is more important to us, because one can be achieved only by sacrificing the other. In computer games, unlike many other networked applications, we may have to give up the consistency requirement to get better responsiveness. Scalability is about dividing the resources among multiple participants, whether they are human players or synthetic players. It begs the questions what parts of the program can be run in serial or parallel and what is the communication capacity of the chosen communication architecture.

Dead reckoning and LPFs provide more responsiveness by sacrificing consistency, whereas synchronized simulation retains consistency at the cost of responsiveness and scalability. Area-of-interest filters aim at providing scalability, but managing the entities' interests reduces the responsiveness as well as the present inconsistencies. Despite all these compensation methods, the fact remains that whatever we do we cannot completely hide the resource limitations – but if we are lucky, we can select the places where they occur so that they cause only a tolerable amount of nuisance.

Exercises

9-1 If we decide to send update messages less often and include several updates to each message, what does it mean in the light of Equation (9.1)? What if we send the messages to only those who are really interested in receiving them?

9-2 Why is processing power included in the network resource limitations?

9-3 Suppose you have 12 computers with equal processing and networking capabilities. You can freely arrange and cable them to peer-to-peer, client–server or server-network (e.g. three servers connected peer-to-peer with three clients each) architecture. With respect to Equation (9.1), compare the resource requirements of these communication architectures. Then, consider how realizable they are in the Internet.

9-4 To achieve consistency, the players have to reach an agreement on the game state. However, this opens a door to distributed consensus problems. Let us look at one of them, called the *two-generals problem*: Two generals have to agree whether to attack a target. They have couriers carrying the messages to and fro, but the delivery of the message is unreliable. Is it possible for them to be sure that they have an agreement on what do? For a further discussion on consensus problems, see Lamport and Lynch (1990).

9-5 Why is it that we can we have sub-linear communication? What are the results of using it?

9-6 Assume that we are sending update messages about the three-dimensional position (x, y, z) to other players. The coordinates are expressed using 32 bits, but the actual changes are of the magnitude $[-10, +10]$. To have more bandwidth, how would you compress this network traffic?

9-7 Assume that we have a centralized architecture, where all players inform their coordinates to a server. Explain how timeout-based and quorum-based message aggregations work in such an environment. Assume we have 12 players and their update interval ranges from $[0.1, 3]$ seconds. Which approach would be recommendable?

9-8 Consider the following entities. How easy or difficult is it to predict their future position in 1 s, in 5 s, and in 1 min?

   (a) A rabbit

   (b) A human being

   (c) A sports car

   (d) A jeep

   (e) An aeroplane.

9-9 Why does a first-order polynomial (e.g. velocity) give better predictions if the second-order derivative (e.g. acceleration) is small or substantial?

9-10 If we do not use a convergence technique, the game character can 'warp', for example, through a wall. Does a convergence technique remove visually impossible moves?

9-11 Compare dead reckoning and LPFs by considering their visual and temporal fidelities.

9-12 What other possibilities are there to define the temporal contour? What would be a theoretically ideal temporal contour?

9-13 In *Pong*, two players at the opposite ends try to hit a ball bouncing between them with a paddle. How can we use LPFs to hide communication delays between the players?

9-14 One way to hide technical limitations is to incorporate them as a part of the game design. Instead of hiding communication delays, LPFs could be used to include temporal distortions. Devise a game design that does so.

9-15 In LPFs, a critical proximity is the distance between players when interaction using entities becomes impossible. Assume that we are using linear temporal contours. Define the critical proximity using the terms of Section 9.4.1.

9-16 Bullet time effect opens the door to temporal cheating. Consider the situation in which players s, n, and t stand in line. Player s shoots at t, who cannot use bullet time. What happens if player n, who is between s and t, uses the bullet time effect?

9-17 Assume we have a game that uses synchronized simulation. If we want to extend the game by including new players, which will become the limiting factor first: the number of human players or the number of synthetic players?

9-18 Area-of-interest filtering reduces update messages between entities that are not aware of one another. Can this lead to problems with consistency?

9-19 In order to use auras, foci, and nimbi, an entity has to be at least aware of the existence of other entities. How can you implement this? (Hint: Select a suitable communication architecture first.)

10

Cheating Prevention

The cheaters attacking networked computer games are often motivated by an appetite for vandalism or dominance. However, only a minority of the cheaters try to create open and immediate havoc, whereas most of them want to achieve a dominating, superhuman position and hold sway over the other players. In fact, many cheating players do so because they want to have an easier game play by lowering the difficulty (e.g. by removing the fog of war) – and they might even maintain that such an act does not constitute cheating. On the other hand, easier game play can be used to gain prestige among peers, since a cheating player may want to appear to be better than his friends in the game. Peer prestige is also a common motivation behind people creating cheating programs (and other 'destructive' coding such as writing virus programs), because they want to excel in their peer group.

As online gaming has grown into a lucrative business, greed has become a driving force behind cheating. Instead of the actual game play, cheating is done because of the financial gain from selling virtual assets (e.g. special items or ready-made game characters). For instance, Castronova (2001) estimates that the gross national product generated by the markets in *EverQuest* makes it the 77th richest 'country' in the world. Naturally, potential financial losses, caused directly or indirectly by cheaters, are a major concern among the online gaming sites and the main motivation to implement countermeasures against cheating. On the other hand, game sites can sometimes even postpone fixing the detected cheating problems, because the possibility of cheating can attract players to participate in the game.

Cheating prevention has three distinct goals (Smed *et al.* 2002; Yan and Choi 2002):

- protect the sensitive information,

- provide a fair playing field, and

- uphold a sense of justice inside the game world.

Each of these goals can be viewed from a technical or social perspective: Sensitive information (e.g. players' accounts) can be gained, for instance, by cracking the passwords or by pretending to be an administrator and asking the players to give their passwords. A fair playing field can be compromised, for instance, by tampering with the network traffic

Algorithms and Networking for Computer Games   Jouni Smed and Harri Hakonen
© 2006 John Wiley & Sons, Ltd

or by colluding with other players. The sense of justice can be violated, for instance, by abusing inexperienced and ill-equipped players or by ganging up and controlling parts of the game world.

In this chapter, we look at different ways to cheat in online multi-player games and review some algorithmic countermeasures that aim at preventing them.

10.1 Technical Exploitations

In a networked multi-player game, a cheater can attack the clients, the servers, or the network connecting them. Figure 10.1 illustrates typical attack types (Kirmse and Kirmse 1997): On the client side, the attacks focus on compromising the software or game data, and tampering with the network traffic. Game servers are vulnerable to network attacks as well as physical attacks such as theft or vandalism. Third party attacks on clients or servers include IP spoofing (e.g. intercepting packets and replacing them with forged ones) and denial-of-service attacks (e.g. blocking networking of some player so that he gets dropped from the game). In the following, we review the common technical exploitations used in online cheating.

10.1.1 Packet tampering

In first-person shooter games, a usual way to cheat is to enhance the player's reactions with *reflex augmentation* (Kirmse 2000). For example, an aiming proxy can monitor the network traffic and keep a record of the opponents' positions. When the cheater fires, the proxy uses this information and sends additional rotation and movement control packets before the fire command, thus improving the aim. On the other hand, in *packet interception* the proxy prevents certain packets from reaching the cheating player. For example, if the packets containing damage information are suppressed, the cheater becomes invulnerable. In a *packet replay* attack, the same packet is sent repeatedly. For example, if a weapon can be fired only once in a second, the cheater can send the fire command packet hundred times a second to boost its firing rate.

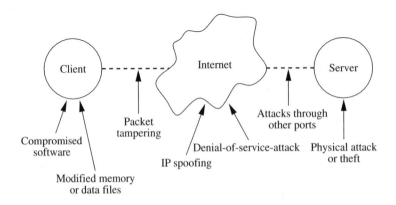

Figure 10.1 Typical attacks in a networked multi-player game.

A common method for breaking the control protocol is to change bytes in a packet and observe the effects. A straightforward way to prevent this is to use checksums. For this purpose, we can use message-digest (MD) algorithms, which are one-way functions that transform a message into a constant length MD (or fingerprint). A widely used variant in computer games is the MD5 algorithm, developed by Rivest (1992), which produces a 128-bit MD from an arbitrary length message. MD algorithms are used to guarantee the integrity of the data as follows: A sender creates a message and computes its MD. The MD (possibly encrypted with the sender's private key or receiver's public key) is attached to the message, and the whole message is sent to a receiver. The receiver extracts the MD (possibly decrypting it), computes the MD for the remaining message, and compares both of them.

Preferably, no one should be able – or at least it should be computationally infeasible – to produce two messages having the same MD or produce the original message from a given MD. However, an MD algorithm has a weakness that if two messages A and B have the same MD, it cannot authenticate which the original message is. If a cheater can find two messages that produce the same MD, he could use a collision attack. In MD5 algorithm, it is possible even to append the same payload P to both the messages M and N ($M \neq N$) so that the MDs remain the same (i.e. MD5($M \parallel P$) = MD5($N \parallel P$)). In addition to these well-known theoretical weaknesses, there is now more and more experimental evidence that finding message collisions is not so hard a task as previously thought, which naturally raises a question about the future of MD algorithms (Wang and Yu 2005).

There are two weaknesses that cannot be prevented with checksums alone: The cheaters can reverse engineer the checksum algorithm or they can attack with packet replay. By encrypting the command packets, the cheaters have a lesser chance to record and forge information. However, to prevent a packet replay attack, it is required that the packets carry some state information so that even the packets with a similar payload appear to be different. Instead of serial numbering, pseudo-random numbers, discussed in Section 2.1, provide a better alternative. Random numbers can also be used to modify the packets so that even identical packets do not appear the same. Dissimilarity can be further induced by adding a variable amount of junk data to the packets, which eliminates the possibility of analysing their contents by the size.

10.1.2   Look-ahead cheating

In peer-to-peer architecture, all nodes uphold the game state, and the players' time-stamped actions must be conveyed to all nodes. This opens a possibility to use look-ahead cheating, where the cheater gains an unfair advantage by delaying his actions – as if he had a high latency – to see what the other players do before choosing his action. The cheater then forges the time-stamped packets so that they seem to be issued before they actually were (see Figure 10.2). To prevent this, we review two methods: the lockstep protocol and active objects.

Lockstep protocol

The lockstep protocol tackles the problem by requiring that each player first announces a commitment to an action; when everyone has received the commitments, the players reveal their actions, which can be then checked against the original commitments (Baughman and Levine 2001). The commitment must meet two requirements: it cannot be used to infer the

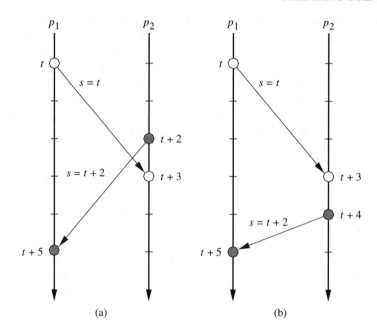

Figure 10.2 Assume the senders must time-stamp (i.e. include the value s) their outgoing messages, and the latency between the players is 3 time units. (a) If both players are fair, p_1 can be sure that the message from p_2, which has the time-stamp $t + 2$, was sent before the message issued at t had arrived. (b) If p_2 has a latency of 1 time unit but pretends that it is 3, look-ahead cheating using forged time-stamps allows p_2 to base decisions on information that it should not have.

action, but it should be easy to compare whether an action corresponds to a commitment. An obvious choice for constructing the commitments is to calculate a hash value of the action.

Algorithm 10.1 describes an implementation for the lockstep protocol, which uses the auxiliary functions introduced in Algorithm 10.2. The details of the function HASH are omitted, but hints for its implementation can be found in Knuth (1998c, Section 6.4).

We can readily see that the game progresses in the terms of the slowest player because of the synchronization. This may suit a turn-based game, which is not time critical, but if we want to use the lockstep protocol in a real-time game, the turns have to be short or there has to be a time limit inside which a player must announce the action or pass that turn altogether.

To overcome this drawback, we can use an *asynchronous lockstep protocol*, where each player advances in time asynchronously from the other players but enters into a lockstep mode whenever interaction is required. The mode is defined by a sphere of influence surrounding each player, which outlines the game world that can possibly be affected by a player in the next turn (or subsequent turns). If two players' spheres of influence do not intersect, they cannot affect each other in the next turn, and hence their decisions will not affect each other when the next game state is computed and they can proceed asynchronously.

Algorithm 10.1 Lockstep protocol.

LOCKSTEP (ℓ, a, P)
   in: local player ℓ; action a; set of remote players P
   out: set of players' actions R
   local: commitment C; action A; set of commitments S
   1: $C \leftarrow \langle \ell, \text{HASH}(a) \rangle$
   2: SEND-ALL(C, P)   ▷ Announce commitment.
   3: $S \leftarrow \{C\}$
   4: $S \leftarrow S \cup$ RECEIVE-ALL(P)   ▷ Get other players' commitments.
   5: SYNCHRONIZE(P)   ▷ Wait until everyone is ready.
   6: $A \leftarrow \langle \ell, a \rangle$
   7: SEND-ALL(A, P)   ▷ Announce action.
   8: $R \leftarrow \{A\}$
   9: $R \leftarrow R \cup$ RECEIVE-ALL(P)   ▷ Get other players' actions.
  10: **for all** $A \in R$ **do**
  11:    $c \leftarrow$ the commitment $c' \in S$ for which $c'_0 = A_0$
  12:    **if** $C_1 \neq \text{HASH}(A_1)$ **then**   ▷ Are commitment and action different?
  13:       **error** player A_0 cheats
  14:    **end if**
  15: **end for**
  16: **return** R

In the *pipelined lockstep protocol*, synchronization is loosened by having a buffer of size p, where the incoming commitments are stored (i.e. in basic lockstep $p = 1$) (Lee *et al.* 2002). Instead of synchronizing at each turn, the players can send several commitments, which are pipelined, before the corresponding opponents' commitments are received. In other words, when player i has received the commitments C_n^j of all other players j for the time frame n, it announces its action A_n^i (see Figure 10.3). The pipeline may include commitments for the frames $n, \ldots, (n + p - 1)$, when player i can announce commitments $C_n^i, \ldots, C_{n+p-1}^i$ before it has to announce action A_n^i. However, this opens a possibility to reintroduce look-ahead cheating: If a player announces its action earlier than required by the protocol, the other players can change both their commitments and actions on the basis of that knowledge. This can be counteracted with an *adaptive pipeline protocol*, where the idea is to measure the actual latencies between the players and to grow or shrink the pipeline size accordingly (Cronin *et al.* 2003).

Active objects

The lockstep protocol requires that the players send two transmissions – one for the commitment and one for the action – in each turn. Let us now address the question, whether we can use only one transmission and still detect look-ahead cheating. Single transmission means that the action must be included in the outgoing message, but the receiver is allowed to view it only after it has replied with its own action. But this leaves open the question how a player can make sure that the exchange of messages in another player's computer

Algorithm 10.2 Auxiliary methods for the lockstep protocol.

SEND-ALL(m, R)
  in: message m; set of recipients R
  1: **for all** $r \in R$ **do**
  2:    send m to r
  3: **end for**

RECEIVE-ALL(S)
  in: set of senders S
  out: set of messages M
  1: $M \leftarrow \emptyset$
  2: **for all** $s \in S$ **do**
  3:    $received(s) \leftarrow$ FALSE
  4: **end for**
  5: **repeat**
  6:    receive message m from $s \in S$
  7:    $received(s) \leftarrow$ TRUE
  8:    $M \leftarrow M \cup \{m\}$
  9: **until** $\forall s \in S : received(s)$
  10: **return** M

SYNCHRONIZE(H)
  in: set of remote hosts H
  1: SEND-ALL($\emptyset$, H)
  2: RECEIVE-ALL(H)

has not been compromised. It is possible that he is a cheater who intercepts and alters the outgoing messages or has hacked the communication system.

We can use active objects to secure the exchange of messages, which happens in a possibly 'hostile' environment (Smed and Hakonen 2005a). Now, the player (or the originator) provides an active object, a *delegate*, which includes a program code to be run by the other player (or the host). The delegate acts then as a trusted party for the originator by guaranteeing the message exchange in the host's system.

Let us illustrate the idea using the game Rock-Paper-Scissors as an example. Player p goes through the following stages:

(i) Player p decides the action 'paper', puts this message inside a box, and locks it. The key to the box can be generated by the delegate of player p, which has been sent beforehand to player r.

(ii) Player p gives the box to the delegate of player r, which closes it inside another box before sending it to player r. Thus, when the message comes out from the delegate, player p cannot tamper with its contents.

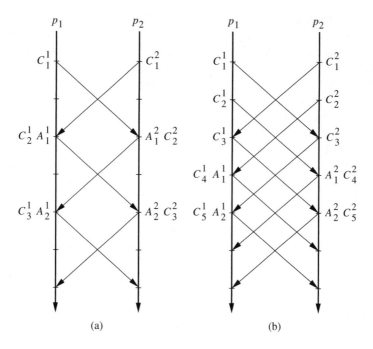

Figure 10.3 Lockstep and pipeline lockstep protocols: (a) The lockstep protocol synchro-
nizes after each turn and waits until everybody has received all commitments. (b) The
pipelined lockstep protocol has a fixed size buffer (here the size is 3), which holds several
commitments.

(iii) Once the double-boxed message has been sent, the delegate of player r generates
a key and gives it to player p. This key will open the box enclosing the incoming
message from player r.

(iv) When player p receives a double-boxed message originating from player r, it can
open the outer box, closed by its own delegate, and the inner box using the key it
received from the delegate of player r.

(v) Player p can now view the action of player r.

At the same time, player r goes through the following stages:

(i) Player r receives a box from player p. It can open the outer box, closed by its own
delegate, but not the inner box.

(ii) To get the key to the inner box, player r must inform its action to the delegate of
player p. Player r chooses 'rock', puts it in a box, and passes it to the delegate.

(iii) When the message has been sent, player r receives the key to the inner box from the
delegate of player p.

(iv) Player r can now view the action of player p.

Although we can trust, at least to some extent, our delegates, there still remains two problems to be solved. First, the delegate must ensure that it really has a connection to its originator, which seems to incur extra talk-back communication. Second, although we have secured one-to-one exchange of messages, there is no guarantee that the player will not alter its action when it sends a message to a third player.

Let us first tackle the problem of ensuring the communication channel. Ideally, the delegate, once started, should contact the originator and convey a unique identification of itself. This identification should be a combination of dynamic information (e.g. the memory address in which the delegate is located or the system time when the delegate was created) and static information (e.g. built-in identification number or the Internet address of the node in which the delegate is being run). Dynamic information is needed to prevent a cheating host from creating a copy of the delegate and using that as a surrogate to work out how it operates. Static information allows to ensure that the delegate has not been moved somewhere else or is replaced after the communication check.

If we could trust the run environment in which the delegate resides, there would be no need to do any check-ups at all. On the other hand, in a completely hostile environment, we would have to ensure the communication channel every time, and there would be no improvement over the lockstep protocol. To reduce the number of check-up messages, the delegate can initiate them randomly with some parameterized probability. In practice, this probability can be relatively low – especially if the number of turns in the game is high. Rather than detecting the cheats, this imposes a threat of being detected: Although a player can get away with a cheat, in the long run attempts to cheat are likely to be noticed. Moreover, as the number of participating players increases, it also increases the possibility of getting caught.

A similar approach helps us to solve the problem of preventing a player from sending differing actions to the other players. Rather than detecting an inconsistent action in the current turn, the players can 'gossip' among themselves about the actions made in the previous turns. These gossips can then be compared with the recorded actions from the previous turns, and any discrepancy indicates that somebody has cheated. Although the gossip can comprise all earlier actions, it is enough to include only a small, randomly chosen subset of them – especially if the number of participants is high. This gossiping does not require any extra transmissions because it can be piggybacked in the ordinary messages. Naturally, a cheater can send a false gossip about other players, which means that if the action and the gossip differ, the veridicality of the gossip has to be confirmed (e.g. by asking randomly selected players).

10.1.3 Cracking and other attacks

Networking is not the only target for attacks but the cheater can affect the game through the software or even through the hardware (Pritchard 2000). A cracked client software may allow the cheater to gain access to the replicated, hidden game data (e.g. the status of other players). On the surface, this kind of passive cheating does not tamper with the network traffic, but the cheaters can base their decisions on more accurate knowledge than they are supposed to have. For example, typical exposed data in real-time strategy games are the variables controlling the visible area on the screen (i.e. the fog of war). This problem is also common in first-person shooters, where, for instance, a compromised graphics rendering driver may allow the player to see through walls.

Strictly speaking, these information exposure problems stem from the software and cannot be prevented with networking alone. Clearly, the sensitive data should be encoded and its location in the memory should be hard to detect. Nevertheless, it is always susceptible to ingenious hackers and, therefore, requires some additional countermeasures. In a centralized architecture, an obvious solution is to utilize the server, which can check whether a client issuing a command is actually aware of the object with which it is operating. For example, if a player has not seen the opponent's base, he cannot give an order to attack it – unless he is cheating. When the server detects cheating, it can drop out the cheating client. A democratized version of the same method can be applied in a replicated architecture: Every node checks the validity of each other's commands (e.g. by using gossiping as in Section 10.1.2), and if some discrepancy is detected, the nodes vote whether its source should be debarred from participating in the game.

Network traffic and software are not the only vulnerable places in a computer game, but design defects can create loopholes, which the cheaters are apt to exploit. For example, if the clients are designed to trust each other, the game is unshielded from *client authority abuse*. In this case, a compromised client can exaggerate the damage caused by a cheater, and the rest accept this information as such. Although this problem can be tackled by using checksums to ensure that each client has the same binaries, it is more advisable to alter the design so that the clients can issue command requests, which the server puts into operation. Naturally, this schema can be hybridized or randomized so that only some operations are centralized using some control exchange protocol.

In addition to a poor design, distribution – especially the heterogeneity of network environments – can be the source of unexpected behaviour. For instance, there may be features that become eminent only when the latency is extremely high or when the server is under a denial-of-service attack (i.e. an attacker sends it a large number of spurious requests).

10.2 Rule Violations

The definition of a game states that the players agree to follow the rules of the game (see Chapter 1). We can then say that all players not adhering to the rules are cheaters. For example, collusion where two or more opposing players play towards a common goal is explicitly forbidden in many games. However, the situation is not always so black and white, because the rules can leave certain questions unanswered. The makers of the rules are fallible and can fail to foresee all possible situations that a complex system like a computer game can generate. If a player then exploits these loopholes, it can be hard to judge whether it is just a good game play or cheating. Ultimately, the question of upholding justice in a game world boils down to the question, what is the ethical code that the players agree and can be expected to follow.

10.2.1 Collusion

The basic assumption of imperfect information games is that each player has access only to a limited amount of information. A typical example of such a game is poker, where the judgements are based on the player's ability to infer information from the bets, thus outwitting the opponents. A usual method of cheating in individual imperfect information games is collusion, where two or more players play together without informing the rest of the participants. Normally this would not pose a problem, since the players are physically present and can (at least in theory) detect any attempts of collusion (e.g. coughs, hand signals, or coded language). For example, in Bridge, all attempts to collude are monitored by the other players as well as by the judges (Yan 2003). However, when the game is played online, the players cannot be sure whether there are colluding players present. This means a serious threat to the e-casinos and other online game sites, because they cannot guarantee a fair playing field (Johansson *et al.* 2003).

Collusion also applies to other types of games, because a gang of cooperating players can share information that they normally would not have or they can ambush and rob other players. Collusion is also possible in tournaments, and the type of tournament dictates how effective it can be (Murdoch and Zieliński 2004). For example, in a scoring tournament, colluding players play normally against other players and agree who is going to win the reciprocal match and score more points (see Table 10.1). In a hill-climbing tournament, colluding players can gain benefit by affecting the result of initial matches (see Figure 10.4).

Only the organizer of an online game, who has the full information on the game, can take countermeasures against collusion. These countermeasures fall into two categories: *tracking* (i.e. determining who the players actually are) and *styling* (i.e. analysing how the players play the game). Unfortunately, there are no pre-emptive or real-time countermeasures against collusion. Although tracking can be done in real time, it is not sufficient by itself. Physical identity does not reflect who is actually playing the game, and a cheater can always avoid network location tracking with rerouting techniques. Styling allows to find out if there are players who participate often in the same games and, over a long period, profit more than they should. For example, online poker sites usually do styling by analysing the betting patterns and investigating the cases in which the overall win percentage is higher than expected. However, this analysis requires a sufficient amount of game data, and collusion can be detected only later.

The situation becomes even worse, when we look at the types of collusion in which the cheating players can engage. In active collusion, cheating players play more aggressively than they normally would. In poker, for example, the colluding players can outbet the

Table 10.1 Winners in a scoring tournament, where all players have equal strength and play optimally. If players c_0 and c_1 collude so that c_0 always wins, player c_0 scores more points than a non-colluding player.

	p	c_0	c_1
p	—	Draw	Draw
c_0	Draw	—	c_0
c_1	Draw	c_0	—

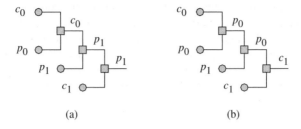

Figure 10.4 Collusion in a hill-climbing tournament, where c_0 and c_1 can win p_0, p_0 can win p_1, and p_1 can win c_0 and c_1. (a) If everyone plays normally, p_1 wins the tournament. (b) If players c_0 and c_1 collude, c_0 can deliberately lose his match so that c_1 will get an easier opponent later in the tournament.

non-colluding ones. In passive collusion, cheating players play more cautiously than they normally would. In poker, for example, the colluding players can let only the one with the strongest hand to continue the play while the rest of them fold. Although styling can manage to detect active collusion, it is hard – if not impossible – to discern passive collusion from a normal play.

10.2.2 Offending other players

Although players may act in accordance with the rules of a game, they can cheat by acting against the spirit of the game. For example, in online role-playing games, killing and stealing from other players are common problems that need to be solved (Sanderson 1999). The players committing these 'crimes' are not necessarily cheating, because they can operate well within the rules of the game. For example, in the online version of *Terminus* different gangs have ended up owning different parts of the game world, where they assault all trespassers. Nonetheless, we may consider an ambush by a more experienced and better-equipped player on a beginner who cheats, because it is neither fair nor justified. Moreover, it can make the challenge of the game impossible or harder than the game designer had originally intended.

There are different approaches to handle this problem. *Ultima Online* originally left the policing to the players, but eventually this led to gangs of player killers that terrorized the whole game. This was counteracted with a rating system, where everybody is initially innocent, but any misconduct against other players (including the synthetic ones) brands the player as a criminal. Each crime increases the bounty on the player's head, ultimately preventing them from entering shops. The only way to clear one's name is not to commit crimes for a given time. *EverQuest* uses a different approach, where the players can mark themselves as being capable of attacking and being attacked by other players, or as being completely unable to engage in such activities. This approach has increasingly become the norm of the online games today.

Killing and stealing are not the only ways to harm another player. There are other, non-violent ways to offend such as blocking exits, interfering with fights, and verbal abuse.

The main methods used against these kinds of attacks are filtering (e.g. banning messages from annoying players), or reporting to the administrator of the game – which of course opens a possibility to collusion, where players belonging to the same clan send numerous and seemingly independent complaints about a player. One can of course ask, whether this kind of behaviour is cheating at all but a feature of the game, and then concede that everything allowed by the game rules is acceptable and cannot be considered as cheating (Kimppa and Bissett 2005).

10.3 Summary

Multi-player computer games thrive on fair play. Nothing can be more off-putting than an unfair game world, where beginners are robbed as soon as they start, where some players have superhuman reflexes, or where an unsuspecting player is cheated out of his money. Cheating prevention is then crucial to guarantee the longevity and 'enjoyableness' of the computer game.

Networked computer games present unique security problems because of the real-time interactivity. Since data needs to be secure for a relatively short period of time, the methods do not have to be as tightly secure as in other contexts. At the same time, the methods should be fast to compute, since all extra computation slows down the communication between the players.

It is impossible to totally prevent cheating. Some forms are so subtle that they are hard to observe and judge using technical methods alone – they might even escape the human moral compass. For good or bad, computer games always reflect the real world behind them.

Exercises

10-1 Is it possible to catch reflex augmentation cheating by monitoring the network traffic and events in the game world alone? Can this lead to problematic situations?

10-2 What data and control architecture is the most susceptible to packet interception? How can it be improved to prevent this kind of cheating?

10-3 The easiest way to prevent packet replay cheating is to include some state information in each packet. Why should this information not be a linearly increasing serial number but a pseudo-random number?

10-4 Describe how the lockstep protocol works when we have three or more players.

10-5 When using active objects, even a small number of gossiping can help catch a cheater. Suppose that a cheater who forges 10% of his messages participates in a game. What is the probability of his getting caught if the other players gossip about the choices made in one previous turn and if there are

(a) 10 players, 60 turns, and 1% gossip

(b) 10 players, 60 turns, and 10% gossip

    (c) 100 players, 60 turns, and 1% gossip

    (d) 10 players, 360 turns, and 1% gossip.

10-6 What countermeasures do we have against using illicit information (e.g. removing the fog of war or using a compromised graphics rendering device) in centralized, distributed and replicated architectures?

10-7 Is it possible to collude in a perfect information game?

10-8 Active collusion means that the cheaters take more risks than they normally would, because they have knowledge that the risk is not as high as it appears to be (e.g. the colluding players raise the stake by outbetting one another). In passive collusion, the cheaters take less risks than they normally would, because they have knowledge that the risk is higher than it appears to be (e.g. colluding players fold when a co-colluder has a better hand). State why active collusion can be recognized, whereas passive collusion is difficult to discern from normal play?

10-9 Consider the following approaches to uphold justice in a game world. What are their good sides? How difficult are they to implement technically? Can a cheater abuse them?

    (a) Human players handle the policing themselves (e.g. forming a militia).

    (b) The game system records misconducts and brands offenders as criminals.

    (c) Players themselves decide whether they can offend and be offended.

10-10 Is it possible to devise an algorithmic method to catch a player acting against the spirit of the game?

Appendix

A

Pseudo-code Conventions

We describe the algorithms using a pseudo-code format, which, for most parts, follows the guidelines set by Cormen *et al.* (2001) closely. The conventions are based on common data abstractions (e.g. sets, sequences, and graphs) and the control structures resemble Pascal programming language (Jensen *et al.* 1985). Since our aim is to unveil the algorithmic ideas behind the implementations, we present the algorithms using pseudo-code instead of an existing programming language. This choice is backed by the following reasons:

- Although common programming languages (e.g. C, C++, Java, and scripting languages) share similar control structures, their elementary data structures differ significantly both on interface level and language philosophy. For example, if an algorithm uses a data structure from STL of C++, a Java programmer has three alternatives: reformulate the code to use Java's collection library, write a custom-made data structure to serve the algorithm, or buy a suitable third-party library. Apart from the last option, programming effort is unavoidable, and by giving a general algorithmic description we do not limit the choices on how to proceed with the implementation.

- Software development should account for change management issues. For instance, sometimes understandability of a code segment is more important than its efficiency. Because of these underlying factors affecting software development, we content ourselves with conveying the idea as clearly as possible and leaving the implementation selections to the reader.

- The efficiency of a program depends on the properties of its input. Often, code optimizations favouring certain kinds of inputs lead to 'pessimization', which disfavours other kinds of inputs. In addition, optimizing a code that is not the bottleneck of the whole system wastes development time, because the number of code lines increases and they are also more difficult to test. Because of these two observations, we give only a general description of a method that can be moulded so that it suits the reader's situation best.

Algorithms and Networking for Computer Games   Jouni Smed and Harri Hakonen
© 2006 John Wiley & Sons, Ltd

- The implementation of an algorithm is connected to its software context not only through data representation but also through control flow. For example, time-consuming code segments are often responsible for reporting their status to a monitoring sub-system. This means that algorithms should be modifiable and easy to augment to respond to software integration forces, which tend to become more tedious when we are closer to the actual implementation language.

- Presenting the algorithms in pseudo-code has also a pedagogic rationale. There are two opposing views on how a new algorithm should be taught: First, the teacher describes the overall behaviour of the algorithm (i.e. its substructures and their relations), which often requires explanations in a natural language. Second, to guide on how to proceed with the implementation, the teacher describes the important details of the algorithm, which calls for a light formalism that can be easily converted to a programming code. The teacher's task is to find a balance between these two approaches. To support both approaches, the pseudo-code formalism with simple data and control abstractions allows the teacher to explain the topics in a natural language when necessary.

The pseudo-code notation tries to obey modern programming guidelines (e.g. avoiding global side effects). To clearly indicate what kind of an effect the algorithm has in the system, we have adopted the functional programming paradigm, where an algorithm is described as a function that does not mutate its actual parameters, and side effects are allowed only in the local structures within a function. For this reason, the algorithms are designed so that they are easy to understand – which sometimes means compromising on efficiency that could be achieved using the imperative programming paradigm (i.e. procedural programming with side effects). Nevertheless, immutability does not mean inefficiency but sometimes it is the key to manage object aliasing (Hakonen *et al.* 2000) or efficient concurrency (Hudak 1989). Immutability does not cause an extra effort in the implementation phase, because a functional description can be converted to a procedural one just by leaving out copy operations. The reader has the final choice on how to implement algorithms efficiently using the programming language of his or her preference.

Let us take an example of the pseudo-code notation. Assume that we are interested in changing a value so that some fraction α of the previous change also contributes to the outcome. In other words, we want to introduce inertia-like property to the change in the value of a variable. This can be implemented as linear momentum: If a change c affects a value v_t at time t, the outcome v_{t+1} is calculated using Equation (A.1).

$$v_{t+1} = v_t + c + \alpha(v_t - v_{t-1}) \iff \Delta v_{t+1} = c + \alpha \Delta v_t. \tag{A.1}$$

$\alpha \in [0, 1]$ is called a momentum coefficient and $\alpha \Delta v_t$ is a momentum term. To keep a record of the generated value, the history can be stored as a tail-growing sequence ⟨the first value, the second value, ..., the most recent value⟩. Algorithm A.1 describes this method as a function in the pseudo-code format.

If the use context of Algorithm A.1 assigns the returned sequence back to the argument variable, for example,

```
1: V ← LINEAR-MOMENTUM(V, c, α)
```

the copying in line 1 can be omitted by allowing a side effect to the sequence V.

Algorithm A.1 Updating a value with a change value and a momentum term.

LINEAR-MOMENTUM(V, c, α)

   in: sequence of n values $V = \langle V_0, V_1, \ldots, V_{n-1} \rangle$ $(2 \leq n)$; change c; momentum co-
          efficient α $(0 \leq \alpha \leq 1)$

  out: sequence of $n + 1$ values W where the first n values are identical to V and the
          last value is $W_n = W_{n-1} + c + \alpha(W_{n-1} - W_{n-2})$

 1: $W \leftarrow$ **copy** V $\triangleright$ Make a local copy from V.

 2: $W \leftarrow W \parallel \langle W_{n-1} + c + \alpha(W_{n-1} - W_{n-2}) \rangle$ $\triangleright$ Append a new value.

 3: **return** W $\triangleright$ Publish W as immutable.

Table A.1   Reserved words for algorithms.

all	div	error	not	repeat	while
and	do	for	of	return	xor
case	else	if	or	then	
copy	end	mod	others	until	

Let us take a closer look at the pseudo-code notation. As in any other formal programming language, we can combine primitive constants and operators to build up expressions,
control the execution flow with statements, and define a module as a routine. To do this,
the pseudo-code notation uses the reserved words listed in Table A.1.

Table A.2 lists the notational conventions used in the algorithm descriptions. The constants FALSE and TRUE denote the truth values, and value NIL is a placeholder for an entity
that is not yet known. The assignment operator $\leftarrow$ defines a statement that updates the structure on the left side by a value evaluated from the right side. Equality can be compared
using the operator $=$. To protect an object from side effects, it can be copied (or cloned) by
the prefix operator **copy**. In a formal sense, the trinity of assignment, equality, and copy
can be applied to the identity, shallow structure, or deep structure of an object. However, a
mixture of these structure levels is possible. Because the algorithms presented in this book

Table A.2   Algorithmic conventions.

Notation	Meaning
FALSE, TRUE	Boolean constants
NIL	Unique reference to non-existent objects
$x \leftarrow y$	Assignment
$x = y$	Comparison of equality
$x \leftarrow$ **copy** y	Copying of objects
$\triangleright$ Read me.	Comment
primitive(x)	Primitive routine for object x
HELLO-WORLD(x)	Algorithmic function call with parameter x
mathematical(x)	Mathematical function with parameter x

Table A.3 Mathematical functions.

Notation	Meaning
$\lfloor x \rfloor$	The largest integer n so that $n \leq x$
$\lceil x \rceil$	The smallest integer n so that $x \leq n$
$\log_b x$	Logarithm in base b
$\ln x$	Natural logarithm ($b = e \approx 2.71828$)
$\lg x$	Binary logarithm ($b = 2$)
$\max C$	Maximum of a collection; similarly for $\min C$
$\tan x$	Trigonometric tangent; similarly for $\sin x$ and $\cos x$
$\arctan \alpha$	Inverse of tangent; similarly for $\arcsin \alpha$ and $\arccos \alpha$

do not have relationships across their software interfaces (e.g. classes in object-oriented languages), we use these operations informally, and if there is a possibility of confusion, we elaborate on it in a comment.

At first sight, the difference between primitive routines and algorithmic functions can look happenstance, but a primitive routine can be likened to an attribute of an object or a trivial operation. For example, when operating with linearly orderable entities, we can define *predecessor*(e) and *successor*(e) for the predecessor and successor of e. The *successor*($\bullet$) – where $\bullet$ denotes a dummy variable – can be seen just as a function that extracts its result from the given argument. A primitive routine that indicates a status can also be seen as an attribute that changes – and can be changed – during the execution of an algorithm. For this reason, we can assign a value to a primitive routine. For example, to mark a town t as visited, we can define a primitive routine *visited*($\bullet$) to characterize this status, and then assign

1: *visited*(t) $\leftarrow$ TRUE

If towns are modelled as software objects, the primitive routine *visited*($\bullet$) can be implemented as a member variable with appropriate get and set functions.

Sometimes, the algorithms include functions originating from elementary mathematics. For example, we denote the sign of x with $\text{sgn}(x)$, which is defined in Equation (A.2).

$$\text{sgn}(x) = \begin{cases} -1, & \text{if } x < 0; \\ 0, & \text{if } x = 0; \\ 1, & \text{if } 0 < x. \end{cases} \qquad (A.2)$$

Table A.3 is a collection of the mathematical functions used throughout this book.

A.1 Changing the Flow of Control

The algorithms presented in this book run inside one control flow or thread. The complete control command of the pseudo-code is a *statement*, which is built from other simpler statements or sub-parts called *expressions*. When a statement is evaluated, it does not yield value but affects the current state of the system. In contrast, the evaluation of an expression produces a value but does not change the visible state of the system.

A.1.1 Expressions

Anything that yields a value after it is evaluated can be seen as an expression. The fundamental expressions are constants, variables, and primitive routines. An algorithm also represents an expression, because it returns a value.

To change, aggregate, and compare values, we need operators (see Table A.4) that can be used to build up more descriptive expressions. Although the pseudo-code operators originate mainly from mathematics, some of them are more related to computer calculations. For example, if we have two integers x and y, expression x **div** y equals the integer part of x/y so that the outcome is truncated towards $-\infty$. Operator **mod** produces the remainder of this division, which means that the Boolean expression $x = (x \textbf{ div } y) \cdot y + (x \textbf{ mod } y)$ is always true. It should be noted that some mathematical conventions are context sensitive. For example, for a value x, the operator $|x|$ denotes its absolute value, but for a set S, the operator $|S|$ means its cardinality (i.e. the number of its members). If the meaning of a notation is ambiguous, we clarify it with a comment.

The value of an arithmetic expression is stored to a variable or compared to another value as a Boolean expression. To construct expressions from truth values, we resort to mathematical logic. We use the logical operators listed in Table A.5 in the main text, and their algorithmic counterparts listed in Table A.6 in pseudo-codes. The conditional logical operators **and then** and **or else** differ in that that their evaluation, proceeding from left to right, is terminated immediately, when the result can be inferred. There are no reserved words for logical implication or equivalence, but, if necessary, they can be formed as $x \Rightarrow y \equiv \neg x \vee y$ and $x \Leftrightarrow y \equiv \neg(x \oplus y)$.

Table A.4   Arithmetic operators.

Notation	Meaning
$x + y$	Addition
$x - y$	Subtraction
x/y	Division ($y \neq 0$)
$x \cdot y$	Multiplication, also denoted as xy
n **div** m	Integer division
n **mod** m	Integer modulo

Table A.5   Logical operators in text.

Notation	Meaning
$\neg x$	Logical negation
$x \wedge y$	Logical and
$x \vee y$	Logical or
$x \oplus y$	Logical exclusive-or
$x \Rightarrow y$	Logical implication
$x \Leftrightarrow y$	Logical equivalence

Table A.6 Logical operators in algorithms.

Notation	Meaning
not x	Logical negation
x **and** y	Logical and
x **or** y	Logical or
x **xor** y	Logical exclusive-or
x **and then** y	Conditional logical and
x **or else** y	Conditional logical or

A.1.2 Control structures

Pseudo-code notations follow the widely accepted idea of structured programming, where the control flow is described using sequence, selection, and repetition structures (Dahl *et al.* 1972; Dijkstra 1968). However, we permit that this rule of 'single entry and single exit points of control' can be broken with an explicit return statement.

Sequence

A sequence of statements is indicated by writing the statements one after the other. If there is more than one statement in the line, the statements are separated by a semicolon (;). For example, swapping the values of variables x and y using a temporary variable t can be written as

1: $t \leftarrow x; x \leftarrow y; y \leftarrow t$

Line numbers are used only for reference purposes, and they do not imply any algorithmic structure.

Many programming languages include a compound structure that combines multiple statements into one. Because we do not scope the variables (e.g. define their lifetimes), this construct is expressed only implicitly: any statement can be replaced with a sequence of statements without stating it explicitly.

Selection

To describe a branch in the control flow, we have two selection structures. The first one, a **if–then–else** structure, proceeds according to the value of a Boolean expression: If the value is TRUE, the control flows to the **then** statements; otherwise, the control flows to the **else** statements. The **else** branch is optional.

```
1: if Boolean expression then
2:     statement₀                    ▷ Executed only for true case.
3: else
4:     statement₁                    ▷ Executed only for false case.
5: end if
```

The **case–of** construct defines a multi-selection that is based on the value of an arithmetic expression. To clearly indicate which control branch is executed, we require that the branches are labelled with disjoint, constant-like values. Unlike in some programming languages, the control does not flow from one branch to another. A label **others** can be used to indicate the branch 'any other value not mentioned'. If the selection expression returns a truth value, we prefer the **if–then–else** structure.

```
1: case expression of
2:    constant₀: statement₀                    ▷ Control branch for value constant₀.
3:    constant₁: statement₁
4:    ⋮
5:    others: default statement
6: end case
```

If none of the branching labels match with the expression, the control moves directly to the next statement following the **case–of** structure.

Repetition

To iterate statements, we introduce one definite loop structure and two indefinite loop structures. The definite loop is called **for–do** structure and it is used when the number of iteration cycles can be calculated before entering the loop body.

```
1: for iteration statement do
2:    statement
3: end for
```

The iteration statement has two variants. First, it can represent an enumeration by introducing a loop variable v that gets values sequentially from a given range $[f, t]$: $v \leftarrow f \ldots t$ (i.e. the initial value of v is f and the final value is t). Second, the iteration statement can represent a sequential member selection over a collection C: **all** $v \in C$. This loop variant bounds v once to each member of C in an unspecified order. To preserve clarity, C cannot be changed until the loop is finished.

As an example of the difference between these two **for** loops, let us find the maximum value from a sequence S of n values. We denote the ith member of S with S_i for $i \in [0, n-1]$. The most concrete algorithm for the problem is to define the order in which the sequence S is traversed:

```
1: c ← S₀
2: for i ← 1 … (n − 1) do
3:    if c < Sᵢ then c ← Sᵢ end if
4: end for
5: ▷ Value in c is the maximum of S.
```

If there is no need to restrict the way the algorithm can traverse S, the iteration statement of the loop can be formed as a member selection:

```
1: c ← some member in S
2: S′ ← S \ {c}
3: for all m ∈ S′ do
4:    if c < m then c ← m end if
5: end for
6: ▷ Value in c is the maximum of S.
```

Of course, finding a maximum from a linear structure is so trivial that we can express it using the mathematical convention $c \leftarrow \max S$.

To find out the position of a maximum value, we can use the primitive function $indices(S)$ that returns the set $\{0, 1, \ldots, |S| - 1\}$ of valid indices in S. The index set can be used for an iteration coordination:

1: $I \leftarrow indices(S)$
2: $c \leftarrow$ some member in I
3: $I' \leftarrow I \setminus \{c\}$
4: **for all** $i \in I'$ **do**
5:     **if** $S_c < S_i$ **then** $c \leftarrow i$ **end if**
6: **end for**
7: ▷ Value S_c is some maximum of S.

Using a mathematical notation, we express the same with $c \leftarrow \arg\max S$.

If we cannot determine a closed form equation for the number of loop cycles, it is preferable to use an indefinite loop structure instead. If it is possible that the loop body is not visited at all, we use the **while–do** structure. The loop exits when the control flow evaluates the Boolean expression to FALSE.

1: **while** *Boolean expression* **do**
2:     *statement*
3: **end while**

If the loop body is executed at least once, we use the **repeat–until** structure. The loop exits when the control flow evaluates the Boolean expression to TRUE.

1: **repeat**
2:     *statement*
3: **until** *Boolean expression*

Control shortcuts

As a general rule, the control structures with single entry and single exit points are easier to maintain than structures that use control shortcuts. For this reason, we use only two statement level mechanisms for breaking the control flow in the middle of an algorithm. Normally, an algorithm ends with a **return** statement that forwards the control back to the invoker of the algorithm possibly including a return value:

1: **return** *expression*

We permit multiple **return** statements to be placed at any pseudo-code line. When the control flow reaches a **return** statement, it exits the algorithm and forwards the evaluated value of the given expression immediately.

Another way to exit the algorithm is when an error has occurred and control flow cannot proceed normally:

1: **error** *description*

Because the algorithm cannot fulfil its operative contract with the invoker, the situation resembles exception handling, as is the way with many programming languages. The invoker can catch errors using a **case–of** structure:

1: $v \leftarrow$ AVERAGE(S)
2: **case** v **of**
3:    **error** empty: $v \leftarrow$ UNDEFINED   ▷ Unexpected situation: $|S| = 0$.
4: **end case**

A.2 Data Structures

Generality of the description of an algorithm follows from proper abstractions, which is why we have abstracted data structures to fundamental data collections such as sets, mappings, and graphs. For accessing data from these data collection, we use primitive routines and indexing abstractions.

A.2.1 Values and entities

The simplest datum is a value. Apart from the constants FALSE, TRUE, and NIL, we can define other literals for special purposes. A value is a result of an expression and can be stored to a variable. The values in the pseudo-code notation do not imply any particular implementation. For example, NIL can be realized using a null pointer, the integer value -1 or a sentinel object.

Values can be aggregated so that they form the attributes of an entity. These attributes can be accessed through primitive routines. For example, to define an entity e with physical attributes, we can attach primitive routines *location*(e), *size*(e) and *weight*(e) to it. Because an attribute concerns only the entity given as an argument, the attribute can also be assigned. For example, to make e weightless, we can assign *weight*$(e) \leftarrow 0$. If an entity is implemented as a software record or an object, the attributes are natural candidates for member variables and the respective get and set member functions.

A.2.2 Data collections

A collection imposes relationships between its entities. Instead of listing all the commonly used data structures, we take a minimalist approach and use only a few general collections. A collection has characteristic attributes and it provides query operations. Moreover, it can be modified if it is a local structure in an algorithm. The elements of a data structure must be initialized, and an element that has not been given a value cannot be evaluated.

Sets

The simplest collection of entities (or values) is a set. The members of a set are unique (i.e. they have different values) and they are not ordered in any way. Table A.7 lists the usual set operations.

The set of natural numbers is $\mathbb{N} = \{0, 1, 2, \ldots\}$, the set of integer numbers is $\mathbb{Z} = \{\ldots, -2, -1, 0, 1, 2, \ldots\}$, and the set of real numbers is $\mathbb{R}$. In a similar fashion, we can define the set $\mathbb{B} = \{0, 1\}$ for referring to binary numbers. We can now express, for example, a 32-bit word by denoting $w \in \mathbb{B}^{32}$, and refer to its ith bit as w_i.

We can also define a set by using an interval notation. For example, if it is clear from the context that a set contains integers, the interval $[0, 9]$ means the set $\{0, 1, \ldots, 9\}$. To

Table A.7   Notations for a set that are used in text and
in pseudo-code.

Notation	Meaning
$e \in S$	Boolean query: is e a member of S
$|S|$	Cardinality (i.e. the number of elements)
$\emptyset$	Empty set
$\{x\}$	Singleton set
$R \cup S$	Union set
$R \cap S$	Intersection set
$R \setminus S$	Difference set
$R \subset S$	Boolean query: is R a proper subset of S
$R \times S$	Cartesian product
S^d	Set $S \times S \times \cdots \times S$ of d-tuples
$\wp(S)$	Power set of S

indicate that an interval notation refers to real numbers, we can denote $[0, 9] \subset \mathbb{R}$. The
ends of the interval can be closed, marked with a bracket [or], or open, marked with a
parenthesis (or).

The cardinality of a set is its attribute. If the final size of a (locally defined) set is known
beforehand, we can emphasize it by stating

1: $|S| \leftarrow n$ ▷ Reserve space for n values.

This idiom does not have any effect in the algorithm; it is merely a hint for implementation.

Sequences

To impose a linear ordering to a collection of n elements we define a sequence as
$S = \langle e_0, e_1, \ldots, e_{n-1} \rangle$. Unlike a set, a sequence differentiates its elements with an index, and, thus, it can contain multiple identical elements. We refer to the elements with
subscripts. For example, the ith element of S is denoted S_i. The indexing begins from
zero – and not from one – and the last valid index is $|S| - 1$. The cardinality of a sequence
equals to its length (i.e. the number of elements in it). In addition to the notations presented
in Table A.8, we have a primitive routine *enumeration*(C), which gives to its argument
collection C some order in a form of a sequence. In other words, *enumeration*(C) returns
a sequence S that is initialized by the following pseudo-code:

1: $|S| \leftarrow |C|$ ▷ Reserve space for $|C|$ elements.
2: $i \leftarrow 0$
3: **for all** $e \in C$ **do**
4:     $S_i \leftarrow e$
5:     $i \leftarrow i + 1$
6: **end for**
7: ▷ Sequence S is initialized.

We can declare the length of a sequence S before it is initialized using a pseudo-code idiom
but – unlike with sets – the assignment affects the algorithm by defining a valid index range
for S.

Table A.8   Notations for a sequence that are used in text and in pseudo-code.

Notation	Meaning
$e \in S$	Boolean query: is e a member of S
$\lvert S \rvert$	Length
$indices(S)$	Set $\{0, 1, \ldots, \lvert S \rvert - 1\}$ of valid indices
S_i	The ith element; $i \in indices(S)$
$\langle\,\rangle$	Empty sequence
$R \parallel S$	Catenation sequence
$sub(S, i, n)$	Subsequence $\langle S_i, S_{i+1}, \ldots, S_{i+n-1} \rangle$; $0 \leq n \leq \lvert S \rvert - i$

1: $\lvert S \rvert \leftarrow n$ ▷ Reserve space for n values.

The context of use can impose restrictions on the sequence structure. A sequence S of n elements can act in many roles:

- If S contains only unique elements, it can be seen as an *ordered set*.

- If the utilization of S does not depend on the element order, S can represent a *multiset* (or bag). A multiset consists possibly multiple identical elements and does not give any order to them.

- If the length of S is constant (e.g. it is not changed by a catenation), S stands for an *n-tuple*. This viewpoint is emphasized if the elements are of the same 'type', or the tuple is a part of a definition of some relation set.

- If S includes sequences, it defines a *hierarchy*. For example, a nesting of sequences $S = \langle a, \langle b, \langle c, \langle d, \langle\,\rangle\rangle\rangle\rangle\rangle$ defines a list structure as recursive pairs $\langle datum, sublist \rangle$. The element d can be accessed with the expression $(((S_1)_1)_1)_0$.

- If a sequence is not stored to a variable but we use it at the left side of the assignment operator, the sequence becomes a *nameless record*. This can be interpreted as a multi-assignment operator with pattern matching. For example, to swap two values in variables x and y, we can write

    1: $\langle x, y \rangle \leftarrow \langle y, x \rangle$

This *unification* mechanism originates from the declarative programming paradigm. However, this kind of use of sequences is discouraged, because it can lead to infinite structures and illegible algorithms. Perhaps, the only viable use for this kind of interpretation is receiving multiple values from a function:

    1: $\langle r, \alpha \rangle \leftarrow$ As-Polar(x, y)
    2:       ▷ Variables r **and** α are assigned **and** can be used separately.

This does away with the need for introducing an extra receiver variable and referring to its elements.

Although a sequence is a one-dimensional structure, it can be extended to implement tables or multidimensional arrays. For example, a hierarchical sequence $T = \langle\langle a, 0\rangle, \langle b, 1\rangle, \langle c, 2\rangle\rangle$ represents a table of three rows and two columns. An element can be accessed through a proper selection of subsequences (e.g. the element c is at $(T_2)_0$). However, this row-major notation is tedious and it is cumbersome to refer to a whole column. Instead of raising one dimension over another, we can make them equally important by generalizing the one-dimensional indexing mechanism of the ordinary sequences.

Arrays

An array allows to index an element in two or more dimensions. An element in a two-dimensional array A is referred as $A_{i,j}$, where $i \in \{0, \ldots, rows(A) - 1\}$ and $j \in \{0, \ldots, columns(A) - 1\}$. A single row can be obtained with $row(A, i)$ and a column with $column(A, j)$. These row and column projections are ordinary sequences. For the sake of convenience, we let $A_{\langle i, j\rangle} = A_{i,j}$, which allows us to refer to an element using a sequence.

For a t-dimensional array $A_{i_0, i_1, \ldots i_{t-1}}$, the size of the array in the dimension d ($0 \le d \le t - 1$) is defined as $domain(A, d)$. Hence, for a two-dimensional array A, we have $rows(A) = domain(A, 0)$ and $columns(A) = domain(A, 1)$. An array $A_{i_0, i_1, \ldots i_{t-1}}$ is always rectangular: if we take any dimension d of A, value $domain(A, d)$ does not change for any valid indices $i_0, i_1, \ldots, i_{d-1}, i_{d+1}, \ldots, i_{t-2}, i_{t-1}$.

Mappings

A mapping is a data structure that behaves like a function (i.e. it associates a single result entity to a given argument entity). To distinguish mappings from primitive functions, algorithms, and mathematical functions, they are named with Greek letters. The definition also includes the domain and codomain of the mapping. For example, $\tau : [0, 7] \times [0, 3] \rightarrow \mathbb{B} \cup \{$ FALSE, TRUE $\}$ defines a two-dimensional function that can contain a mix of bits and truth values (e.g. $\tau(6, 0) = 1$ and $\tau(4, 2) = $ FALSE). It is worth noting that a sequence S that has elements from the set R can be seen as a mapping $S : [0, |S| - 1] \rightarrow R$. In other words, we denote $S : i \mapsto r$ simply with an access notation $S_i = r$. Similarly, arrays can be seen as multi-argument functions. However, the difference between $\tau(\bullet, \bullet)$ and an array with eight rows and four columns is that the function does not have to be rectangular.

Because a mapping is a data structure, it can be accessed and modified. A mapping $\mu(k) = v$ can be seen as an associative memory, where μ binds a search key k to the resulting value v. This association can be changed by assigning a new value to the key. This leads us to define the following three categories of functions: A function $\mu : K \rightarrow V$ is *undefined* if it does not has any associations, which means that it cannot be used. When μ is a local structure of an algorithm and its associations are under change, μ is *incomplete*. A function is *complete* after it is returned from an algorithm in which it was incomplete.

To define *partial functions*, we assume that NIL can act as a placeholder for any entity but cannot be declared into the codomain set explicitly. If mapping $\mu : K \rightarrow V$ is undefined, it can be made 'algorithmically' partial:

```
1: for all k ∈ K do
2:     μ(k) ← NIL
3: end for
```

Now, each search key is bound to NIL but not to any entity in the codomain V. The separation of undefined and partial functions allows us to have explicit control over incomplete functions: accessing an unbound search key implies fault in the algorithm, but we can refer to the members of the set $\{ k \mid k \in K \wedge \mu(k) = \text{NIL} \}$.

Mappings are useful when describing self-recursive structures. For example, if we have $V = \{a, b, c, d\}$, a cycle can be defined with a successor mapping $\sigma : V \rightarrow V$ so that $\sigma(a) = b$, $\sigma(b) = c$, $\sigma(c) = d$, and $\sigma(d) = a$.

Graphs

To describe discrete elements and their relationships, we use graphs. Graphs provide us with a rich terminology that can be used to clarify a vocabulary for problem and solution descriptions. Informally put, an *undirected graph* $G = (V, E)$ (or a graph for short) comprises a finite set of vertices V and a set of edges $E \subseteq V \times V$. A vertex is illustrated with a circle and an edge with a line segment. An edge $e = (u, v) \in E$ is undirected and it is considered identical to (v, u). An edge (v, v) is called a *loop*. The ends of an edge $e = (u, v) \in E$ are returned by the primitive routine $ends(e) = \{u, v\}$. If a vertex u is connected to another vertex v ($u \neq v$) by an edge, u is said to be *adjacent* to v. The set of adjacent vertices of a vertex v is called a *neighbourhood*, and it is returned by the routine $neighbourhood(v)$. A sequence $W = \langle e_0, e_1, \ldots, e_{n-1} \rangle$ is called a *walk* of length n if $e_i = (v_i, v_{i+1}) \in E$ for $i \in [0, n-1]$. If we are not interested in the intermediate edges of a walk but only in its starting vertex and ending vertex, we denote $v_0 \rightsquigarrow v_n$. If $v_0 = v_n$, the walk W is *closed*. The walk W is called a *path* if all of its vertices differ (i.e. $v_i \neq v_j$ when $i \neq j$) and it does not contain loops. A closed walk that is a path, except for $v_0 = v_n$, is a *cycle*. A graph without cycles is *acyclic*.

A *directed graph* (or digraph) changes the definition of the edge: An edge has a direction, which means that $(u, v) \neq (v, u)$ when $u \neq v$. In this case, an edge $e = (u, v)$ is illustrated with an arrow from u to v. Vertex v is the *head* and u is the *tail* of the edge, and we have routines $head(e)$ and $tail(e)$ to retrieve them. Naturally, $ends(e) = \{head(e)\} \cup \{tail(e)\}$. In a directed graph, the successors of vertex v are in a set returned by routine $successors(v)$, and if v has no successors, then $successors(v) = \emptyset$. Similarly, the predecessors of vertex v are given by $predecessors(v)$. The neighbourhood is the union of adjacent vertices: $neighbourhood(v) = successors(v) \cup predecessor(v)$. Because we allow loops, a vertex can be its own neighbour. The definition of the concepts *directed walk*, *directed path*, and *directed cycle* are similar to their respective definitions in the undirected graphs.

In a *weighted graph*, derived from an undirected or a directed graph, each edge has an associated weight given by a weight function $weight : E \rightarrow \mathbb{R}_+$. We let $weight(e)$ and $weight(u, v)$ to denote the weight of the edge $e = (u, v) \in E$.

A *tree* is an undirected graph in which each possible vertex pair u and v is connected with a unique path. In other words, the tree is acyclic and $|E| = |V| - 1$. A *forest* is a disjoint collection of trees. We are often interested in a *rooted tree*, where one vertex is called a *root*. We can call a vertex of a rooted tree as a *node*. The root can be used as a base for traversing the other nodes and the furthermost nodes from the root are *leaves*. The non-leaf nodes, the root included, are called *internal nodes*. The adjacent nodes of node n away from the root are called the *children* of node n, denoted by $children(n)$. The unique node in $neighbourhood(n) \setminus children(n)$ is called the *parent* of node n. If $parent(n) = \emptyset$, n is the root node.

A.3   Format of Algorithms

Algorithm A.2 is an example of an algorithm written using pseudo-code. The algorithm iteratively solves the Towers of Hanoi, and the solution can be generated with the following procedure:

TOWERS-OF-HANOI(n)
  in: number of discs n ($0 \le n$)
  out: sequence S of states from the initial state to final state

  1: $S \leftarrow \langle \text{INITIAL-STATE}(n) \rangle$
  2: **while** $turn(S) \ne 2^n - 1$ **do**
  3:    $S \leftarrow S \parallel \langle \text{NEXT-MOVE}(S) \rangle$
  4: **end while**
  5: **return** S

The details of how this algorithm works are left as an exercise for the interested reader. However, we encourage the casual reader to study the used notations and identify the conventions described in this appendix.

The *signature* of an algorithm includes the name of the algorithm and the arguments passed to it. It is followed by a *preamble*, which may include the following descriptions:

in: This section describes the call-by-value arguments passed to the algorithm. The most important preconditions concerning an argument are given in parenthesis. Because an algorithm behaves as a function from the caller's perspective, there is no need for preconditions about the state of the system. If the algorithm has multiple arguments, their descriptions are separated by a semicolon.

out: This section outlines the result passed to the caller of the algorithm. In most cases, it is sufficient to give the post-condition in a natural language. Because the algorithms are functions, each algorithm must include a description about its return values.

constant: If an algorithm refers to constant values or structures through a symbolic name, they are described in this section. The constraints are given in parentheses, and multiple constants are separated by a semicolon. The difference between an argument and a constant of an algorithm depends on the point of view, and the constants do not necessarily have to be implemented using programming language constants.

local: Changes are allowed only to the entities created inside the local scope of the algorithm. This section describes the most important local variables and structures.

The preamble of an algorithm is followed by enumerated lines of pseudo-code. The line numbering serves only for reference purposes and it does not impose any structure on the pseudo-code. For example, we can elaborate that line 3 of NEXT-MOVE in Algorithm A.2 can be implemented in $O(1)$ time by introducing an extra variable.

Algorithm A.2 An iterative solution to Towers of Hanoi.

INITIAL-STATE(n)

   in: number of discs n ($0 \le n$)

   out: triplet $S = \langle s_0, s_1, s_2 \rangle$ representing the initial state

  1: $s_0 \leftarrow \langle n, n-1, \ldots, 1 \rangle$; $s_1 \leftarrow s_2 \leftarrow \langle \, \rangle$

  2: $S \leftarrow \langle s_0, s_1, s_2 \rangle$ ▷ Start s_0, goal s_1, aid s_2.

  3: $turn(S) \leftarrow 0$

  4: $direction(S) \leftarrow 1$ ▷ Clockwise rotation.

  5: **if** n is even **then**   ▷ Counter-clockwise rotation.

  6:    $direction(S) \leftarrow -1$

  7: **end if**

  8: **return** S

NEXT-MOVE(S)

   in: triplet $S = \langle s_0, s_1, s_2 \rangle$ representing the current game state

   out: triplet $R = \langle r_0, r_1, r_2 \rangle$ representing the new game state

   local: pole indices $a, b, z \in \{0, 1, 2\}$; disc numbers $g, h \in [2, n]$; $last(Q) = Q_{|Q|-1}$, if

           $1 \le |Q|$, otherwise, $last(Q) = +\infty$

  1: $R \leftarrow$ **copy** S ▷ Now $r_i = s_i, 0 \le i \le 2$.

  2: $direction(R) \leftarrow direction(S)$

  3: $a \leftarrow$ the index of the pole where $1 \in r_a$

  4: $b \leftarrow (3 + a + direction(R))$ mod 3

  5: $z \leftarrow (3 + a - direction(R))$ mod 3

  6: **if** $turn(R)$ is even **then**   ▷ Move the smallest disc.

  7:    $r_b \leftarrow r_b \, \| \, \langle 1 \rangle$

  8:    $r_a \leftarrow sub(r_a, 0, |r_a| - 1)$

  9: **else**   ▷ Move the non-smallest disc.

10:    $g \leftarrow last(r_b)$ ▷ $+\infty$, if $|r_b| = 0$.

11:    $h \leftarrow last(r_z)$ ▷ $+\infty$, if $|r_z| = 0$.

12:    **if** $g < h$ **then**

13:       $r_z \leftarrow r_z \, \| \, \langle g \rangle$

14:       $r_b \leftarrow sub(r_b, 0, |r_b| - 1)$

15:    **else if** $h < g$ **then**

16:       $r_b \leftarrow r_b \, \| \, \langle h \rangle$

17:       $r_z \leftarrow sub(r_z, 0, |r_z| - 1)$

18:    **else**

19:       **error** already in the final state

20:    **end if**

21: **end if**

22: $turn(R) \leftarrow turn(S) + 1$

23: **return** R

A.4   Conversion to Existing Programming Languages

To concretize how an algorithm written in pseudo-code can be implemented with an existing programming language, let us consider the problem of converting a given Arabic number to the equivalent modern Roman number. Modern Roman numerals are the letters M (for the value 1000), D (500), C (100), L (50), X (10), V (5), and I (1). For example, $1989 = 1000 + (1000 - 100) + 50 + 3 \cdot 10 + (10 - 1)$ is written as MCMLXXXIX. Algorithm A.3 solves the conversion problem by returning a sequence R of multipliers of 'primitive' numbers in $P = \langle 1000, 900, 500, 400, 100, 90, 50, 40, 10, 9, 5, 4, 1 \rangle$. In our example, 1989 becomes $R = \langle 1, 1, 0, 0, 0, 0, 1, 0, 3, 1, 0, 0, 0 \rangle$.

Algorithm A.3 Conversion from an Arabic number to a modern Roman number.

ARABIC-TO-ROMAN(n)

    in: decimal number n $(0 \le n)$

    out: sequence $R = \langle s_0, s_1, \ldots, s_{12} \rangle$ representing the structure of the Roman num-
                 ber (R_i = number of primitives V_i in n for $i \in [0, 12]$)

    constant: sequence $P = \langle 1000, 900, 500, 400, 100, 90, 50, 40, 10, 9, 5, 4, 1 \rangle$ of primi-
                 tive Roman numbers

    local: remainder x to be converted $(0 \le x \le n)$; coefficient c for a primitive Roman
                 numbers (for other than P_0, $0 \le c \le 3$)

  1: $|R| \leftarrow |P|$ ▷ Reserve space for $|P| = 13$ values.

  2: $x \leftarrow n$

  3: **for** $i \leftarrow 0 \ldots (|P| - 1)$ **do**

  4:    $c \leftarrow x$ **div** P_i ▷ Number of multiplicands P_i in x.

  5:    $R_i \leftarrow c$

  6:    $x \leftarrow x - c \cdot P_i$

  7: **end for**

  8: **return** R

A Java programmer could implement Algorithm A.3 by first modelling the primitive numbers with the enumeration type `RomanNumeral`. Each **enum** constant (I, IV, ..., M) is declared with its decimal value, which can be accessed with the function `getValue()`.

```
public enum RomanNumeral {
    I(    1),
    IV(   4), V(    5), IX(   9), X(   10),
    XL( 40), L(   50), XC(  90), C(  100),
    CD(400), D(  500), CM(900), M(1000);

    private int value;
    private RomanNumber(int v) { value = v; }

    public int getValue() { return value; }
}
```

The actual conversion is implemented as a static function toRoman(**int**) in the class ArabicToRomanNumber. Note that the original algorithm has been modified as follows:

- The conversion returns a string instead of a sequence of integers. Because a Roman number does not include zeros, the for-loop at lines 3–7 is replaced by two nested while-loops. The inner loop takes care of possible repetitions of the same primitive number.

- The precondition is strengthened to $1 \leq n$.

- To emphasize that the values $4000 \leq n$ are cumbersome to express in Roman numerals, the post-condition gives an estimate of how long the result string will be.

The actual Java code looks like this:

```
public class ArabicToRomanNumber {
    /** Convert an Arabic number to a modern Roman number.
     *    @.pre   1 <= n
     *    @.post  result.length() <= (n div 1000) + (3 * 4)
     */
    public static String toRoman(int n) {
        RomanNumeral[] primitives = {
            RomanNumeral.M,   RomanNumeral.CM, RomanNumeral.D,
            RomanNumeral.CD, RomanNumeral.C,   RomanNumeral.XC,
            RomanNumeral.L,   RomanNumeral.XL, RomanNumeral.X,
            RomanNumeral.IX, RomanNumeral.V,   RomanNumeral.IV,
            RomanNumeral.I
        };
        int remainder = n;
        StringBuffer result = new StringBuffer();
        int i = 0;
        while ( remainder != 0 ) {
            while ( primitives[i].getValue() <= remainder ) {
                result.append(primitives[i]);
                remainder -= primitives[i].getValue();
            }
            ++i;
        }
        String res = result.toString();
        return res;
    }
}
```

A programmer more accustomed to the quirks of C programming language could implement Algorithm A.3 following the original form more closely. However, the primitive sequence P has a regular structure and it can be compressed to four values by introducing a scaling variable. To include a possibility for memory allocation optimizations, the caller must provide the storage buffer for the Roman number.

```c
#include <string.h>

/* Convert an Arabic number to a modern Roman number.
 * Pre:   (the length of buffer is at least 13) and (0 <= n).
 * Post:  (result == buffer) and (result[0..12] represents
 *        Roman number).
 */
int* arabicToRoman(int* buffer, int n) {
   memset(buffer, 0, 13 * sizeof(int));
   /* Here: For all i: buffer[i] == 0. */
   int conversions[] = { 1000, 900, 500, 400 };
   int divider = 1;
   int i = 0;
   int value;
   while ( n != 0 ) {
      value = conversions[i % 4] / divider;
      buffer[i] = n / value;
      n -= buffer[i] * value;
      ++i;
      if ( i % 4 == 0 ) divider *= 10;
      }
   return buffer;
   }
```

As we can see, the Java and C implementations include numerous language-specific details that can be omitted from the pseudo-code representation. When the syntax and semantics of C, C++, and Java seem as peculiar as Algol68, Cobol, and Fortran do today, descriptions resembling Algorithm A.3 are likely to remain understandable in the future too and can be re-implemented using the favourite programming language of that time.

Bibliography

Abramson B 1989 Control strategies for two-player games. *ACM Computing Surveys* **21**(2), 137–161.

Albers S and Mitzenmacher M 1998 Average case analyses of list update algorithms, with applications to data compression. *Algorithmica* **21**(3), 312–329.

Aldous D and Diaconis P 1986 Shuffling cards and stopping times. *American Mathematical Monthly* **93**(5), 333–348.

Alexander T 2002 GoCap: Game observation capture. In *AI Game Programming Wisdom* (ed. Rabin S), pp. 579–589. Charles River Media, Hingham, MA, USA.

Aylett R and Louchart S 2003 Towards a narrative theory of virtual reality. *Virtual Reality* **7**(1), 2–9.

Bachrach R and El-Yaniv R 1997 Online list accessing algorithms and their applications: Recent empirical evidence. *Proceedings of the 8th Annual ACM-SIAM Symposium on Discrete Algorithms (SODA'97)*, pp. 53–62. Society for Industrial and Applied Mathematics, Philadelphia, PA, USA.

Ballard BW 1983 The *-minimax search procedure for trees containing chance nodes. *Artificial Intelligence* **21**(3), 327–350.

Bartle R 1990 Interactive multi-user computer games. Technical report, British Telecom. ⟨http://www.mud.co.uk/richard/imucg.htm⟩.

Baughman NE and Levine BN 2001 Cheat-proof playout for centralized and distributed online games. *Proceedings of the Twentieth IEEE Computer and Communication Society INFOCOM Conference*, Anchorage, AK, USA.

Bayer D and Diaconis P 1992 Trailing the dovetail shuffle to its lair. *Annals of Applied Probability* **2**(2), 294–313.

Bellman RE and Zadeh LA 1970 Decision-making in a fuzzy environment. *Management Science* **17**(4), 141–164.

Benford S, Bowers J, Fahlén LE, Mariani J and Rodden T 1994 Supporting cooperative work in virtual environments. *Computer Journal* **37**(8), 653–668.

Benford S, Greenhalgh C, Reynard G, Brown C and Koleva B 1998 Understanding and constructing shared spaces with mixed-reality boundaries. *ACM Transactions on Computer-Human Interaction* **5**(3), 185–223.

Benford S, Greenhalgh C, Rodden T and Pycock J 2001 Collaborative virtual environments. *Communications of the ACM* **44**(7), 79–85.

Berglund EJ and Cheriton DR 1985 Amaze: A multiplayer computer game. *IEEE Software* **2**(3), 30–39.

Bettner P and Terrano M 2001 1500 archers on a 28.8: Network programming in Age of Empires and beyond. *Gamasutra*. ⟨http://www.gamasutra.com/features/20010322/terrano_01.htm⟩.

Box GEP and Muller ME 1958 A note on the generation of random normal deviates. *The Annals of Mathematical Statistics* **29**(2), 610–611.

Bratley P, Fox BL and Schrage LE 1983 *A Guide to Simulation*. Springer-Verlag, New York, USA.

Bringsjord S 2001 Is it possible to build dramatically compelling interactive digital entertainment? *Game Studies* **1**(1). ⟨http://www.gamestudies.org/0101/bringsjord/⟩.

Buschmann F, Meunier R, Rohnert H, Sommerland P and Stal M 1996 *Pattern-Oriented Software Architecture: A System of Patterns*, vol. 1 of *Software Design Patterns*. John Wiley & Sons, West Sussex, UK.

Cai W, Lee FBS and Chen L 1999 An auto-adaptive dead reckoning algorithm for distributed interactive simulation. *Proceedings of the Thirteenth Workshop on Parallel and Distributed Simulation*, pp. 82–89, Atlanta, GA, USA.

Castronova E 2001 Virtual worlds: A first-hand account of market and society on the cyberian frontier. CESifo Working Paper Series No. 618. ⟨http://ssrn.com/abstract=294828⟩.

Chang YI 1996 A simulation study on distributed mutual exclusion. *Journal of Parallel and Distributed Computing* **33**(2), 107–121.

Charles F, Mead SJ and Cavazza M 2002 Generating dynamic storylines through characters' interactions. *International Journal of Intelligent Games & Simulation* **1**(1), 5–11.

Chazelle B 1991 Triangulating a simple polygon in linear time. *Discrete & Computational Geometry* **6**(5), 485–524.

Cormen TH, Leiserson CE, Rivest RL and Stein C 2001 *Introduction to Algorithms*, second edn. MIT Press, Cambridge, MA, USA.

Costikyan G 2002 I have no words & I must design: Toward a critical vocabulary for games. In *Computer Games and Digital Cultures Conference Proceedings* (ed. Mäyrä F), pp. 9–33, Tampere University Press, Tampere, Finland.

Crawford C 1984 *The Art of Computer Game Design*. Osborne/McGraw-Hill, Berkeley, CA, USA. ⟨http://www.vancouver.wsu.edu/fac/peabody/game-book/Coverpage.html⟩.

Cronin E, Filstrup B and Jamin S 2003 Cheat-proofing dead reckoned multiplayer games. In *Proceedings of the 2nd International Conference on Application and Development of Computer Games* (eds. Sing LW, Man WH and Wai W), pp. 23–29. Hong Kong SAR, China.

Dahl OJ, Dijkstra EW and Hoare CAR 1972 Structured Programming, number 8 in *A.P.I.C. Studies in Data Processing*. Academic Press, London, UK.

Defense Advanced Research Projects Agency 1981 Internet protocol Internet RFC 791. ⟨http://www.faqs.org/rfcs/rfc791.html⟩.

Dewdney AK 1984 Computer recreations: In the game called Core War hostile programs engage in a battle of bits. *Scientific American* **250**(5), 14–22.

Dijkstra EW 1968 Letters to the editor: Go to statement considered harmful. *Communications of the ACM* **11**(3), 147–148.

Diot C and Gautier L 1999 A distributed architecture for multiplayer interactive applications on the Internet. *IEEE Networks Magazine* **13**(4), 6–15.

Dubois D, Fargier H and Prade H 1996 Possibility theory in constraint satisfaction problems: Handling priority, preference and uncertainty. *Applied Intelligence* **6**, 287–309.

Dybsand E 2004 GDC 2004 AI Roundtables Moderator Report. ⟨http://www.gameai.com/cgdc04notes.dybsand.html⟩.

Encyclopædia Britannica 2005 Game Encyclopædia Britannica Online. ⟨http://search.eb.com/eb/article-9035963⟩.

Entacher K 1999 Parallel streams of linear random numbers in the spectral test. *ACM Transactions on Modeling and Computer Simulation* **9**(1), 31–44.

Evans R 2002 Varieties of learning. In *AI Game Programming Wisdom* (ed. Rabin S), pp. 567–578. Charles River Media Hingham, MA, USA.

Fairclough C and Cunningham P 2002 An interactive story engine. In *Proceedings of the 13th Irish International Conference on Artificial Intelligence and Cognitive Science* (eds. O'Neill M, Sutcliffe RFE, Ryan C, Eaton M and Griffith NJL), vol. 2464 of *Lecture Notes in Artificial Intelligence*, pp. 171–176. Springer-Verlag, Limerick, Ireland.

Federation Internationale de Football Association 2003 Laws of the Game. ⟨http://www.fifa.com/ref/laws_E.html⟩.

Finkel RA and Fishburn JP 1982 Parallelism in alpha-beta search. *Artificial Intelligence* **19**(1), 89–106.

Fishburn JP 1983 Another optimization of alpha-beta search. *ACM SIGART Bulletin* **84**, 37–38.

Fournier A, Fussell D and Carpenter L 1982 Computer rendering of stochastic models. *Communications of the ACM* **26**(6), 371–384.

Frécon E and Stenius M 1998 DIVE: A scaleable network architecture for distributed virtual environments. *Distributed Systems Engineering* **5**(3), 91–100.

Freeman JA and Skapura DM 1991 *Neural Networks: Algorithms, Applications, and Programming Techniques*. Addison-Wesley, Redwood City, CA, USA.

Fullér R and Carlsson C 1996 Fuzzy multiple criteria decision making: Recent developments. *Fuzzy Sets and Systems* **78**, 139–153.

Game Developers' Association of Australia 2003 Game Industry Fact Sheet. ⟨http://www.gdaa.asn.au/about/gdaaindustryfactsheetoct2003.pdf⟩.

Gamma E, Helm R, Johnson R and Vlissides J 1995 *Design Patterns: Elements of Reusable Object-Oriented Software*, Addison-Wesley Professional Computing Series. Addison-Wesley, Reading, MA, USA.

Glover F 1989 Tabu search–part I. *ORSA Journal of Computing* **1**(3), 190–206.

Goldberg DE 1989 *Genetic Algorithms in Search, Optimization and Machine Learning*. Addison-Wesley, Reading, MA, USA.

Graetz JM 1981 The origin of Spacewar. *Creative Computing* pp. 56–67. ⟨http://www.wheels.org/spacewar/creative/SpacewarOrigin.html⟩.

Greenhalgh C 1998 Awareness-based communication management in the MASSIVE systems. *Distributed Systems Engineering* **5**(3), 129–137.

Guesgen HW 1994 A formal framework for weak constraint satisfaction based on fuzzy sets. *Proceedings of ANZIIS-94*, pp. 199–203, Brisbane, Australia.

Gustafson JL 1988 Reevaluating Amdahl's law. *Communications of the ACM* **31**(5), 532–533.

Hakonen H, Leppänen V and Salakoski T 2000 Object integrity while allowing aliasing. In *Proceedings of Conference on Software: Theory and Practice* (eds. Feng Y, Notkin D and Gaudel MC), pp. 91–96, 16th IFIP WCC2000, Publishing House of Electronics Industry, Beijing, China.

Harel D 1987 *Algorithmics: The Spirit of Computing*. Addison-Wesley, Wokingham, UK.

Hauk T, Buro M and Schaeffer J 2005 Rediscovering *-minimax search. *Proceedings of the Fourth International Conference on Computers and Games*, Forthcoming in *Lecture Notes in Computer Science*. Springer-Verlag.

Hellekalek P 1998 Good random number generators are (not so) easy to find. *Mathematics and Computers in Simulation* **46**(5–6), 485–505.

Herrera F and Verdegay JL 1997 Fuzzy sets and operations research. Perspectives. *Fuzzy Sets and Systems* **90**, 207–218.

Hertel S and Mehlhorn K 1985 Fast triangulation of the plane with respect to simple polygons. *Information and Control* **64**(1–3), 52–76.

Higgins D 2002 Pathfinding design architecture. In *AI Game Programming Wisdom* (ed. Rabin S), pp. 122–132. Charles River Media, Hingham, MA, USA,

Hudak P 1989 Conception, evolution, and application of functional programming languages. *ACM Computing Surveys* **21**(3), 359–411.

Huizinga J 1955 *Homo Ludens: A Study of the Play-Element in Culture*. The Beacon Press, Boston, MA, USA.

Intel Platform Security Division 1999 *Intel Random Number Generator*. Intel Corporation.

International Game Developers Association 2003 IGDA Curriculum Framework: The Study of Games and Game Development. ⟨http://www.igda.org/academia/IGDA_Curriculum_Framework_Feb03.pdf⟩.

International Game Developers Association 2004 Foundations of Interactive Storytelling. ⟨http://www.igda.org/writing/InteractiveStorytelling.htm⟩.

Jensen K, Wirth N, Mickel AB and Miner JF 1985 *Pascal–User Manual and Report*, third edn. Springer-Verlag, New York, NY, USA.

Johansson U, Sönströd C and König R 2003 Cheating by sharing information – the doom of online poker? In *Proceedings of the 2nd International Conference on Application and Development of Computer Games* (eds. Sing LW, Man WH and Wai W), pp. 16–22. Hong Kong SAR, China.

Johnson G 2003 Avoiding dynamic obstacles and hazards. In *AI Game Programming Wisdom 2* (ed. Rabin S), pp. 161–170. Charles River Media, Hingham, MA, USA.

Kaukoranta T, Smed J and Hakonen H 2003 Understanding pattern recognition methods. In *AI Game Programming Wisdom 2* (ed. Rabin S), pp. 579–589. Charles River Media, Hingham, MA, USA.

Keil JM 1985 Decomposing a polygon into simpler components. *SIAM Journal on Computing* **14**(4), 799–817.

Kelley AD, Malin MC and Nielson GM 1988 Terrain simulation using a model of stream erosion. *Computer Graphics* **22**(4), 263–268.

Kennedy J, Eberhart RC and Shi Y 2001 *Swarm Intelligence*. Morgan Kaufmann, San Francisco, CA, USA.

Kimppa KK and Bissett A 2005 Is cheating in network computer games a question worth raising? In *Ethics of New Information Technology: Proceedings of the Sixth International Conference of Computer Ethics* (eds. Brey P, Grodzinsky F and Introna L), pp. 261–267. Center for Telematics and Information Technology (CTIT), Enschede, The Netherlands.

Kirkpatrick S, Gelatt CD and Vecchi MP 1983 Optimization by simulated annealing. *Science* **220**(4598), 671–680.

Kirmse A 2000 A network protocol for online games. In *Game Programming Gems* (ed. DeLoura M), pp. 104–108. Charles River Media, Hingham, MA, USA.

Kirmse A and Kirmse C 1997 Security in online games. *Game Developer* **4**(4), 20–28.

Knuth DE 1998a *Fundamental Algorithms*, vol. 1 of *The Art of Computer Programming*, third edn. Addison-Wesley, Reading, MA, USA.

Knuth DE 1998b *Seminumerical Algorithms*, vol. 2 of *The Art of Computer Programming*, third edn. Addison-Wesley, Reading, MA, USA.

Knuth DE 1998c *Sorting and Searching*, vol. 3 of *The Art of Computer Programming*, second edn. Addison-Wesley, Reading, MA, USA.

Knuth DE 2005 *Combinatorial Algorithms: Graph and Network Algorithms*, vol. 4B of *The Art of Computer Programming*. Pre-fascicle. ⟨http://www-cs-faculty.stanford.edu/~knuth/taocp.html⟩.

Knuth DE and Moore RW 1975 An analysis of alpha-beta pruning. *Artificial Intelligence* **6**(4), 293–326.

Kohonen T 1995 *Self-Organizing Maps*. Springer-Verlag, Berlin, Germany.

Krasner GE and Pope ST 1988 A cookbook for using the model-view-controller user interface paradigm in Smalltalk-80. *Journal of Object-Oriented Programming* **1**(3), 26–49.

Kronmal RA and Peterson AV 1979 The alias and alias-rejection-mixture methods for generating random variables from probability distributions. *Proceedings of the 11th Conference on Winter Simulation (WSC'79)*, vol. 1, pp. 269–280. IEEE Press, Piscataway, NJ, USA.

Lamport L and Lynch N 1990 Distributed computing: Models and methods. In *Handbook of Theoretical Computer Science* (ed. van Leeuwen J), vol. B: *Formal Models and Semantics*, pp. 1157–1199. Elsevier, Amsterdam, The Netherlands.

Lecky-Thompson GW 1999 Algorithms for infinite universe. *Gamasutra*. ⟨http://www.gamasutra. com/features/19990917/infinite_01.htm⟩.

L'Ecuyer P 1988 Efficient and portable combined random number generators. *Communications of the ACM* **31**(6), 742–749,774.

L'Ecuyer P 1999 Tables of linear congruential generators of different sizes and good lattice structure. *Mathematics of Computation* **68**(225), 249–260.

L'Ecuyer P, Blouin F and Couture R 1993 A search for good multiple recursive random number generators. *ACM Transactions on Modeling and Computer Simulation* **3**(2), 87–98.

L'Ecuyer P and Côté S 1991 Implementing a random number package with splitting facilities. *ACM Transactions on Mathematical Software* **17**(1), 98–111.

Lee H, Kozlowski E, Lenker S and Jamin S 2002 Multiplayer game cheating prevention with pipelined lockstep protocol. In *Entertainment Computing: Technologies and Applications, IFIP First International Workshop on Entertainment Computing* (eds. Nakatsu R and Hoshino J), pp. 31–39. Kluwer, Makuhari, Japan.

Lewis JP 1987 Generalized stochastic subdivision. *ACM Transactions on Graphics* **6**(3), 167–190.

Lewis PA, Goodman AS and Miller JM 1969 A pseudo-random number generator for the System/360. *IBM Systems Journal* **8**(2), 136–146.

Lindley CA and Eladhari M 2002 Causal normalization: A methodology for coherent story logic design in computer role-playing games. In *Proceedings of the Third International Conference on Computers and Games* (eds. Schaeffer J, Müller M and Björnsson Y), vol. 2883 of *Lecture Notes in Computer Science*, pp. 292–307. Springer-Verlag, Edmonton, Canada.

Mackenzie D 2002 The mathematics of... shuffling: The Stanford flip. *Discover* **23**(10), 22–23. ⟨http://www.discover.com/oct_02/featmath.html⟩.

Marsland TA and Campbell M 1982 Parallel search of strongly ordered game trees. *ACM Computing Surveys* **14**(4), 533–551.

Matias Y, Vitter JS and Ni WC 1993 Dynamic generation of discrete random variates. *Proceedings of the 4th Annual ACM-SIAM Symposium on Discrete Algorithms (SODA'93)*, pp. 361–370. Society for Industrial and Applied Mathematics, Philadelphia, PA, USA.

McLeod AI 1985 Remark AS R58: A remark on algorithm AS 183. An efficient and portable pseudo-random number generator. *Applied Statistics* **34**(2), 198–200.

Meyer B 1997 *Object-Oriented Software Construction*, second edn. Prentice Hall, Upper Saddle River, NJ, USA.

Michie D 1966 Game-playing and game-learning automata. In *Advances in Programming and Non-Numerical Computation* (ed. Fox L), pp. 183–200. Pergamon Press, Oxford, UK.

Miller GSP 1986 The definition and rendering of terrain maps. *Computer Graphics* **20**(4), 39–48.

Morse KL, Bic L and Dillencourt M 2000 Interest management in large-scale virtual environments. *Presence* **9**(1), 52–68.

Murdoch SJ and Zieliński P 2004 Covert channels for collusion in online computer games. In *Information Hiding: 6th International Workshop* (ed. Fridrich J), vol. 3200 of *Lecture Notes in Computer Science*, pp. 355–369. Springer-Verlag, Toronto, Canada.

Neyland DL 1997 *Virtual Combat: A Guide to Distributed Interactive Simulation*. Stackpole Books, Mechanicsburg, PA, USA.

Object Management Group 2005 *Unified Modeling Language: Superstructure, Version 2.0.* Formal/05-07-04. ⟨http://www.uml.org⟩.

Park KS and Kenyon RV 1999 Effects of network characteristics on human performance in a collaborative virtual environment. *Proceedings of IEEE International Conference on Virtual Reality*, Houston, TX, USA.

Park SK and Miller KW 1988 Random number generators: Good ones are hard to find. *Communications of the ACM* **31**(10), 1192–1201.

Patel AJ 2003 Amit's thoughts on Path-Finding. ⟨http://theory.stanford.edu/~amitp/GameProgramming/⟩.

Pearl J 1986 Fusion, propagation, and structuring in belief networks. *Artificial Intelligence* **29**(3), 241–364.

Peinado F and Gervás P 2004 Transferring game mastering laws to interactive digital storytelling. In *Technologies for Interactive Digital Storytelling and Entertainment* (eds. Göbel S, Spierling U, Hoffman A, Iurgel I, Schneider O, Dechau J and Feix A), vol. 3105 of *Lecture Notes in Computer Science*, pp. 48–54. Springer-Verlag, Darmstadt, Germany.

Perlin K 1985 An image synthesizer. *Computer Graphics* **19**(3), 287–296.

Pottinger DC 2000 Terrain analysis in realtime strategy games. *2000 Game Developer Conference Proceedings*, San Jose, CA, USA. ⟨http://www.gdconf.com/archives/2000/pottinger.doc⟩.

Pritchard M 2000 How to hurt hackers: The scoop on Internet cheating and how you can combat it. *Gamasutra*. ⟨http://www.gamasutra.com/features/20000724/pritchard_01.htm⟩.

Propp V 1968 *Morphology of the Folktale*. University of Texas Press, Austin, TX, USA.

Rabiner LR and Juang BH 1986 An introduction to hidden Markov models. *IEEE Acoustics, Speech, and Signal Processing Magazine* **3**(1), 4–16.

Reynolds CW 1987 Flocks, herds, and schools: A distributed behavioral model. *Computer Graphics* **21**(4), 25–34.

Rivest R 1992 The MD5 Message Digest Algorithm Internet RFC 1321. ⟨http://theory.lcs.mit.edu/~rivest/Rivest-MD5.txt⟩.

Ryan MD and Sharkey PM 1999 The causal surface and its effect on distribution transparency in a distributed virtual environment. *Proceedings of IEEE International Conference on Systems, Man, and Cybernetics*, vol. 6, pp. 75–80, Tokyo, Japan.

Salen K and Zimmerman E 2004 *Rules of Play: Game Design Fundamentals*. MIT Press, Cambridge, MA, USA.

Samuel AL 1959 Some studies in machine learning using the game of checkers. *IBM Journal of Research and Development* **3**(3), 210–229. Reprinted in *IBM Journal of Research and Development* **44**(1/2), 206–226, 2000.

Samuel AL 1967 Some studies in machine learning using the game of checkers. II–recent progress. *IBM Journal of Research and Development* **11**(6), 601–617.

Sanderson D 1999 Online justice systems. *Game Developer* **6**(4), 42–49.

Schmidt D, Stal M, Rohnert H and Buschmann F 2000 *Pattern-Oriented Software Architecture: Patterns for Concurrent and Networked Objects* vol. 2 of *Software Design Patterns*. John Wiley & Sons, West Sussex, UK.

Sedgewick R 1977 Permutation generation methods. *Computing Surveys* **9**(2), 137–164.

Seidel R 1991 A simple and fast incremental randomized algorithms for computing trapezoidal decompositions and for triangulating polygons. *Computational Geometry* **1**(1), 51–64.

Shafer G 1990 Perspectives on the theory and practice of belief functions. *International Journal of Approximate Reasoning* **4**(5–6), 323–362.

Sharkey PM, Ryan MD and Roberts DJ 1998 A local perception filter for distributed virtual environments. *Proceedings of IEEE Virtual Reality Annual International Symposium*, pp. 242–249, Atlanta, GA, USA.

Shirmohammadi S and Georganas ND 2001 An end-to-end communication architecture for collaborative virtual environments. *Computer Networks* **35**(2–3), 351–367.

Siira A 2004 *Automatic commentators*, Master's thesis, University of Turku, Department of Information Technology, Turku, Finland.

Singhal SK 1996 *Effective Remote Modeling in Large-Scale Distributed Simulation and Visualization Environments*, PhD thesis, Standford University, Standford, CA, USA.

Singhal SK and Zyda MJ 1999 *Networked Virtual Environments: Design and Implementation*. Addison Wesley, Reading, MA, USA.

Slany W 1994 *Fuzzy Scheduling*, PhD thesis, Technische Universität Wien, Vienna, Austria. CD-Technical Report 94/66.

Slany W 1995 Comparing partial constraint satisfaction models. *Workshop Notes of the CP'95 Workshop on Over-Constraint Systems*, pp. 151–159, Cassis, France.

Smed J and Hakonen H 2003 Towards a definition of a computer game. Technical Report 553, Turku Centre for Computer Science, Turku, Finland.

Smed J and Hakonen H 2005a Preventing look-ahead cheating with active objects. *Proceedings of the Fourth International Conference on Computers and Games*, Forthcoming in *Lecture Notes in Computer Science*. Springer-Verlag.

Smed J and Hakonen H 2005b Synthetic players: A quest for artificial intelligence in computer games. *Human IT* **7**(3), 57–77.

Smed J, Kaukoranta T and Hakonen H 2002 Aspects of networking in multiplayer computer games. *The Electronic Library* **20**(2), 87–97.

Smed J, Kaukoranta T and Hakonen H 2003 Networking and multiplayer computer games–the story so far. *International Journal of Intelligent Games & Simulation* **2**(2), 101–110.

Smed J, Niinisalo H and Hakonen H 2005 Realizing the bullet time effect in multiplayer games with local perception filters. *Computer Networks* **49**(1), 27–37.

Snook G 2000 Simplified 3D movement and pathfinding using navigation meshes. In *Game Programming Gems* (ed. DeLoura M), pp. 288–304. Charles River Media, Hingham, MA, USA.

Spierling U 2002 Editorial: Digital storytelling. *Computers & Graphics* **26**(1), 1–2.

Spierling U, Grasbon D, Braun N and Iurgel I 2002 Setting the scene: Playing digital director in interactive storytelling and creation. *Computers & Graphics* **26**(1), 31–44.

Street G, Petersen S and Kidd M 2001 How to balance a real time strategy game: Lessons from the Age of Empires series. ⟨http://www.gdconf.com/archives/2001/gstreetprintable3.ppt⟩.

Tozour P 2003 Search space representations. In *AI Game Programming Wisdom 2* (ed. Rabin S), pp. 85–102. Charles River Media, Hingham, MA, USA.

van der Sterren W 2003 Path look-up tables–small is beautiful. In *AI Game Programming Wisdom 2* (ed. Rabin S), pp. 115–129. Charles River Media, Hingham, MA, USA.

Verna D, Fabre Y and Pitel G 2000 Urbi et Orbi: Unusual design and implementation choices for distributed virtual environments. In *VSMM 2000: Sixth International Conference on Virtual Systems and Multimedia* (ed. Thwaites H), pp. 714–724. IOS Press, Amsterdam, The Netherlands, Gifu, Japan.

Wang X and Yu H 2005 How to break MD5 and other hash functions. In *Advances in Cryptology–EUROCRYPT 2005: 24th Annual International Conference on the Theory and Applications of Cryptographic Techniques* (ed. Cramer R), vol. 3494 of *Lecture Notes in Artificial Intelligence*, pp. 19–25. Springer-Verlag, Aarhus, Denmark.

Watt A 2000 *3D Computer Graphics*, third edn. Addison-Wesley, Harlow, UK.

Wichmann BA and Hill ID 1982 Algorithm AS 183: An efficient and portable pseudo-random number generator. *Applied Statistics* **31**(2), 188–190. See also McLeod (1985); Wichmann and Hill (1984); Zeisel (1986).

Wichmann BA and Hill ID 1984 Correction: Algorithm AS 183: An efficient and portable pseudo-random number generator. *Applied Statistics* **33**(1), 123.

Witten IH, Moffat A and Bell TC 1999 *Managing Gigabytes: Compressing and Indexing Documents and Images*, second edn. Morgan Kaufmann, San Francisco, CA, USA.

Woodcock S 2002 Recognizing strategic dispositions: Engaging the enemy. In *AI Game Programming Wisdom* (ed. Rabin S), pp. 221–232. Charles River Media, Hingham, MA, USA..

Wu J and Sheng L 2001 An efficient sorting algorithm for a sequence of kings in a tournament. *Information Processing Letters* **79**(6), 297–299.

Yager RR 1981 A new methodology for ordinal multiobjective decisions based on fuzzy sets. *Decision Sciences* **12**, 589–600.

Yager RR 1988 On ordered weighted averaging aggregation operators in multicriteria decision making. *IEEE Transactions on Systems, Man, and Cybernetics* **18**(1), 183–190.

Yager RR and Filev DP 1994 *Essentials of Fuzzy Modeling and Control*. John Wiley & Sons, New York, NY, USA.

Yan J 2003 Security design in online games. *Proceedings of the 19th Annual Computer Security Applications Conference (ACSAC'03)*, pp. 286–297, Las Vegas, NV, USA.

Yan JJ and Choi HJ 2002 Security issues in online games. *The Electronic Library* **20**(2), 125–133.

Yob G 1975 Hunt the Wumpus. *Creative Computing* **1**(5), 51–54. ⟨http://atariarchives.planetmirror. com/ bcc1/showpage.php?page=247⟩.

Yu SJ and Choy YC 2001 A dynamic message filtering technique for 3D cyberspaces. *Computer Communications* **24**(18), 1745–1758.

Zadeh LA 1965 Fuzzy sets. *Information and Control* **8**(3), 338–353.

Zeisel H 1986 Remark ASR61: A remark on algorithm AS 183. An efficient and portable pseudo-random number generator. *Applied Statistics* **35**(1), 89.

Zobrist AL 1969 A model of visual organization for the game of Go. *Proceedings of AFIPS Spring Joint Computer Conference*, pp. 103–112, Boston, MA, USA.

Ludography

Atari, *Pong*. Atari, 1972.

Berglund EJ and Cheriton DR, *Amaze*. 1985.

Bioware, *Neverwinter Nights*. Infogrames, 2002.

Blizzard North, *Diablo II*. Blizzard Entertainment, 2000.

Braben D and Bell I, *Elite*. Firebird, 1984.

Bungie Software, *Halo: Combat Evolved*. Microsoft Games, 2003.

DevTeam, *NetHack 3.4.3*. ⟨http://www.nethack.org/⟩, 2005.

Dewdney AK, *Core War*. 1984.

DMA Design, *Grand Theft Auto III*. Rockstar Games, 2001.

Ensemble Studios, *Age of Empires II: The Age of Kings*. Microsoft Games, 1999.

Epyx, *Pitstop II*. U.S. Gold, 1984.

Frontier Developments, *Frontier: Elite II*. Gametek, 1993.

Graetz JM, Russell SR and Witanen W, *Spacewar!*. 1962.

id Software, *Doom*. id Software, 1993.

id Software, *Quake*. id Software, 1996.

Lionhead Studios, *Black & White*. Electronic Arts, 2001.

Maxis, *The Sims*. Electronic Arts, 2000.

MicroProse Software, *Formula One Grand Prix*. MicroProse Software, 1991.

Monolith Productions, *No One Lives Forever 2: A Spy in H.A.R.M.'s Way*. Fox Interactive, 2002.

Namco, *Pac-Man*. Midway Games West, 1981.

Nishikado T, *Space Invaders*. Taito, 1978.

Origin, *Ultima Online*. Electronic Arts, 1997.

Pandemic Studios, *Star Wars: Battlefront*. LucasArts, 2004.

Raven Software, *Jedi Knight II: Jedi Outcast*. LucasArts, 2002.

Relic Entertainment, *Homeworld*. Sierra Studios, 1999.

Remedy Entertainment, *Max Payne*. Gathering of Developers, 2001.

Rotobee, *Singles: Flirt Up Your Life*. Deep Silver, 2004.

Sphere, *Falcon A.T.*. Spectrum Holobyte, 1988.

Sullivan Bluth, *Dragon's Lair*. ReadySoft, 1989.

Valve Software, *Half-Life*. Sierra Studios, 1998.

Verant Interactive, *EverQuest*. 989 Studios, 1999.

Vicarious Visions, *Terminus*. Vicarious Visions, 2001.

Yob G, *Hunt the Wumpus*. 1975.

Index

2n-Gong, *181*

A* algorithm, 103–107, *112*
A-STAR, **107**
Acceptor, 124, *144*
Action, 125
Active collusion, 222, *225*
Active object, 217–220, *224*
Adaptation, 121–122, *143*, 157
Adaptive pipeline protocol, 217
Admissibility, 104, 107, *112*
Aesthetics, 108, *113*
Age of Empires II: The Age of Kings, 6, 119, 139, 205
Aggregation, 163–164
AI processor, 110
Algol68, 246
Algorithm format, 242–244
Algorithmic function, 232
Alignment, 135, 137
ALIGNMENT, **138**, *147*
ALL-PERMUTATIONS, **29**, *44*
Alluringness, 139
Ally, 6
Alpha-beta pruning, 82–86, 88, 89, *94*
    analysis, 84–86
    rules, 83
Amaze, *181*
Amdahl's law, 187
Anthropocentrism, 5, 8, *12*
ARABIC-TO-ROMAN, **244**
Area-of-interest filtering, 205–209, *211*
Armwrestling, 47
Array, 240
Aspiration search, 86
Asynchronous lockstep protocol, 216
Augmented reality, 171
Aura, 206, 208, *211*

Autonomy, 143
Avatar, 9
Avoidance, 108, 135
AVOIDANCE, **138**

B-spline, 108
Backgammon, 73
Bandwidth, 173, 176, 183, 185, 190–193, 205, *210*
Bayes' theorem, 149–151
Bayesian network, 151, *166*
Beam search, 102
Belief, 149, 152–153, *167*
Best-first search, 102, 104
Best-of-m match, 53, 60, *70*
Bézier curve, 108
Binary, 237
Binary tree, 56
Binomial distribution, 25
Bit reversal, 18, 57
BIT-REVERSE, **60**
Black & White, 118
Boid, 135, *147*
Boxing, 118, 119
Bracket, 56, *69*, *71*
Branching factor, 78, 81, 82, 85, 88, *93*
Breadth-first search, 102, 104, *111*
Bridge, 222
Broadcasting, 174, 175, *180*
Brownian movement, 35
Bullet time effect, 202–205, *211*
Bye, 57–58, 60–62

C programming language, 229, 245, 246
C++, 229, 246
Card trick, 28, *44*
Centralized architecture, 177, *181*, 186, 221, *225*